Financing SMEs and Entrepreneurs 2012

AN OECD SCOREBOARD

OECD

This work is published on the responsibility of the Secretary-General of the OECD. The opinions expressed and arguments employed herein do not necessarily reflect the official views of the Organisation or of the governments of its member countries.

This document and any map included herein are without prejudice to the status of or sovereignty over any territory, to the delimitation of international frontiers and boundaries and to the name of any territory, city or area.

Please cite this publication as:
OECD (2012), *Financing SMEs and Entrepreneurs 2012: An OECD Scoreboard*, OECD Publishing.
http://dx.doi.org/10.1787/9789264166769-en

ISBN 978-92-64-02802-9 (print)
ISBN 978-92-64-16676-9 (PDF)

Photo credits: Cover © Shutterstock/Roman Gorielov.

Corrigenda to OECD publications may be found on line at: *www.oecd.org/publishing/corrigenda*.
© OECD 2012

Foreword

Small and medium-sized enterprises (SMEs) are important engines of growth, jobs and social cohesion. However, the creation, survival and growth of SMEs is often hampered by access to finance, a challenge that is at the core of this Scoreboard on Financing SMEs and Entrepreneurs.

The global crisis has exacerbated the financing constraints on SMEs. They have suffered a double shock: a drastic drop in the demand for the goods and services they provide and a credit crunch. These events have had a severe effect on SMEs' cash flows and liquidity, forcing many into bankruptcy and contributing to record levels of unemployment in many OECD countries. Since the onset of the crisis, governments have responded with a number of different measures to support sales, prevent the depletion of SMEs' working capital and enhance access to credit for SMEs.

The importance of SME finance is now widely recognised. At the Pittsburgh Summit in 2009, G20 Leaders acknowledged that access to finance provides growth opportunities for businesses and the economy as a whole. Financial Inclusion is a pillar of the G20 Multi-Year Action Plan on Development, and the G20 Global Platform for Financial Inclusion (GPFI) was launched in Korea in December 2010. The need to address the financing hurdles to SME growth was also underlined by G8 Leaders at the 2011 Deauville Summit, where the OECD was invited, in co-operation with other relevant international institutions, to identify impediments to SME growth, including the issue of private funding.

The OECD has pioneered efforts to develop data and statistical information on SMEs' and entrepreneurs' access to finance in response to the G20 call for more and better data, and international benchmarks on the financial situation of SMEs. Better data can improve our understanding of business financing needs and provide a sound basis for informed policy discussions, as well as giving the suppliers of finance a more comprehensive assessment of their clients' needs that enables them to design better products and services. In 2010, the OECD Working Party on SMEs and Entrepreneurship (WPSMEE) launched a Pilot OECD Scoreboard on SME and Entrepreneurship Financing Data and Policies. During the course of the pilot, 13 indicators on debt, equity and general market conditions were selected and tested, and measures and policies to promote SME and entrepreneurship financing were reviewed.

This first edition of Financing SMEs and Entrepreneurs: An OECD Scoreboard is an important step in filling the information gap on SME finance. It provides an original framework to monitor trends in SMEs' and entrepreneurs' access to finance – at the country level and internationally – and a tool to support the formulation and evaluation of policies. As country coverage expands and progress is made on methodological issues, this OECD Scoreboard is expected to become an international reference for monitoring developments and trends in SME finance.

This OECD Scoreboard aims at contributing to country-specific policy strategies that result in better SME policies for better lives!

Angel Gurría
OECD Secretary-General

Acknowledgements

*F*inancing SMEs and Entrepreneurs: An OECD Scoreboard is the result of the combined efforts and strong co-operation between representatives and country experts from OECD member and non-member countries, international organisations and other stakeholders participating in the Informal Steering Group on SME and Entrepreneurship Financing of the OECD Working Party on SMEs and Entrepreneurship (WPSMEE). This Informal Steering Group, chaired by Professor Salvatore Zecchini, has proved essential in the identification, collection and analysis of the data used in the SME Scoreboard.

COUNTRY EXPERT TEAM

Canada	Richard Archambault	Industry Canada
	Adèle McCracken	Industry Canada
Chile	Ximena Clark Núñez	Vice Ministry of Economy and Small Enterprises
	Katia Makhlouf Issid	Vice Ministry of Economy and Small Enterprises
	Oscar Rojas	Vice Ministry of Economy and Small Enterprises
Denmark	Rasmus Pilegaard	Ministry of Economic and Business Affairs
Finland	Jari Huovinen	Confederation of Finnish Industries
	Pertti Valtonen	Ministry of Employment and the Economy
France	Elisabeth Kremp	Banque de France
	Cécile Golfier	Banque de France
Hungary	Peter Pogacsas	Ministry for National Economy
Italy	Salvatore Zecchini	Ministry of Economic Development
	Sabrina Pastorelli	Bank of Italy
Korea	Dongsoo Kang	Korea Development Institute
	Changwoo Nam	Korea Development Institute
Netherlands	Dinand Maas	Ministry of Economic Affairs
New Zealand	Michael James Shaffrey	Ministry of Economic Development
	Caleb Johnstone	Ministry of Economic Development
Portugal	Nuno Goncalves	Office of the Secretary of State of Economy and Regional Development
Slovak Republic	Daniel Pitonak	National Agency for SME Development
Slovenia	Tine Janzek	Bank of Slovenia
Sweden	Henrik Levin	Ministry of Enterprise, Energy and Communications
	Peter Vikstrom	Swedish Agency for Growth Policy Analysis, Entrepreneurship and Enterprise
	Johan Harvard	Swedish Agency for Growth Policy Analysis, Entrepreneurship and Enterprise
Switzerland	Marianne Neuhaus	State Secretariat for Economic Affairs
	Markus Willimann	State Secretariat for Economic Affairs
Thailand	Salinee Wangtal	Bank of Thailand
	Dhidaporn Dharmasaroja	Bank of Thailand
	Varangkana Thamrongrat	Bank of Thailand
United Kingdom	Daniel Van der Schans	Department for Business, Innovation and Skills
United States	Giuseppe Gramigna	US Small Business Administration
	Alicia Robb	Kauffman Foundation

The contributions of Veronique Genre (European Central Bank), Helmut Kraemer-Eis (European Investment Fund) and Mark Pevsner (European Investment Bank), as members of the WSPMEE's Informal Steering Group on SME and Entrepreneurship Financing, have also been extremely valuable. In addition, thanks go to Paul Atkinson (Group on Global Economy/Sciences Po) for his contributions to the thematic chapter on Basel III and SME lending. Mariarosa Lunati and Eric Gonnard (OECD Statistics Directorate) provided valuable comments and inputs for identification and collection of venture capital statistics.

This report was prepared under the supervision of Ms. Miriam Koreen, Deputy Director of the OECD Centre for Entrepreneurship, SMEs and Local Development (CFE). Ms. Lorraine Ruffing (Consultant, CFE), Ms. Lucia Cusmano (SMEs and Entrepreneurship Division, CFE) and Mr. Benjamin Dean (Consultant, CFE) compiled and reviewed the report. Mme Elsie Lotthé provided technical support.

Finally, sincere thanks go to Mme Marie-Florence Estimé, former Deputy Director of the OECD Centre for Entrepreneurship, SMEs and Local Development, for her role and dedication in launching this study, as well as to the Delegates of the OECD WPSMEE for their numerous comments and inputs during the compilation of this report.

Table of Contents

Tables

11

This book has...

StatLinks

**A service that delivers Excel® files
from the printed page!**

Look for the *StatLinks* at the bottom right-hand corner of the tables or graphs in this book.
To download the matching Excel® spreadsheet, just type the link into your Internet browser,
starting with the *http://dx.doi.org* prefix.
If you're reading the PDF e-book edition, and your PC is connected to the Internet, simply
click on the link. You'll find *StatLinks* appearing in more OECD books.

Acronyms and abbreviations

BIS	Bank for International Settlements
CAD	Canadian dollar
CHF	Swiss franc
CLP	Chilean peso
DKK	Danish krone
EC	European Commission
ECB	European Central Bank
EU	European Union
EUR	Euro
EVCA	European Venture Capital Association
FDI	Foreign direct investment
G8	Group of 8
G20	Group of 20
GBP	British pound
GDP	Gross domestic product
GPFI	Global Platform for Financial Inclusion
GSIFI	Global systemically important financial institution
HUF	Hungarian forint
IRB	Internal ratings-based method
KRW	Korean won
LCR	Liquidity coverage ratio
MFI	Monetary financial institution
NPL	Non-performing loan
NSF	Net stable funding
NZD	New Zealand dollar
RWA	Risk weighted asset
SEK	Swedish krona
SME	Small and medium-sized enterprise
THB	Thai baht
UEAPME	European Association of Craft, Small and Medium-sized Enterprises
USD	United States dollar
VAT	Value added tax
VC	Venture capital
WPSMEE	Working Party on SMEs and Entrepreneurship

Chapter 1

Financing SMEs and Entrepreneurs: Understanding and Developing an OECD Scoreboard

This chapter provides the users of the Scoreboard on SME and entrepreneurship finance with tools to interpret the data. It introduces the methodology and presents the core indicators used in the country profiles. The chapter explains the criteria for the selection of indicators and discusses the limitations to cross-country comparability. It highlights areas for advancement and concludes with recommendations to improve SME finance data so as to enable better cross-country comparisons in the future.

Introduction

The OECD Scoreboard on SME and entrepreneurship finance establishes a comprehensive framework for monitoring SMEs' and entrepreneurs' access to finance over time. Information at the national level is provided in the form of country profiles, which present data for a number of debt, equity and financing framework condition indicators. Taken together, they provide governments and other stakeholders with a tool to understand SME financing needs, to support the design and evaluation of policy measures and to monitor the implications of financial reforms on SME access to finance.

This first edition of the Scoreboard on SME and entrepreneurship finance includes information for 18 countries: Canada, Chile, Denmark, Finland, France, Hungary, Italy, Korea, the Netherlands, New Zealand, Portugal, the Slovak Republic, Slovenia, Sweden, Switzerland, Thailand, the United Kingdom and the United States.

Indicators

SME and entrepreneurship financing trends are monitored through 13 core indicators, which tackle specific questions related to access to finance (Table 1.1). For example, the changes in the share of SME loans in total business loans show how the allocation of credit is evolving at the country level and how well SMEs are doing in accessing finance compared to larger firms. Likewise, the changes in the share of short-term loans in SME loans show the evolution of the debt structure of SMEs and whether the loans are used to fund current operations or expansion. Indicators on credit conditions, such as loans authorised divided by loans requested, interest rate spreads and collateral, show if the credit market is tightening. The indicators on payment delays and bankruptcies complete the picture on cash flow constraints and implications for SME survival. On the equity side, trends in venture and growth capital provide insights into the ability of entrepreneurs to access external equity for start-up, early development and expansion stages.

The selection of indicators was based on the following criteria:

- *Usefulness*: the indicators must be an appropriate instrument to measure how easy or difficult it is for SMEs and entrepreneurs to access finance and to help policy makers formulate or adjust their policies and programmes.
- *Availability*: the data for constructing the indicators should be *readily available* in order not to impose new burdens on governments or firms.
- *Feasibility*: if the information for constructing the indicator is not publicly available, it should be *feasible* to make it available at a modest cost, or to collect it during routine data exercises or surveys.
- *Timeliness*: the information should be collected in a *timely* manner so that the evolving conditions of SME access to finance can be monitored. This means that annual or quarterly data are needed. In many cases, turning points can be better captured by quarterly data.

● *Comparability*: the indicators should be relatively uniform across countries in terms of the population surveyed, content, method of data collection and periodicity or timeliness.

Table 1.1. **Core indicators of the OECD Scoreboard on SME and entrepreneurship finance**

Core indicators	What they show
1. Share of SME loans in business loans	SMEs' access to finance compared to larger firms
2. SME short-term loans in SME loans	Debt structure of SMEs; % used for operations and % used for expansion
3. SME loan guarantees	Extent of public support for SME finance
4. SME guaranteed loans	Extent of public support for SME finance
5. SME direct government loans	Extent of public support for SME finance
6. SME loans authorised/SME loans requested or	Tightness of credit conditions and willingness of banks to lend
SME loans used/SME loans authorised	Proxy for above indicator; however a decrease indicates credit conditions are loosening
7. SME non-performing loans/SME loans	When compared to the ratio of non-performing loans (NPLs) for all business loans it indicates if SMEs are less creditworthy than larger firms
8. SME interest rates	Tightness of credit conditions and risk premium charged to SMEs
9. Interest rate spreads between large and small enterprises	Tightness of credit conditions; indicates how closely interest rates are correlated with firm size
10. Per cent of SMEs required to provide collateral on their last bank loan	Tightness of credit conditions
11. Venture capital and growth capital	Ability to access external equity for start-up, early development and expansion stages
12. Payment delays	Indicator of cash flow problems; difficulty in paying and being paid
13. Bankruptcies	Rough indicator of ability to survive during a crisis

Data collection

The data in the present report cover the period 2007 to 2010, which comprises three distinct economic stages: pre-crisis (2007), crisis (2008-09) and recovery (2010). The year 2007 serves as the benchmark year from which changes in SME access to finance are measured in 2008-10.

For most of the countries in the report, the indicators have been developed using a "target" SME population that consists of non-financial "employer" firms, that is, firms with at least one employee besides the owner/manager. This is consistent with the methodology adopted by the OECD-Eurostat Entrepreneurship Indicators Programme, which also calculates its indicators on the basis of "employer" enterprises.

Most of the indicators are built on supply-side data, that is, financial institutions and other government agencies represent the main source of information. Ideally, quantitative demand-side data, as collected by SME surveys, would complement the picture and improve the interpretative power of this framework. However, whereas a plethora of *qualitative* SME surveys (*i.e.* opinion surveys) exist, *quantitative* demand-side surveys are rare. Experience shows that *qualitative* information based on opinion survey responses must be used cautiously. Furthermore, comparability of national surveys is limited, as survey methodologies differ from country to country. Annex B provides references to surveys and statistical resources on SME and entrepreneurship finance in several countries. Annex C presents an example of a simplified quantitative demand-side survey by Industry Canada on Small Business Credit Conditions in 2010, which constitutes a good practice for demand-side surveys, yielding high quality data while limiting costs to administrators and burdens to respondents.

Cross-country comparability

At the individual country level, the Scoreboard on SME and entrepreneurship finance allows indicators to be examined as a set and to draw a coherent picture of SME access to finance. On the other hand, differences in definition and coverage between countries for many indicators limit cross country comparisons. The biggest challenge remains the lack of comparability in the statistical definitions of an SME. Greater harmonisation continues to prove difficult due to the different economic, social and political concerns of individual countries (see Annex A). The most commonly used definition among participating countries is the one used in the European Union, although it is set to be reviewed in 2012. Furthermore, the national statistical definition often differs from the one used by banks and financial institutions to collect data on SME financing. In addition, in a number of cases, it was not possible to adhere to the "preferred definition" of the core indicators. In these instances, a proxy was adopted. For these reasons, in each country profile, the data are complemented with a table of definitions, which reports, for each indicator, the definition adopted and the reference to the data source. Details are provided on the definition of SMEs used by governments or statistical offices and the definition adopted by financial institutions.

Despite these limitations, it is possible to observe general trends across countries. Chapter 2 provides an overview of the situation internationally and highlights the value of comparative analysis in shedding light on the changing conditions for SME financing around the world.

Definition of indicators and data collection: Current challenges and recommendations

To enable better cross-country comparison in the future, better monitor SME and entrepreneur access to finance and increase the usefulness of the Scoreboard as a framework for policy makers there are several areas where improvements are needed. There is a need for OECD and non-OECD countries to collect data on SME financing in a more timely fashion. In addition, it is necessary for countries to advance in the harmonisation of data content and in the standardisation of methods of data collection.

SME population covered

Currently, the composition of the SME population for data collection differs across countries, and this limits comparisons. For the indicators in the OECD Scoreboard on SME and entrepreneurship finance, the target population is composed of "employer" firms, that is, firms with at least one employee besides the owner/manager, operating a non-financial business. Accordingly, the population covered does not include financial enterprises. However, not all countries collect data at the source and compile them in accordance with these criteria. Therefore, in a few cases data include financial firms and/or self-employed individuals.

SME loan data: definitions and contents

Differences emerge across countries in the composition of business loans and SME business loans. This report aims to collect business loan data that include overdrafts, lines of credit, short-term loans and long-term loans, regardless of whether they are performing or non-performing loans. Additionally, it aims to exclude personal credit card debt and residential mortgages. In some cases leasing, factoring and trade credit are included, although they are difficult to capture if they are not provided by financial institutions that report to central authorities. Future efforts should be directed towards the collection of more complete information and standardisation of the precise content of the loans reported.

The differences in the definition of an SME loan by banks or other national organisations represent an important limitation to cross-country comparisons. In many cases (thirteen countries), the national authorities adopted the national or EU definition for an SME, based on firm size. In other cases (five countries), the SME loan was based not on the size of the firm but on the size of the loan. In this case, the size of the SME loan differed among countries and sometimes even among banks within the same country. Several challenges to the collection of SME loan data by firm size have emerged. These challenges include the following:

- banks do not collect data by firm size;
- it is too expensive to collect such data; and
- breaking down loan data by firm size would jeopardise confidentiality.

Experience gained from this Scoreboard suggests that loan data broken down by firm size are already in the financial system but are not extracted unless banks are under a regulatory obligation to provide them. Experience also suggests that the challenges mentioned above could be addressed quite easily. For instance, confidentiality requirements in theory could be met through the use of judicious sub-grouping. In this case, resolution of the issue could be found if national regulatory authorities were to make the provision of this information mandatory for banks.

Data on government loan guarantees

The coverage of government loan guarantees to SMEs differs across countries. This includes information on both the value of the loan guarantee fund and the value of the loan amounts guaranteed. When partial coverage exists, policy makers are limited in their capacity to assess the uptake of their programmes. The coverage could be increased by centralising information on the various guarantee funds available in instances where different organisations provide guarantees. As a first step, efforts could be directed towards encouraging lending institutions to indicate the *amount guaranteed* or *amount of government support received* out of the total value of their SME loans.

Venture capital data

Data collection for venture capital and growth capital encounters particular problems related to different and inconsistent definitions and sources across countries and, in some cases, even within countries. Furthermore, differences exist in the timing and coverage/ sample size of venture capital associations' surveys of members, the main source of data across the countries in this report. There is a need for greater standardisation of venture capital data reporting, in terms of both the definition used for the different stages of investment and the methodology employed to collect data. At present, the selected indicator of equity financing includes venture and growth capital, that is, it covers also *later stage development capital* or *expansion capital*, but it excludes buyouts, turnarounds and replacement capital.

Demand-side data collection

Demand-side data are collected by surveys undertaken by both public and private institutions and as a result, there is little standardisation in terms of the timing, the sample population, the sampling method, the interview method, and the questions asked. To address this issue, governments are encouraged to increase co-operative efforts between public and private institutions in order to increase coverage and comparability of results of different surveys covering the same phenomenon. The survey on SME access to finance developed by the European Commission and the European Central Bank provides a good example of the benefits that can come from standardised definitions and methodology across countries. At the country level, the experience of Canada shows that such quantitative surveys can have good coverage, be limited in the number of questions and relatively inexpensive to carry out, while yielding high quality data (see Annex C).

Recommendations for data improvements

The following steps should be considered by governments to improve SME finance data and information:

- require financial institutions to use the national definition for an SME based on firm size;
- require financial institutions to report on a timely basis to their regulatory authorities SME loans, interest rates, collateral requirements, by firm size and broken down into the appropriate size subcategories, as well as those SME loans that have government support;
- encourage international, regional and national authorities as well as business associations to work together to harmonise quantitative demand-side surveys in terms of survey population, questions asked and timeframes; encourage the competent organisations to undertake yearly surveys; and
- promote the harmonisation of the definition of venture capital in terms of stages of development.

By taking these steps, more timely and comparable data would become available to policy makers and support them in the design, implementation and assessment of policies aimed at improving SMEs' and entrepreneurs' access to finance.

Chapter 2

Emerging Trends in SME and Entrepreneurship Finance

This chapter analyses trends in SME and entrepreneurship finance for participating countries, based on data collected in the Scoreboard on financing SMEs and entrepreneurs and information from demand-side surveys. An overview of the global business environment and economic prospects sets the framework for the analysis of trends in lending to SMEs and equity financing over the period 2007 to 2010. The pre-crisis (2007) year serves as a benchmark to assess changes in SMEs' access to finance during the crisis (2008-09) and the recovery (2010). The chapter concludes with an overview of government policy responses to improve SMEs' and entrepreneurs' access to finance during the crisis.

Introduction

The objective of this chapter is to highlight emerging trends in SME and entrepreneur access to finance during the period 2007 to 2010, which covers three distinct economic stages: pre-crisis (2007), crisis (2008-09) and recovery (2010). 2007 serves as the benchmark year from which changes in SME access to finance are measured in 2008-10.

The analysis is based on the comparative assessment of trends in the core indicators of the report, which address, at country level, specific questions related to SME and entrepreneur access to finance (see Chapter 1). Most of the indicators are built on supply-side data. When appropriate, these are supplemented with information from demand-side surveys of SMEs undertaken by the European Central Bank and the European Commission. These surveys adopt a consistent methodology across countries and cover questions on SMEs' access to finance which are related to the indicators in the OECD Scoreboard on SME and entrepreneurship finance (see Box 2.1).

Box 2.1. **ECB/EC Survey on SME access to finance**

The survey on access to finance includes between 5 000 and 7 500 SMEs from the euro area. This survey was developed by the European Commission (EC) and the European Central Bank (ECB). A joint ECB/EC survey round is conducted every two years for all the EU member states and some additional countries. Every six months the ECB repeats part of the survey in order to assess the latest developments in the financing conditions for firms in the euro area. It has been undertaken four times: first half 2009 (1H2009), second half 2009 (2H2009), first half 2010 (1H2010) and second half 2010 (2H2010). Some of the questions covered are directly comparable with the supply side evidence provided by the OECD Scoreboard on SME and entrepreneurship finance. In particular:

● The % of SMEs whose need for a bank loan increased/decreased.

● The % of SMEs that feel the availability of bank loans has improved/deteriorated.

● The % of SMEs that feel the banks' willingness to lend has improved/deteriorated.

● The % of SMEs that sought a bank loan in the last 6 months.

● The % of SMEs that obtained all the financing they sought.

● The % of SMEs whose request was rejected.

Business environment and economic prospects

The 2008-09 financial crisis was the most severe in decades and its costs have been enormous. GDP contracted by about 3.5% in the OECD area as a whole in 2009 and unemployment reached a post-war high of close to 9% on average. The longer-term legacy of the crisis is also heavy. Public debt in OECD countries was expected to be 100%

of GDP at the end of 2011, some 30 percentage points higher than before the crisis. OECD countries may have lost about 3% of potential output. In 2012, world GDP is projected to increase by 3.4%, whereas across OECD countries GDP is projected to rise by 1.6% (OECD, 2010a, 2011a). However, uncertainty surrounding projections is high.

While the recovery may be underway in many OECD countries, it is uneven, and significant downside risks continue to cloud the growth horizon. In several OECD economies, the recovery came to a halt in the second quarter of 2011, earlier improvements in the labour market have been fading, and there appear to be greater risks that high unemployment could become entrenched. Economic growth slowed down also in non-OECD countries, including China, where manufacturing production weakened in the first half of 2011.

In particular, financial vulnerability remains, in spite of the strong adjustment efforts underway in several countries. Heightened risk aversion in financial markets is reflected in wide sovereign risk spreads in the euro area, tumbling share prices and increasing yields on higher-risk corporate bonds. Furthermore, renewed concerns over the balance sheets of banks point to possible further tightening of credit conditions (OECD, 2011b). At the same time, faster private sector balance sheet adjustment and bank de-leveraging could exert a significant drag on growth.

The crisis had a strongly negative impact on real economic performance of SMEs. Over 2008-09, output, sales, employment and exports were all adversely impacted. In line with the general decline in GDP, SMEs reported that final demand began to contract sharply in mid- to late-2008. This contraction accelerated in early 2009 and lasted until the second or third quarter, with the decline being sharpest in the first half of 2009 in most cases. Across OECD countries, indices of SME confidence fell well below their previous historic lows, which in most cases were reached in the early 1990s. Companies that were heavily engaged in exports experienced a sharper contraction than those mainly engaged in domestic production due to plunges in the levels of world trade.

Table 2.1. **Bankruptcies,**[1] **2007-10**
Various measures, all enterprises

	Unit	2007	2008	2009	2010
Canada	Per 1 000 firms	3.1	3.1	2.9	2.2
Denmark	Number	2 401	3 709	5 710	6 461
Finland	% of firms in bankruptcy proceedings	0.9	1.0	1.2	1.0
France[2]	Number	48 111	52 104	58 930	56 883
Hungary	Per 10 000 firms	566	624	726	805
Italy	Number	6 165	7 521	9 429	11 289
Korea	Number	2 294	2 735	1 998	1 570
Netherlands	Number	4 602	4 635	8 040	7 211
Portugal	Number	26 446	31 167	24 917	26 990
Slovak Republic	Number	169	251	276	344
Sweden	Number	5 791	6 298	7 638	7 274
Switzerland	Number	4 314	4 221	5 215	6 255
United Kingdom	Number	12 507	15 535	19 077	16 045
United States	Number	28 322	43 546	60 837	56 282

1. Definitions differ across countries. Refer to the table of definitions in each respective country profile in Chapter 4.
2. Only SMEs.

StatLink ⫘ *http://dx.doi.org/10.1787/888932579341*

In 2010, conditions generally stabilised, and in most cases, a recovery began, although gains have generally been considerably less than those observed at comparable stages of earlier recoveries. The weak economic recovery and the credit crunch continued to take their toll on SME cash flows and survival.

The OECD Scoreboard on SME and entrepreneurship finance reveals that, in several countries, payment delays (however measured) increased during the recession (2009) and remained high or even increased during the recovery. The evidence on bankruptcies is unambiguous (Table 2.1). They were on the rise in 2009 in all countries monitored in this report except Canada, Korea and Portugal. They also continued to rise in 2010 in Denmark, Hungary, Italy, the Slovak Republic and Switzerland. While bankruptcies in Finland, France, the Netherlands, Sweden, and the United Kingdom declined during the recovery, they remained considerably higher than their 2007 levels.

Lending to SMEs in 2007-10

In the wake of the crisis, the financial situation of SMEs broadly deteriorated. This report shows that in most countries, business loans and SME loans declined markedly during the recession and, while they recovered somewhat in 2010, they did not reach their 2007 levels (Table 2.2). Lending to SMEs continued to decline during the recovery in Finland, New Zealand, Portugal, Slovenia, the United Kingdom and the United States. The exceptions were Canada, Chile, France, Italy, Korea, Switzerland and Thailand, which enjoyed positive, though slowing, SME loan growth throughout the entire period.

Loan authorisation rates for SMEs decreased considerably in a number of countries due to tighter credit standards and more negative prospects as a result of the crisis. According to the ECB/EC survey, in the euro area, rejection rates rose from 12% to 18% between the first and second half of 2009. The sole exception was France, where rejection rates decreased from 12% to 7%. During 2010 the rejection rate for the euro area declined to 11%.

Table 2.2. **Growth of SME business loans,**[1] **2008-10**

Year-on-year growth rate, as a percentage

	2008	2009	2010
Canada	-0.1	3.7	-0.9
Chile	11.3	6.9	8.8
Denmark	-13.7	-19.2	22.9
Finland	2.6	-16.3	-22.0
France	4.3	1.0	5.7
Hungary	4.9	-6.8	1.3
Italy	2.1	1.2	6.6
Korea	14.1	5.5	-1.0
Netherlands	-5.0	-24.2	5.1
Portugal	9.2	1.8	-2.0
Slovak Republic	34.1	-0.3	..
Slovenia	16.7	-0.9	-8.8
Sweden	7.2	20.4	..
Switzerland	5.9	5.3	1.3
Thailand	9.5	7.4	7.2
United Kingdom	8.2	1.4	-6.1
United States	3.6	-2.3	-6.2

1. Definitions differ across countries. Refer to the table of definitions in each respective country profile in Chapter 4.
StatLink http://dx.doi.org/10.1787/888932579360

SME loan shares across countries varied between 12% and 30%, well below the respective contribution by SMEs to national income and employment. During the recession, this share decreased even further, as SME lending declined more than lending to large enterprises. SME loan shares in Finland continued to suffer declines during the recovery, and in Denmark and the United States, they did not return to pre-crisis levels. (Table 2.3).

Table 2.3. **SME loan share of total business loans,**[1] **2007-10**

As a percentage of total business loans

	2007	2008	2009	2010
Canada	17	16	18	18
Chile	17	15	18	18
Denmark	12	9	9	11
Finland	27	22	20	14
France	26	26	26	26
Hungary	59	58	58	60
Italy	19	18	18	19
Korea	87	83	84	81
Portugal	78	78	78	77
Slovak Republic	63	74	76	. .
Slovenia	57	56	55	50
Sweden	89	89	92	. .
Switzerland	81	. .	. .	. .
Thailand	28	27	27	38
United Kingdom	11	11	12	12
United States	30	28	28	29

1. Definitions differ across countries. Refer to the table of definitions in each respective country profile in Chapter 4.

StatLink ⬚⬚⬚ http://dx.doi.org/10.1787/888932579379

However, in a number of countries, the SME loan shares were significantly higher than on average, exceeding 50%. A number of specific factors can explain these "outliers":

● large companies found external finance elsewhere, such as in the bond markets;

● intercompany loans may have been under-reported;

● government policy and commercial banks catered to the SME sector; and

● loan data are derived from balance sheets and may include more than credit from financial institutions.

Short-term loans vs. loans for investment

During a recession, the share of short-term loans could be expected to increase relative to long-term or investment loans, because short-term borrowing is needed to solve cash flow problems. Such a shift occurred in four countries in 2008 and reflects changes on the demand side, as SMEs sought working capital to offset declining revenues and increased payments delays, while cutting back on investment outlays. However, this trend has not been consistent across countries and over time. In five countries, the share of short-term loans decreased in 2009 and the downward trend continued in 2010 (Table 2.4).

The decline in short-term loans in a time of a recession could be the result of policies, such as those introducing or strengthening guarantee programmes. In fact, loan guarantees, which are usually granted on long-term loans, were extensively supported during the crisis. At the same time, however, this evidence could reflect the type of data collected at the country level. In the case of stock data, as opposed to flow data, the indicator includes prior years' investments, whereas it excludes the short-term loans that mature and/or are not being renewed. In fact, evidence points to a decline of short-term loan shares in countries such as France, Switzerland and the United States, which collected stock data.

Table 2.4. **Share of short-term SME loans,**[1] **2007-10**

As a percentage of total SME loans

	2007	2008	2009	2010
Canada	42	..	43	36
Chile	..	..	..	60
Denmark	65	75	79	65
Finland	21	28	30	26
France	22	21	18	18
Italy	34	32	29	27
Korea	69	68	69	..
Netherlands	56	55	57	48
Portugal	32	31	33	31
Slovak Republic	51	39	41	..
Slovenia	43	47	43	38
Sweden	14	12	12	..
Switzerland	83	79	77	74
Thailand	43	44	44	58
United States	31	32	27	24

1. Definitions differ across countries. Refer to the table of definitions in each respective country profile in Chapter 4.

StatLink http://dx.doi.org/10.1787/888932579398

SME credit conditions compared to larger enterprises

Overall, SMEs faced more severe credit conditions than did large enterprises, in the form of higher interest rates, shortened maturities and increased requests for collateral. Over 2007-10, the SME interest rates trended downward but the interest rate spread between SMEs and large enterprises increased over the entire period, including during the recovery, indicating that large enterprises faced easier credit terms, and suggesting that smaller firms were considered to be higher-risk companies due to their poorer business prospects.

Data on collateral requirements were more difficult to obtain. Nevertheless, most countries reported that the percentage of SMEs required to provide collateral rose.

Demand vs. supply of financing

The downward trend of SME lending over 2008-09 was confirmed by both direct surveys of SMEs and surveys of bank lending officers (OECD, 2010b). However, whereas the former were largely negative in the assessment of the credit conditions, the latter generally pointed to declines in "credit demand" as the reason for the fall off in bank lending.

The evidence in the euro area from the ECB/EC demand survey is consistent with the findings in this report, especially with regard to stiffer credit conditions and a decline or a slowdown in lending in early 2010 (Table 2.5). In particular, the slowdown in lending recorded on the supply side is matched by SMEs' perceptions of availability of credit and the banks' willingness to lend. Of SMEs surveyed, 25% said that their need for a bank loan had increased during the crisis (2H2009), compared to 18% whose need increased during the recovery (2H2010). On the question of the availability of bank loans, the percentage of SMEs with negative views declined over the period (from 43% in 1H2009 to 23% in 2H2010). Over the first half of 2010, however, SMEs' perception of banks' willingness to lend did not improve greatly.

According to the survey, the percentage of SMEs that applied for a bank loan decreased slightly during the recovery, but those applying for a bank loan were more likely to receive the amount they requested, rising from 56% (2H2009) to 66% (2H2010). This might indicate that more credit-worthy SMEs had applied. However, SMEs reported that the terms of finance were stiffer, in particular interest rates. While low, they continued to rise. The view on the increase in collateral requirements did not change significantly over time. Indeed, the share of firms indicating less stringent collateral conditions decreased in 2010.

It is important to note, however, that SMEs indicated "finding customers" as their most pressing problem, both during the recession and the recovery. In particular, access to finance dropped from the second most pressing problem to third between 1H2009 and 2H2010. This also underscores that the recovery was weak in 2010. Furthermore, according to the ECB/EC survey, the use of overdrafts and credit lines outstripped the use of term bank loans (42% vs. 36%) during the recovery period, indicating that liquidity remained an important problem in the euro area. This is the only discrepancy with the OECD Scoreboard on SME and entrepreneurship finance, which shows that in some countries, such as France, the Slovak Republic and Switzerland, short-term lending declined.

Table 2.5. **European Central Bank/European Commission survey on SME access to finance**

As a percentage of total SMEs surveyed

Category	1H2009	2H2009	1H2010	2H2010
SME need for bank loan				
Increased	19	25	15	18
Decreased	9	9	12	11
Most pressing problem				
Finding customers	27	28	28	25
Competition	14	13	15	14
Finance	17	19	15	16
Availability of bank loans				
Improved	10	10	12	14
Deteriorated	43	42	24	23
Willingness of banks to lend				
Improved	17	8	13	13
Deteriorated	32	33	29	29
Applied for a bank loan	28	29	24	25
Outcome				
Granted in full	60	56	63	66
Rejected	12	18	11	11
Interest rate				
Increased	34	35	38	54
Decreased	29	27	20	10
Collateral				
Increased	34	39	37	34
Decreased	8	6	3	3

Source: ECB/EC.

StatLink http://dx.doi.org/10.1787/888932579417

Stiffer credit terms, combined with weak sales, could have deterred some SMEs from seeking finance, especially for expansion purposes. There is evidence that, faced with declining demand for their output, SMEs largely responded by taking steps to lessen external borrowing rather than by seeking new external funding. In France, for instance, net credit demand (percentage of firms requesting increases in credit minus the percentage requesting less credit) fell from +40% in 3Q08 to –70% in 2Q09. In the United States, the *Federal Reserve Survey of Senior Loan Officers* indicated that SME demand for loans, which had been trending downward since 2007, fell precipitously in early 2009. The net percentage of respondents reporting stronger demand for Commercial and Industrial (C&I) loans fell to –60%, roughly equal to its earlier historic low in 2002. As an explanation, loan officers cited both sharply reduced demand for investment capital and less demand to finance inventories and accounts receivable (OECD, 2010b). Whether SME loan demand rebounded in the United States during the recovery is not clear as the surveys conducted by the Federal Reserve and the National Federation of Independent Businesses showed conflicting results.

Equity financing

The OECD Scoreboard on SME and entrepreneurship finance includes an indicator on equity financing, more precisely, venture capital and, for some countries, growth capital. Venture capital includes seed, start-up and early development capital. Growth capital includes later stage expansion capital, but generally excludes buy-outs, turnarounds, replacement capital.[1] The capital provided by business angels is not included in the equity section of the Scoreboard, since only a few countries can currently report on business angel investments.

This report shows a sharp decline in venture capital and growth capital between 2008 and 2009. In 2010 these types of funding had not recovered to their 2007 levels. A number of countries had government programmes promoting early stage and expansion capital, including Canada, Chile, Denmark, Finland, France, Italy, the Netherlands, New Zealand, Sweden and the United Kingdom.

It should be noted, however, that accurate and comparable reporting on equity financing was particularly difficult for the countries monitored. Specific challenges to the development of indicators on venture and growth capital have been identified in the framework of the OECD-Eurostat *Entrepreneurship Indicators Programme* (OECD, 2011c), namely:

● At the country level, venture capital data are not always broken down by stage of development. When this happens, definitions of the investment stages are not harmonised across countries.

● In some countries, venture capital figures may also include later stage expansion capital, referred to hereafter as "growth capital".

● The data are not usually collected by the government, but rather by private bodies such as venture capital associations, which rely on the voluntary reporting of their members through periodic surveys.

● Depending on the methodology for data collection, a country's data may capture only the portion of the market surveyed by venture capital associations and may therefore be incomplete.

The demand-side data provide further support to the view that the venture capital market was particularly affected during the crisis. The ECB/EC survey found that very few SMEs had used equity in the second half of 2010. Only 6% of the SMEs surveyed accessed external equity. 78% said that this source of financing was not relevant to their enterprise. As mentioned, SMEs were more likely to use bank overdrafts or a line of credit in 2H2010. SMEs that accessed external equity were more likely to be innovative firms with high growth potential.

Government responses

Governments were sensitive to the increasing difficulties faced by SMEs in accessing finance and responded by injecting capital into their loan guarantee programmes and direct lending programmes, two indicators collected in the Scoreboard on SME and entrepreneurship finance. Almost every country had a loan guarantee programme and/or direct lending programme that could be ramped up during the crisis, in terms of the total amount of guarantee funds and direct lending available, the percentage of the loan guaranteed, the size of the guaranteed or direct loan and the number of eligible enterprises. However, new elements were added to these programmes, or new instruments were created outside the traditional guarantee programmes (Table 2.6). These included:

- guaranteeing short-term loans and counter-cyclical loans;
- combining guaranteed loans with business advice services (get started loans);
- increasing the coverage of guarantees sometimes to 100%;
- postponing the repayment of guaranteed loans;
- using pension funds to augment loan guarantee schemes;
- guaranteeing equity capital;
- assisting mutual guarantee associations; and
- increasing co-financing by public agencies and banks.

Table 2.6. **Government policy responses to improve SME access to finance during the 2008-09 crisis**

Policy response	Countries
Increased amount government loan guarantees and/or % guaranteed, number of firms eligible, countercyclical loans	Canada, Chile, Denmark, Finland, France, Hungary, Italy, Korea, the Netherlands, Portugal, the Slovak Republic, Slovenia, Switzerland, Thailand, the United Kingdom, the United States
Special guarantees and loans for start ups	Denmark, the Netherlands
Increased government export guarantees	Denmark, Finland, the Netherlands, New Zealand, Portugal, Sweden, Switzerland
Government co-financing	Sweden
Increased direct lending to SMEs	Chile, Hungary, Korea, Slovenia
Subsidised interest rates	Portugal, Thailand
Venture capital, equity funding and guarantees	Canada, Chile, Denmark, Finland, France, Italy, the Netherlands, New Zealand, Sweden, the United Kingdom
New programmes: business advice	Denmark, New Zealand, Sweden
Tax exemptions, deferments	France, Italy, New Zealand, Sweden
Credit mediation	France

Source: OECD, 2010b.

Among the new programmes or programme elements were Canada's Business Credit Availability Programme, which allowed the Business Development Bank and Export Development Canada to provide financing support to businesses with viable models, whose access to financing would otherwise be restricted. Denmark created "get started loans", which combined loan guarantees and consultancy schemes for new businesses. Finnvera, a financing company owned by the government of Finland, introduced counter-cyclical loans and guarantees to finance working capital. Counter-cyclical loans were intended for small enterprises whose profitability or liquidity declined because of the crisis. The Enterprise Finance Guarantee Scheme of the United Kingdom also supported counter-cyclical lending and assisted viable enterprises that in normal circumstances would be able to secure lending from banks but could not because of the credit crunch.

Some governments also intervened in the private equity market. For example, the Netherlands created a "Growth Facility", which offered banks and private equity enterprises a 50% guarantee on newly issued equity or mezzanine loans. Canada, Chile, Denmark, Finland, France, Italy, the Netherlands, New Zealand, Sweden and the United Kingdom also provided assistance to equity financing.

The other emergency responses especially tailored to remedy the deterioration in SME finance included:

- deferring tax payments temporarily;
- capping interest rates;
- rolling over SME loans;
- converting short-term loans into long-term loans or overdrafts into loans;
- refraining from declaring loans non-performing; and
- setting up credit mediation systems.

A number of these measures were time-bound and were intended to be phased out. However, as the recession has continued in some countries, many of these measures have been extended. In countries that have exited from recession, the measures have been phased out or made more selective. Overall, a formal evaluation of these measures would have to be undertaken to determine their effectiveness in easing access to finance.

Notes

1. In the case of the Netherlands and Switzerland, the Scoreboard data for growth capital also include buy-outs, turnarounds and replacement capital.

References

European Commission (2010), *Monthly Note on Economic Recovery in Manufacturing, Construction and Services Industries*, April 2010, European Commission, Brussels.

OECD (2010a), *OECD Economic Outlook 87*, May 2010, OECD Publishing.

OECD (2010b), *Assessment of Government Support Programmes for SMEs' and Entrepreneurs' Access to Finance in the Global Crisis*, OECD, Paris.

OECD (2011a), *OECD Economic Outlook 90*, November 2011, OECD Publishing.

OECD (2011b), *OECD Economic Outlook. Interim Assessment*, September 2011, OECD, Paris.

OECD (2011c), *Entrepreneurship at a Glance 2011*, OECD Publishing.

Chapter 3

Basel III and SME Lending: Thematic Focus

This chapter describes the "Basel III" reforms to the global financial system and discusses the possible impacts on lending to SMEs and entrepreneurs. Particular attention is given to the impact that the risk weighting system for assets could have on lending to SMEs. The discussion mainly draws from early evaluations and forecasts developed by countries and international institutions. The perspectives of experts from countries participating in the OECD Scoreboard on SME and entrepreneurship finance are also presented.

Introduction

The need to reform the global financial system to prevent another crisis of the same scope and scale as the recent one has been widely recognised. This thematic chapter describes the reforms regarding minimum capital requirements and the design of new rules for liquidity management – commonly known as "Basel III" – and examines the possible impacts on lending to SMEs and entrepreneurs. The implications of these reforms have been the object of discussion and analytical assessment in different countries and by different international institutions. This chapter discusses the main arguments proposed in these early evaluations and forecasts. The discussion also draws on the perspectives of experts from countries participating in the OECD Scoreboard on SME and entrepreneurship finance, as collected through a survey on the expected impacts of these reforms on access to finance for SMEs and entrepreneurs.

Background on Basel III capital and liquidity standards

The main regulatory reforms developed in response to the recent financial crisis consist of revisions to the rules relating to minimum capital requirements, and the introduction of new ones relating to liquidity management, as defined by the Basel Committee of Bank Supervisors. The objective of the reforms/new standards, widely known as "Basel III", is to improve the banking sector's ability to absorb shocks arising from financial and economic stress, whatever the source, thus reducing the risk of spill-over from the financial sector to the real economy. Basel III extends and complements Basel II by strengthening capital adequacy rules and introducing a new regulatory framework which will apply to liquidity management.

The rationale for these rules stems from the financial crisis that began in 2007, when it became apparent that many banks, despite adequate capital levels, experienced difficulties because they did not manage their liquidity in a prudent manner. Prior to the crisis, asset markets were buoyant and funding was readily available at low cost. The rapid reversal in market conditions illustrated how quickly liquidity can evaporate and that illiquidity can last for an extended period of time (BIS, 2010).

The basics of Basel II and III

Capital adequacy ratio

The most important change affecting capital requirements arising from Basel III is that the minimum capital adequacy ratio, or the ratio of core Tier 1 capital (common equity and retained earnings) to "risk-weighted" assets, will increase from 2% to 7% (Table 3.1). This will comprise a minimum common equity requirement, to be phased in by 2015, and a "capital conservation buffer", to be phased in by 2019.[1]

The "risk-weights" are parameters intended to measure the "riskiness" of assets in bank portfolios, which, under Basel II, are determined by one of two methods: the "standardised" method or the "internal ratings-based method" (IRB), intended for use

Table 3.1. **Minimum capital adequacy ratios**
Ratio of Core Tier 1 capital to risk-weighted assets, per cent

Minimum common equity component	4.5
Capital conservation buffer	2.5
Minimum and conservation buffer	**7**
Countercyclical buffer according to national circumstances	0-2.5
Range for all banks	**7-9.5**
Proposed surcharge for GSIFIs	1-2.5
Range for GSIFIs	**8-12**

mainly by the largest banks. In addition, where national circumstances are believed to warrant it in order to protect the financial system against large swings in asset prices, a counter-cyclical buffer of 0%-2.5% may be added to the ratio. In the case of global systemically important financial institutions (GSIFIs) an additional surcharge of 1%-2.5% has been proposed. Applicability and the amount to be added would depend on the bank's size, interconnectedness, global activity, complexity and availability of competitors to pick up their business in a crisis. This would mean that all banks would have to reach minimum core Tier 1 ratios of 7%-9.5% and the GSIFIs could have even higher ratios.

Banks can meet their ratios by increasing their capital, reducing the average risk-weights that apply to their assets or decreasing their total assets. Given that capital adequacy ratios are to be met by 2019, banks have eight years to gradually build up capital or divest themselves of non-strategic assets.

There are two ways to determine the value of risk-weighted assets (RWAs):

- the standardised approach based on external credit ratings; banks classify their exposures to risk according to various asset classes and, where possible, establish weights based on the credit rating given to the entity by an external credit assessment institution;

- internal ratings-based (IRB) approach: large, sophisticated banks use their own internal risk models to determine appropriate minimum capital depending on estimates of a loan's probability of default, exposure to loss, etc. This gives a modest reduction in capital compared to the standardised approach and risk modelling can be expensive.

The standardised approach uses certain pre-determined weights depending on the entities' external credit rating. For example, the following weights are used against assets that represent claims against corporations and commercial real estate.

Credit rating	AAA to AA-	A+ to A-	BBB+ to B-	Below BB-	Unrated
Risk weight	20%	50%	100%	150%	100%

For retail exposures, that is, loans to individuals and small businesses, the risk weight is 75% if the bank's retail portfolio is diverse and no loan exceeds EUR 1 million, otherwise the risk weight is 100%. In contrast, claims against sovereign governments and central banks with an AAA to AA- rating have a 0% risk weight.

It is likely that smaller banks will opt for the standardised approach rather than the more complicated and costly internal ratings based approach. However, the standardised approach depends on the work of the external credit rating agencies which have come under scrutiny because on their failure to properly assess risk prior to the financial crisis. Some have questioned whether private sector entities, which are dependent on client fees and whose accountability is under scrutiny, should be endorsed in this way by the regulatory system.

Liquidity management rules

While many banks had adequate capital during the recent financial crisis, they did not have adequate liquidity or cash, or the ability to raise cash quickly. In response, rules applying to two new measures of liquidity are being introduced to reinforce the Basel Committee's 2008 principles for sound liquidity risk management and supervision: the *liquidity coverage ratio* and the *net stable funding ratio*.

The liquidity coverage standard requires banks to maintain an adequate level of unencumbered, high-quality liquid assets that can be converted into cash to meet their liquidity needs for a 30 calendar-day time horizon under a significantly severe liquidity stress scenario specified by bank supervisors. Rules will apply to the liquidity coverage ratio, defined as the stock of high-quality liquid assets over total net cash outflows of 30 days. The standard requires that the value of the ratio be no lower than 100%. The liquidity coverage standard will come into effect by 2015.

The net stable funding (NSF) ratio measures the amount of longer-term, stable sources of funding employed by banks, relative to the liquidity profiles of the assets funded and the potential for contingent calls on funding liquidity arising from off-balance sheet commitments and obligations. Rules for the NSF ratio are designed to promote stable sources of funding. Although calibration of these rules is not yet finalised, the time horizon of one year is expected to provide a sustainable maturity structure of assets and liabilities. Rules will become effective in 2018.

The leverage ratio

The *leverage ratio of 3%* is a non-risk-weighted supplementary measure to the risk-based capital adequacy ratios. The ratio of Tier 1 capital to total, *i.e.* un-weighted assets, will be tested in parallel with the risk-based system with a view to making it binding in 2018, based on appropriate review and calibration. If fully implemented, it will provide a simple, easy-to-understand "sanity check" for the results produced by the risk-based framework. The leverage ratio is an additional test of capital adequacy to serve as a "safety net" to protect against problems with risk weightings. It requires a 100% risk-weight treatment of all balance sheet items[2] and includes certain off-balance sheet exposures.

Potential impact on SME lending

The purpose of Basel III is to mitigate and possibly avoid future financial crises. It should be noted that at the time of the recent financial crisis, Basel II had only recently been implemented, and not in all countries. Therefore, its rules had never been tested on a broad scale in a non-crisis environment. If Basel III is implemented, it could have a positive effect on both growth and, as a result, on SME lending. Some argue that SMEs are affected more by financial instability than large firms or households. SMEs are less able to hedge against a financial crisis than large firms, and they cannot rely on public safety nets as households do. SMEs are highly dependent on external finance. Thus, their prosperity might be relatively more dependent on economic and financial stability. According to the 2009 EC/ECB Flash Eurobarometer, almost 60% of SMEs used at least one source of external financing in the previous six months. For example, Figure 3.1 shows that in 2010, 36% of SMEs accessed bank loans and 42% relied on overdrafts/credit lines.

Nevertheless, a number of critics are certain that Basel III will have an impact on enterprise lending. "It is beyond serious dispute that loans and other banking services will become more expensive and harder to obtain under Basel III. The real argument is about the degree, not the direction" (Elliott, 2010). Others are not convinced that this would be so, because central banks could always mitigate the higher interest rates.

Figure 3.1. **Sources of SME external finance, 2010**

As a percentage

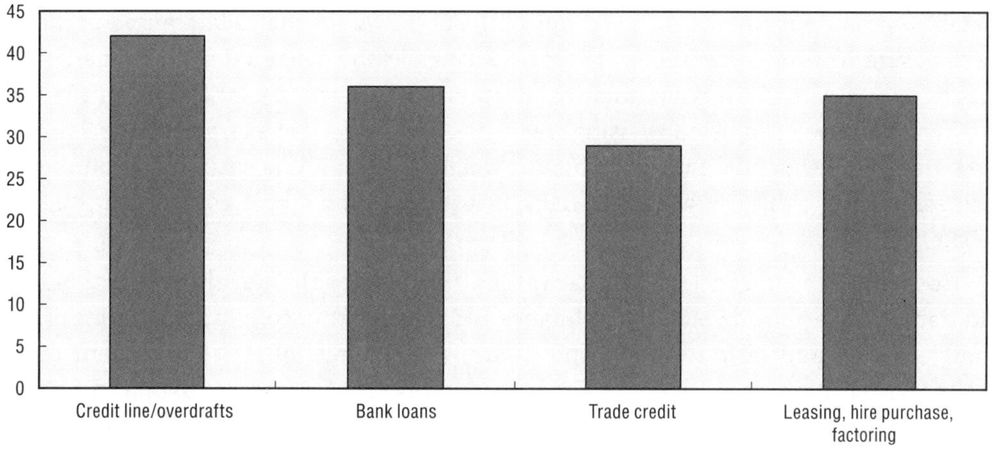

Note: Base = all SMEs (6 941).

Source: ECB/EC Survey on SME access to finance, 2H2010.

StatLink 🔗 http://dx.doi.org/10.1787/888932578600

If the Basel III rules affect enterprise lending, they will affect euro zone enterprises more than US enterprises, since the former rely on banks for 74% of their funding compared to 24% for the latter (ABI, 2011). Problems could arise from the manner in which banks achieve their capital adequacy ratios. Either they can increase capital or decrease their risk-weighted assets. It might be difficult for some banks to raise capital after the financial crisis, and so they might sell off or reduce high risk-weighted or non-strategic assets in order to reduce their total risk-weighted assets (*Financial Times*, 16/11/10). Thus, they would engage in arbitrage, swapping high risk-weighted assets, mainly lending to businesses, for lower ones such as sovereign debt, inter-bank claims and residential mortgages. It should be noted that this scope for arbitraging the risk weights downward implies that there could be no floor for the minimum capital requirements (Atkinson, 2011b).

Impact of the risk weighting system

As Basel III carries over the risk weighting system for assets from Basel II, it retains the capital requirements that are sensitive to risk, which increases the risk premium that banks charge for SMEs. As a result, it exacerbates their well-known financial difficulties (Cardone-Riportella and Trujillo-Ponce, 2007). According to Blundell-Wignall and Atkinson

(2010a, 2010b) the proposals for capital reform – the new Basel III – do not address the fundamental problems with the risk-weighting approach. Since the particular credit risk associated with individual borrowers in different businesses and regions is not well catered for in the analytical framework, it leaves Basel III with the same problem as Basel II: undue reliance on cumbersome supervisory override that has not worked well in the past.

The Basel Committee on Banking Supervision has taken this issue into consideration and made revisions in the formulas for calculating the regulatory capital associated with SME lending.[3] The main modification is that the retail risk rating (75%) can be used to weight SME loans, provided the bank's portfolio is diverse and the bank's loan to an SME borrower is less than EUR 1 million.

Basel III regulations also allow enterprises to make use of collateral and collateral substitutes such as government guarantees, which can reduce or "mitigate" the risk weights. Under the standardised approach the credit rating of the collateral or the guarantor will be substituted for the rating of the borrower for the collateralised portion of the exposure, if certain conditions are met. Specifically, the collateral must be marked-to-market and re-valued every six months. Furthermore, there is a 20% floor on the risk-weight that has been adjusted by using credit-risk mitigation. For example, if the SME loan is secured by a residential property, the risk weight is 35%; if it is secured by commercial business property, the risk weight is 100%; if it is guaranteed by a government, the risk weight could be 0%.

Government guarantees or guarantees from Mutual Guarantee Associations traditionally have helped SMEs access finance and obtain better conditions in terms of rate, credit amount, and term (Camino and Cardone-Riportella, 1999). The current report documents the increase in guarantee funds that has eased SMEs' access to finance in some countries both during and after the crisis. The new banking regulation could increase the use of guarantees. Guaranteed loans can be backed by reduced amounts of regulatory capital when compared with those loans collateralised by assets (financial or not). In fact, guarantees issued by entities with a lower risk weight than the SME can lead to reduced regulatory capital since the protected portion of the SME exposure is assigned the risk weight of the guarantor and the uncovered portion retains the risk weight of the SME. For example, where the guarantor is a sovereign government with an AAA rating, the risk weight for the guaranteed portion of the SME loan would be zero. However, a revision in these ratings to lower levels is under way in some countries, which means that guaranteed SME loans would have to be backed by increased amounts of capital.

The question remains to what degree banks will make increased use of government guarantees as a credit-risk mitigation technique. In the past, government guarantees have been used as a substitute for collateral and, as such, partially improved SME access to credit. However, this report shows that only a small fraction of SME loans have government guarantees. In countries such as the United States, banks have been reluctant to participate in the Small Business Administration's loan guarantee programme, leaving at times large amounts of guarantee funds unused. This could reflect their reluctance in general to service SMEs even when their risks are reduced by guarantees. Basel III could provide an incentive to participate in such programmes, since guarantees would serve the additional purpose of reducing the amount of capital a bank has to hold against an SME loan (see Box 3.1).

Box 3.1. **Credit risk mitigation**

By reducing the risk weight attached to SME loans, guarantees can reduce the amount of capital a bank has to hold against these loans. For instance:

- **Without a guarantee,** a USD 100 000 loan to an SME, with a 75% risk weight, would need to be matched by USD 5 250, that is:

  Value of risk weighted asset (RWA) = USD 100 000 loan × 0.75 = USD 75 000

  Amount of capital the bank has to hold = USD 75 000 RWA × 0.07 (capital adequacy ratio) = USD 5 250

- **With a guarantee for 90% of the loan** from a sovereign government with an AAA rating, the capital the bank is required to hold against the SME loan reduces to USD 525, that is:

  Value of RWA = USD 90 000 guaranteed loan × 0 + USD 10 000 non-guaranteed loan × 0.75 = USD 7 500

  Amount of capital the bank has to hold = USD 7 500 × 0.07 (capital adequacy ratio) = USD 525

However, even with risk mitigation techniques, Basel III still carries over the problems of Basel II in terms of risk weightings. Previous OECD analysis found that the Basel risk-weighting approach in fact encourages portfolio concentrations in low-weighted assets like government bonds, mortgages and lending between banks. There is a continuing incentive to economise on capital and expand business into lower-weighted areas (Blundell-Wignall and Atkinson, 2010a, 2010b). Risk weighting for assets are skewed in favour of sovereign debt, which has a risk weighting of 0% (if rated AAA). This could generate a crowding out effect on private loans, as banks are encouraged to lend to governments rather than to enterprises.

The weighting system also favours many large enterprises over small ones: large companies with good external credit ratings (AAA) are assigned a 20% risk weight, whereas SMEs that are unrated have risk weightings of 100% or 75%. Under Basel III, the difference in core Tier 1 capital the bank needs to hold against their loans is remarkable: 7% of the loan for SMEs with 100% risk weighting, as opposed to 1.4% (7% × 20%) for a large company with an AAA rating.

The Bank Lending Survey undertaken by the European Central Bank (July 2011) finds that banks are already adjusting their capital position or their risk-weighted asset position. Figures 3.2 and 3.3 show that, in 2012, banks intend to build their capital position via retained earnings and divest themselves of the riskier assets.

The Basel Committee's definition of off-balance sheet items includes open lines of credit and trade credit. Under Basel II, such off-balance sheet items are currently put on the balance sheet at 20%. For example, a short term self-liquidating trade letter of credit collateralised by the goods being shipped is put on the balance sheet at 20%. Basel III would raise this conversion factor to 100%. This fivefold increase in the credit conversion factor for trade credit instruments neglects the fact that they are supported by underlying transactions. The most probable result will be a significant restriction in access to trade finance.

Figure 3.2. **Bank adjustments implemented to meet Basel III:**
Capital position, 2011

In net percentage of responding banks

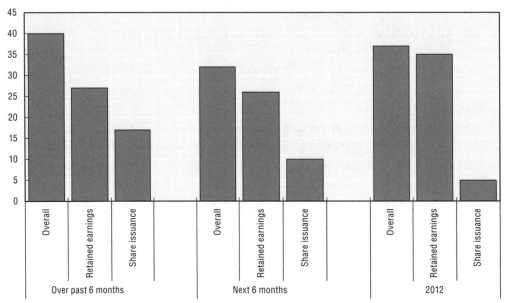

Note: The net percentage is defined as the difference between the shares of banks that reported increasing "considerably" or "somewhat" and the shares of those that reported decreasing "somewhat" or "considerably".

Source: ECB, Bank Lending Survey, July 2011.

StatLink http://dx.doi.org/10.1787/888932578619

Figure 3.3. **Bank adjustments implemented to meet Basel III:**
Risk-weighted assets, 2011

In net percentage of responding banks

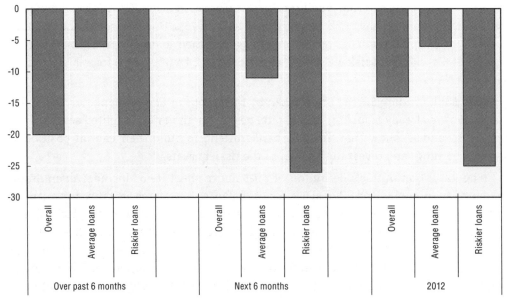

Note: The net percentage is defined as the difference between the shares of banks that reported increasing "considerably" or "somewhat" and the shares of those that reported decreasing "somewhat" or "considerably".

Source: ECB, Bank Lending Survey, July 2011.

StatLink http://dx.doi.org/10.1787/888932578638

Impact of the liquidity coverage ratio

According to liquidity coverage rules, banks must hold sufficient easy-to-sell assets. This will increase the cost of business lines that tie up liquid assets like payment services and foreign trade finance which is low risk (*Financial Times*, 31/12/2010).

The liquidity coverage ratio (LCR) could also push banks to hold more sovereign debt (BIS, December 2010). According to Blundell-Wignall and Atkinson (2010a, 2010b), like the risk weighting system, the LCR has a bias towards government bonds. While budget deficits are large and it may be handy from the viewpoint of interest rate risk to have captured buyers, this process will work against lending to the private sector and particularly to SMEs.

Furthermore, according to the LCR standard, banks must hold liquid assets equal to 100% of undrawn lines of credit that are used for liquidity purposes; 100% liquidity coverage for revolving credit could make this facility more expensive (*Financial Times*, 10/09/10). Business representatives in different countries expressed the business community's concern that liquidity issues will force banks to be more restrictive in terms of credit (*e.g. Financial Times*, 09/08/10; ABI 2011).

A similar concern was expressed by UEAPME, the European Association of Craft, Small and Medium-sized Enterprises, in its comments on the Basel III agreement. While it welcomed the principles underlying the reform, the association warned about the risk of procyclical effects of the regulation. It also urged, when moving to the implementation of Basel III, to respect the specificities of co-operatives and savings banks as regards their capital, in order to limit problems for access to finance for SMEs in many regions of Europe.

The European Union has developed guidelines for the implementation of Basel III, which must be approved by its member countries. These guidelines would apply to 8 200 banks and investment firms. If applied now, the European Commission estimated that there would be a capital shortfall of EUR 460 billion; the cost of borrowing would increase by 0.29% and loan stocks would decline by 1.8%.

The debate at the national level: perspectives from countries in the OECD Scoreboard on SME and entrepreneurship finance

Discussions on the impact of Basel III have been taking place in many countries, informed by quantitative studies that have been undertaken to understand the impacts of the reform on the economy and lending. An OECD questionnaire submitted to experts from the countries participating in this exercise revealed different views on the implications of Basel III for SMEs' access to bank finance. While the sample for this survey was relatively small, its findings nevertheless help to shed light on the potential effects of Basel III on SME lending in the countries monitored.

While some experts expected little or even a positive impact on SME lending, others foresaw more severe effects, particularly on SMEs that are heavily indebted or dependent on bank credit. There was some expectation that the negative effects might be attenuated by a number of factors or would gradually dissipate. For example, the new rules maintain the Basel II risk weightings, under which the banks might be subject to smaller capital charges for loans to small enterprises compared to large enterprises. Since large banks would be most affected, and since SMEs are less likely to use large banks, they may not be overly penalised if small and medium-sized banks continued to lend. Most small and medium-sized banks, with their local roots and close relationships with customers, have a large enough capital base to maintain an adequate flow of funds to their customers. One country expert believed that commercial banks would continue to lend to SMEs because margins were higher than on loans to large enterprises. Finally, some experts stated that their banks were well capitalised and already met the core Tier 1 capital ratio, so that any deposit-taking institutions that needed to raise more capital would likely rely on prudent earnings retention.

In terms of action being taken by banks, on the basis of early assessments and monitoring at the national level, it was reported that they are acting in advance of the promulgation of any national rules implementing Basel III, in effect shortening the transition period. Most are strengthening capital by issuing shares, retaining profits, reducing dividends and disposing of non-strategic assets.

Box 3.2. **The impact of Basel III in Denmark**

The extent to which the new standards will affect Danish credit institutions cannot be precisely calculated before the standards have been finally adopted by the EU. However, IMF studies indicate that the introduction of the Basel III standards could have a relatively large, adverse effect on lending in Denmark going forward. This is due partly to relatively high interest rate elasticity in lending demand and partly to the high net costs associated with raising capital in Denmark. However, Danmarks Nationalbank assesses the capital ratios of Danish credit institutions to be above average compared with the countries included in the analyses, and given the lengthy transitional period, Danmarks Nationalbank assesses that there is scope for the necessary adjustment.

Source: Ministry of Economics and Business Affairs, *Memorandum on Developments in credit availability in Denmark in the second half of 2010*, 29 June 2011.

While none of the governments surveyed have enacted rules to implement Basel III, they have undertaken a number of Basel-related actions. Some have or intend to enact higher capital requirements than required for banks that pose systemic risks. Others are engaging in mitigating the possible negative impacts on SME lending by retaining crisis measures particularly in the area of government guarantees. Some thought that the national financial reforms might have a bigger impact on SME lending than Basel III particularly if the move to separate retail banking from investment banking succeeded.

The results of this small survey are similar to those of other recent reports. Rather than taking the allowed eight years to meet requirements, banks seem to be competing with each other to boost capital and liquidity, possibly in order to retain a good credit rating. Accumulating reserves in the midst of a weak recovery, when bankruptcies are still rising in some countries, could have negative impacts on the growth of the real economy and job creation. Policy makers might want to consider exerting pressure to promote a more gradual approach by banks to meet Basel III standards as specified in the Basel timelines themselves. Even the Basel Macro Assessment Group has suggested that for bank-dependent sectors (like SMEs), a longer implementation period could allow for the development of non-bank lending channels, thus improving the impact of new rules on lending (ACCA, 2011).

Notes

1. Additional requirements will also apply for Tier 1 and total regulatory capital, which include lower quality types of capital, generally debt with "equity-like" characteristics. Once core Tier 1 requirements are met these seem unlikely to pose difficulties for banks or clients such as SMEs.

2. This is subject to the qualification that many derivative positions, mainly for banks using IFRS accounting, can be netted out in a way consistent with Basel II rules.

3. Under the Basel Capital Accords, a company is identified as an SME when the reported sales for the consolidated group of which the firm is part are less than EUR 50 million (Cardone-Riportella *et al.*, 2011).

References

ABI (2011), "Basel 3: corrections needed to avoid the risk of credit restrictions", Associazione Bancaria Italiana, Press release, 20 June.

ACCA (2011), *Framing the debate: Basel III and SMEs*, Association of Chartered Certified Accountants, London.

Atkinson, P. (2011a), "Possible Impact of Basel III on SME Lending", WPSMEE Informal Steering Group on SME and Entrepreneurship Financing and Country Experts, OECD, Paris, 16 September.

Atkinson, P. (2011b), "Basel III in the Global Regulatory Framework", presentation to Banca IMI conference *The Debt Crisis: Different Rules for a Different World*, New York, 20 May.

BIS (2010), *Basel III: International framework for liquidity risk measurement, standards, and monitoring*, Bank for International Settlements, December.

Blundell-Wignall, A. and P. Atkinson (2010a), "Thinking Beyond Basel III: Necessary Solutions for Capital and Liquidity", *OECD Journal*, Vol. 2010, Issue 1.

Blundell-Wignall, A. and P. Atkinson (2010b), "What Will Basel III Achieve", German Marshall Fund of the United States and Groupe d'Économie Mondiale de Sciences Po, November, *http://gem.sciences-po.fr/ content/publications/pdf/Blundell_Atkinson_Basel_III_achievements112010.pdf*.

Camino, D. and C. Cardone-Riportella (1999), "The Valuation and Cost of Credit Insurance Schemes for SME's: the Role of the Loan Guarantee Associations", *International Small Business Journal* 17, 13-31, 1999.

Cardone-Riportella, C. and A. Trujillo-Ponce (2007), "Efectos del aval de las SGRs en la financiación de las PYME y los requerimientos de capital de Basilea II", *Revista Española de Financiación y Contabilidad* 36, 753-85.

Cardone-Riportella, C., A. Trujillo-Ponce and A. Briozzo (2011), "What do Basel Capital Accords Mean for SMEs?", *Working Paper* 10, Business Economics Series 04, University Carlos III de Madrid, April.

Caruana, J. (2003), "Consequences of Basel II for SMEs", *BIS Review* 32/2003.

De Larosiere, J. (2011), "Don't punish the banks that performed best", *Financial Times*, 04/03/11, p. 11.

Dun and Bradstreet (2010), "The Business Impact of Basel III", *Special Report*, October.

Elliott, D., Basel III (2010), "The Banks and the Economy", *Brookings Paper*, July.

Financial Times, "Basel rules spark mitigation drives", 16/11/10, p. 16.

Financial Times, "Liquidity rules to squeeze smaller banks on processing of payments", 31/12/2010, p. 1.

Financial Times, "Basel threat on borrowing", 10/09/10, p. 13.

Financial Times, "Smaller enterprises fear a further retreat in banks' readiness to lend", 10/08/10, p. 7.

Genre, V. (2011), "Impact of Basel III on the lending to SMEs: a first assessment", WPSMEE informal Steering Group on SME and entrepreneurship financing, OECD, Paris, 16 September.

Jenkins, P., "For their health, banks need a holiday away from Basel", *Financial Times*, 09/08/11, p. 14.

Natter, R. (2004), *The Basel II Standardized Approach, Partner*, Barnett Sivon and Natter, Washington, DC.

Parisot, L., "View from the top", *Financial Times*, 09/08/10.

UEAPME (2010), "New Capital Requirements for Banks (Basel III)", Comments from UEAPME, European Association of Craft, Small and Medium-Sized Enterprises, Brussels, 27 October.

Chapter 4

Country Profiles of SME Financing 2007-10

This chapter presents data for debt, equity and financing framework conditions for 18 countries: Canada, Chile, Denmark, Finland, France, Hungary, Italy, Korea, the Netherlands, New Zealand, Portugal, the Slovak Republic, Slovenia, Sweden, Switzerland, Thailand, the United Kingdom and the United States. The chapter is structured around individual country profiles, which include core indicators and the definitions adopted for each indicator at the country level. The statistical information is complemented by a description of trends in SMEs' and entrepreneurs' access to finance and information on government policies addressing SME financing constraints.

Canada

Small business lending

The Canadian statistics are based on SMEs when possible, but in many instances, due to data limitations, the country profile reports on only small businesses with 1-99 employees which represent 98.0% of businesses. As medium-sized enterprises, those with 100-499 employees, only represent 1.7% of Canadian businesses, their exclusion does not have a significant impact on the data or results. In 2010, the Canadian small businesses employed 48.3% of the private sector. Among those employees, 76.3% are employed in the services sector and 23.7% in the goods sector.

Table 4.1. **Distribution of establishments in Canada, 2010**

By size of establishment

Establishment size	Number	%
All establishments	1 096 365	100.0
SMEs (1-499)	1 093 837	99.8
Micro (1-9)	826 775	75.4
Small (10-99)	248 129	22.6
Medium (100-499)	18 933	1.7
Large (500+)	2 528	0.2

Notes: Data exclude the financial sector (NAICS code 52).
Source: Statistics Canada, Business Register, December 2010.

StatLink ᴍᴤ🔊 http://dx.doi.org/10.1787/888932579436

Figure 4.1 shows the major suppliers of small business financing in 2010. Most small business financing (78%) was provided by banks (domestic and foreign), credit unions and caisses populaires. The remainder came from finance companies, financial funds and insurance companies.

Data from supply-side surveys show that while debt outstanding to all businesses peaked in 2008 at CAD 480 billion, lending to SMEs slightly declined that year to CAD 83.3 billion. As a result, the share of outstanding loans to SMEs, which stood at 15.6%, hit the lowest point since 2000. In contrast, in 2009, while total debt outstanding fell, outstanding debt owed by SMEs increased. This resulted in re-establishing the share of SME outstanding debt to 17.9%, a level slightly higher than before the financial crisis. In 2010, there were few changes in levels of both total and SME outstanding debt. When looking at the period 2000-10, debt financing for large businesses grew, while it remained relatively flat for SMEs as seen in Figure 4.2.

Figure 4.1. **Debt financing by source of funding, 2010**

As a percentage

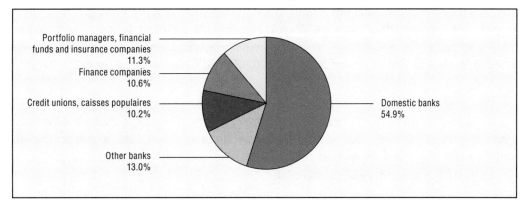

Source: Statistics Canada, Survey of Suppliers of Business Financing 2010.

StatLink ⋙ http://dx.doi.org/10.1787/888932578657

Figure 4.2. **Business debt outstanding in Canada, 2000-10**

In CAD millions

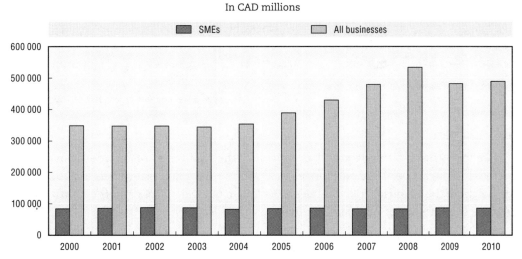

Note: 2000-07 data have been recalculated to ensure comparability with 2008-10 figures following a change in survey methodology.

Source: Statistics Canada, Survey of Suppliers of Business Financing, 2000-10; and Industry Canada.

StatLink ⋙ http://dx.doi.org/10.1787/888932578676

Small business loans authorised vs. requested

Statistics Canada's *Survey on Financing of Small and Medium Enterprises* was conducted in 2007, and was supplemented by Industry Canada's *Credit Conditions Survey* in 2009 and 2010. The results of these demand-side small business financing surveys show that credit conditions improved from 2009 to 2010, with increases recorded in all key indicators: request rate for debt financing (14% to 18%), approval rate (79% to 88%), and ratio of amounts authorised to those requested (76% to 93%).

Small business credit conditions

Despite these favourable indicators from the surveys, other indicators in the Scoreboard on SME and entrepreneurship financing show that small businesses clearly experienced tightened credit conditions during and after the crisis. The average business prime rate, which is typically the rate charged to the most creditworthy borrowers, declined from 6.1% (2007) to 2.6% (2010), while the interest rate for SMEs remained high at 7.5% (2007) and 5.8%[1] (2010). More importantly, the business risk premium (the difference between the average small business interest rate and the business prime rate) increased sharply from 1.4% in 2007 to 3.2% in 2010. The percentage of small businesses that were asked for collateral also increased from 47.7% to 66.7% during the same period.

Equity financing

As in most other OECD countries in this report, equity provided in the form of venture capital decreased between 2007 and 2009 and rose slightly in 2010. The figures for Canada contain early stage and expansion capital. The later stage of acquisition/buyout, turn-around and other stage have been excluded.

Table 4.2. **Venture and growth capital in Canada, 2007-10**

In CAD

Stage	2007	2008	2009	2010
Seed	62 325 000	50 965 000	18 095 000	16 367 000
Start up	201 694 000	151 402 000	211 977 000	119 685 000
Other early stage	500 206 000	383 676 000	228 061 000	317 143 000
Expansion/later stage	1 067 749 000	755 555 000	498 206 000	634 199 000
Total	**1 831 974 000**	**1 341 598 000**	**956 339 000**	**1 087 394 000**

Source: Thomson Reuters, VC Reporter, 2011.

StatLink ᵐᵍ⁵ http://dx.doi.org/10.1787/888932579455

Business insolvencies

Despite these difficult credit conditions, the incidence of business insolvency decreased from 3.1 per 1 000 enterprises in 2008 to 2.2 per 1 000 enterprises in 2010. During the height of the financial crisis, between the fourth quarter of 2008 and the fourth quarter of 2009, the number of business insolvency cases actually decreased by 14.7%. This is contrary to economic expectations. However, this phenomenon can be partially explained by the fact that the demand slump faced by SMEs was less severe than in many other countries. In general, Canadian SMEs are less export-oriented than larger firms, and domestic demand remained relatively strong during the financial and economic crisis, increasing at an average annual rate of 4.2% between 2007 and 2009. This strength in domestic demand benefited SMEs.

It is worth noting that, during the recession, business insolvencies increased in most export-oriented sectors: mining, oil and gas extraction and manufacturing. Additionally, SMEs are traditionally more flexible than large businesses, allowing them to organise different aspects of work more easily to achieve cost reductions. In sum, the flexibility found in the Canadian economy allowed businesses to make gradual adjustments in their cost structure, thereby helping to avoid insolvency.

Government policy response

Together, the Business Development Bank of Canada (BDC), Export Development Canada (EDC) and the Canada Small Business Financing Program (CSBFP) provided financing support to small businesses in the form of direct loans and guaranteed loans of

CAD 5.6 billion in 2007, CAD 5.4 billion in 2008, CAD 6.7 billion in 2009 and CAD 6.0 billion in 2010.

One of the ways the government mitigated the impact of the credit crunch on SMEs was through the creation of the Business Credit Availability Program (BCAP), which allowed the BDC and EDC to provide financing support to businesses with viable business models whose access to finance would otherwise be restricted. By working closely with private sector lenders, this programme filled gaps in market access and leveraged additional lending by private sector institutions. Some of the activities under BCAP include:

- *Export guarantee programme* – A risk-sharing programme introduced in 2009 whereby Export Development Canada (EDC) provides a guarantee to financial institutions in support of the client's financing requirements. The programme addresses various financing needs including working capital, contract specific and capital expenditures.

- *Economic Recovery Loans Programme* – A programme introduced by the BDC in 2010 to provide smaller working capital loans (up to CAD 100 000). This programme expired on 31 October 2010 but drove much of BDC's BCAP activity in 2010.

- *Vehicle Equipment Financing Partnership* – Following the expiry of the BDC's Canadian Secured Credit Facility in March 2010, which helped establish a floor in the asset-backed security (ABS) market, it was found that some smaller finance and leasing companies could not obtain enough financing to meet the growing needs of their customers. In response, the Vehicle Equipment Financing Partnership was implemented by the BDC, with an initial allocation of CAD 500 million in funding. This was done in partnership with experienced lenders and investors in the private market for asset-based financing. The partnership seeks to expand financing options for small and medium-sized finance and leasing companies, increasing the availability of credit at market rates for dealers and users of vehicles and equipment.

From its inception in 2009 to 31 December 2010, EDC and BDC reported CAD 10.12 billion in total activity under the Business Credit Availability Program (BCAP). In the calendar year 2009, the EDC and BDC reported CAD 5.07 billion in BCAP activity and CAD 5.05 billion in 2010, helping businesses across the country and in all sectors of the economy, with a particular focus on small businesses. During 2009 and 2010, nearly all BCAP transactions, 17 718 out of 17 986 total transactions, supported SMEs with less than CAD 25 million in revenues. By value, BCAP deals worth CAD 3.44 billion have been made to SMEs with less than CAD 25 million in revenues. A recent report from the Conference Board of Canada concluded that having the EDC and BDC work closely with private financial institutions under BCAP helped build a bridge to more normal credit conditions.

In addition to increased funding to the EDC and BDC through BCAP, the government has also implemented other measures to help ease the impact of the credit crunch on SMEs, and help SMEs invest for growth during the period of recovery. For example, the maximum eligible loan amount and the ceiling on claims for eligible loan losses were increased under the Canada Small Business Financing Program (CSBFP), a loan loss-sharing programme. The National Research Council's Industrial Research Assistance Program (IRAP) was provided with an additional CAD 200 million over two years to temporarily expand its initiatives for technology-based SMEs and contribute to an innovation-led economic recovery. This included CAD 170 million for contributions to firms, and CAD 30 million to help companies hire over 1 000 new post-secondary graduates in business and science over two years. The BDC was also provided with an additional CAD 475 million over three years for its venture capital activities to allow it to make additional direct investments in technology companies and invest in private, independent Canadian venture capital funds.

Box 4.1. **Definition of small businesses used in Canada's SME and entrepreneurship finance Scoreboard**

Country definition

The national definition is used for certain indicators in the OECD Scoreboard on financing SMEs and entrepreneurs for Canada. It is based on the number of employees: 1-99 employees for small enterprises; 100-499 for medium-sized enterprises; 500 and greater for large enterprises. All data from the demand side are defined based on the number of employees, less than 100.

The SME definition used by financial institutions

The financial definition used in Statistics Canada's *Survey of Suppliers of Business Financing* is based on loan size of less than CAD 1 000 000 for SMEs and more than CAD 1 000 000 for large businesses. This definition is used for the authorised outstanding business loans, total and for SMEs.

Table 4.3. **Financing SMEs and entrepreneurs: Scoreboard for Canada, 2007-10**

Indicators	Units	2007	2008	2009	2010
Debt					
Business loans, SMEs	CAD millions	83 422	83 363	86 428	85 676
Business loans, total	CAD millions	479 793	533 951	482 290	489 480
Business loans, SMEs	% of total business loans	17.4	15.6	17.9	17.5
Short-term loans, small businesses	CAD millions	15 056	..	..	16 230
Long-term loans, small businesses	CAD millions	21 118	..	..	28 470
Total short and long-term loans, small businesses	CAD millions	36 174	..	..	44 700
Short-term loans, small businesses	% of total authorised loans	41.6	..	43.4	36.3
Government guaranteed loans, SMEs	CAD billions	1.2	1.3	1.2	1.3
Direct government loans, SMEs	CAD billions	4.4	4.1	5.5	4.7
Loans authorised, small businesses	CAD millions	34 525	..	..	44 700
Loans requested, small businesses	CAD millions	36 174	..	..	48 100
Ratio of loans authorised to requested, small businesses	%	85	..	76	93
Interest rate, average	%	7.5	..	6.2	5.8
Interest rate, business prime	%	6.1	..	3.1	2.6
Risk premium for small businesses	%	1.4	..	3.1	3.2
Collateral, small businesses	% of SMEs required to provide collateral on last loan	47.7	..	56.1	66.7
Equity					
Venture and growth capital, Investments	CAD billions	1.8	1.3	0.9	1.0
Venture and growth capital, Investments	Year-on-year growth rate, %	n.a.	−33.3	−28.6	11.1
Other					
Bankruptcies, total	Per 1 000 firms	3.1	3.1	2.9	2.2

Sources: Refer to Table 4.4 "Definitions and sources of indicators for Canada's Scoreboard".

StatLink http://dx.doi.org/10.1787/888932579474

Figure 4.3. **Trends in SME and entrepreneurship finance in Canada**

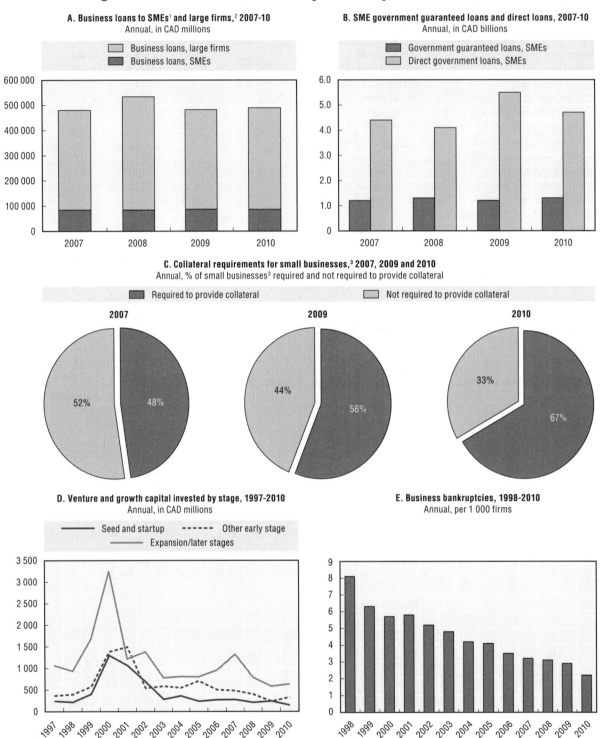

A. Business loans to SMEs[1] and large firms,[2] 2007-10
Annual, in CAD millions

- Business loans, large firms
- Business loans, SMEs

B. SME government guaranteed loans and direct loans, 2007-10
Annual, in CAD billions

- Government guaranteed loans, SMEs
- Direct government loans, SMEs

C. Collateral requirements for small businesses,[3] 2007, 2009 and 2010
Annual, % of small businesses[3] required and not required to provide collateral

- Required to provide collateral
- Not required to provide collateral

2007: 52% / 48%
2009: 44% / 56%
2010: 33% / 67%

D. Venture and growth capital invested by stage, 1997-2010
Annual, in CAD millions

- Seed and startup
- Other early stage
- Expansion/later stages

E. Business bankruptcies, 1998-2010
Annual, per 1 000 firms

1. SME loans defined as loans authorised up to CAD 1 million.
2. Large firm loans defined as those greater than CAD 1 million.
3. Small businesses are defined as firms with 1-99 employees.

Sources: Charts A and C: Statistics Canada. Chart B: Export Development Canada, Business Development Bank of Canada and the Canada Small Business Financing Program. Chart D: Industry Canada VC Monitor. Chart D: Office of the Superintendent of Bankruptcy Canada.

StatLink 🔗 http://dx.doi.org/10.1787/888932578695

Table 4.4. **Financing SMEs and entrepreneurs: Definitions and sources of indicators
for Canada's Scoreboard**

Indicator	Definitions	Sources
Debt		
Business loans, SMEs	Commercial loans to SMEs (defined as the value of amounts authorised up to CAD 1 million), amount outstanding (stocks)	Statistics Canada, 2007-10 Survey of Suppliers of Business Financing
Business loans, total	Commercial loans to all enterprises, amounts outstanding (stocks)	Statistics Canada, 2007-10 Survey of Suppliers of Business Financing
Short-term loans, small businesses	Operating line (short-terms loans, 12 months or less, lines of credit, credit cards), flows. Small businesses are enterprises with 1-99 employees.	Statistics Canada, 2007 Survey on Financing of Small and Medium Enterprises and Industry Canada, 2009 and 2010 Supplementary Survey on Credit Conditions
Long-term loans, small businesses	Term loan (more than 12 months) or mortgage, flows. Small businesses are enterprises with 1-99 employees.	Statistics Canada, 2007 Survey on Financing of Small and Medium Enterprises and Industry Canada, 2009 and 2010 Supplementary Survey on Credit Conditions
Government guaranteed loans, SMEs	Guaranteed loans for SMEs, flows from central government. SMEs are defined as enterprises with annual sales (turnover) lower than CAD 5 million.	Administrative data from Export Development Canada, Business Development Bank of Canada and the Canada Small Business Financing Program
Direct government loans, SMEs	Direct loans to SMEs, flows from central government. SMEs are defined as enterprises with annual sales (turnover) lower than CAD 25 million.	Administrative data from Export Development Canada and Business Development Bank of Canada
Loans authorised, small businesses	Flows – all small business loans. Small businesses are enterprises with 1-99 employees.	Statistics Canada, 2007 Survey on Financing of Small and Medium Enterprises and Industry Canada, 2009 and 2010 Supplementary Survey on Credit Conditions
Loans requested, small businesses	Flows –all small business loans. Small businesses are enterprises with 1-99 employees.	Statistics Canada, 2007 Survey on Financing of Small and Medium Enterprises and Industry Canada, 2009 and 2010 Supplementary Survey on Credit Conditions
Interest rate, average	Average annual interest rate for all new small business loans, base rate plus risk premium; includes credit card.	Statistics Canada, 2007 Survey on Financing of Small and Medium Enterprises and Industry Canada, 2009 and 2010 Supplementary Survey on Credit Conditions
Interest rate, business prime	The chartered banks' rates on prime business loans are the interest rates charged to the most creditworthy borrowers.	Bank of Canada, Banking and Financial Statistics
Risk premium for small businesses	Difference between interest rate paid by small business and business prime. Small businesses are enterprises with 1-99 employees.	Bank of Canada, Banking and Financial Statistics
Collateral, small businesses	Percentage of small businesses that were required to provide collateral to secure their latest loan. Small businesses are enterprises with 1-99 employees.	Statistics Canada, 2007 Survey on Financing of Small and Medium Enterprises and Industry Canada, 2009 and 2010 Supplementary Survey on Credit Conditions
Equity		
Venture and growth capital	Actual amounts of venture and growth capital invested. Includes seed, start up, early stage and expansion. All enterprises.	Thompson Reuters Canada, Industry Canada VC Monitor
Other		
Bankruptcies, total	Business insolvency is defined as the number of bankruptcy and proposal cases. All enterprises.	Office of the Superintendent of Bankruptcy Canada

Notes

1. Average interest rate paid by small businesses between January 2010 and December 2010.

Chile

SME lending

In Chile, 99% of all enterprises are SMEs. They employ 57% of the business sector labour force, and 77% of SMEs are microenterprises, 19% are small and 3% are medium-sized.[1] Although the usual definition of an SME is based on the annual sales of the enterprise, the financial sector uses a definition based on the loan amount, as indicated in Box 4.2. The share of SME loans in total business loans increased during the years 2007-10, from 16.7% to 18.2%. The share of SMEs' short-term loans in total SME loans was 60% (2010), indicating that loans were mainly being used to resolve cash flow problems in the production cycle or during the course of business. There was a noticeable decrease in the proportion of SMEs' non-performing loans in total SME loans, from 7.1% (2009) to 6.6% (2010).

Table 4.5. **Distribution of enterprises in Chile, 2010**
By size of enterprise

Enterprise size (annual sales)	Number	%
All enterprises	**798 073**	**100.0**
SMEs (up to UF 100 000)	**786 940**	**98.6**
Micro (up to UF 2 400)	616 702	77.3
Small (UF 2 400 to UF 25 000)	148 194	18.6
Medium (UF 25 000 to UF 100 000)	22 044	2.8
Large (UF 100 000+)	11 133	1.4

Note: Data include all industries and non-employer enterprises.
Source: Ministerio de Economia de Chile, 2012.

StatLink ⟪🖳⟫ http://dx.doi.org/10.1787/888932579493

Loans utilised compared to authorised

The indicator "loans utilised *vs.* loans authorised" is calculated with the information from the *Longitudinal Survey of Enterprises* and it provides data on the number of enterprises that received and requested one or more loans during the years 2006-08.[2] The ratio of loans authorised to loans requested for SMEs was 61.1%, and for large firms 98.8%, indicating the existence of a gap between SMEs' and large firms' access to credit. SMEs faced credit rationing because they could not meet the credit requirements of financial institutions.

SME credit conditions

In October 2008, banks tightened lending conditions (higher spreads on loans, higher collateral requirements and smaller loans) due to the international financial crisis, and they gradually normalised them by mid-2009 (Cowan and Marfan, 2010). According to the last supply-side survey on *General Conditions and Standards in the Credit Market*, conducted by the Central Bank of Chile in June 2011, business loans for all enterprises have more flexible conditions. Of the banks surveyed, 23% reported better credit conditions for SMEs: lower spreads and an increase in the financing credit lines for these clients. However, for large firms, 18% of the banks increased their collateral requirements. Also, 70% of the banks surveyed said that there was an increase in the demand for new business loans due to the greater need for working capital and higher fixed asset investments, both for SMEs and large enterprises.

There were no data on interest rates for the years 2007-09, and the only data available were for the year 2010, when the nominal interest rate spread between SMEs and large enterprises in 2010 was 5.4% for short-term loans, and 8.3% for long-term loans.[3] There are no data available on collateral requirements for the whole period.

Equity financing

Total equity financing investment fell drastically between 2008 and 2009 due to the negative effects of the global financial crisis. Most of this decrease was in later stage investment. In Chile, the private equity market has different sources of funding for the different stages of investment. Seed capital, angel investment (currently there are six networks of angel investors in Chile), and expansion capital receive support from CORFO (the Corporation for the Development of Production or the government economic development agency), through different support programmes of CORFO-Innova. The maturity stage is financed by the private sector, and it was most affected by the financial crisis. In 2010, the government launched a new programme to provide CLP 40 000 in start-up equity to entrepreneurs with new business ideas.

Table 4.6. **Formal flows of venture and growth capital investment in Chile, 2007-09**

By stage of investment, in CLP billions

Stages	2007	2008	2009
Seed capital	3.4	3.9	2.8
Angel investors	1.8	1.9	1.8
Expansion	24.7	23.6	21.0
Subtotal for venture capital	*29.8*	*29.4*	*25.5*
Maturity	24.3	51.7	9.5
Total	**54.1**	**81.1**	**35.0**

Source: Innova Chile, CORFO, SVS. Extracted from Echecopar and Rogers (2011).

StatLink ⬛ᵐˢ▱ *http://dx.doi.org/10.1787/888932579512*

Payment delays

Payment delays are low in Chile, and they improved between 2009 and 2010 for both SMEs and large firms. The average number of days of payment delays reduced for SMEs from 5 to 4.4 days, and for large firms from 1.2 to 0.8 days.

Government policy response

SME government loan guarantees and government guaranteed loans

Government loan guarantees are offered by two institutions: Banco Estado, a commercially-oriented government bank, and CORFO, which depends on the Ministry of Economy. Banco Estado provides a public guarantee fund named FOGAPE (guarantee fund for small business) for micro and small enterprises. CORFO also provides different lines of financing for SMEs through its microcredit and loan guarantee programmes: FOGAIN (a guarantee fund for investment loans), COBEX (guarantee for exports) and SME debt restructuring.[4] These loan guarantees partially guarantee credits issued by commercial banks. Credit evaluation is fully delegated to the banks by Banco Estado and CORFO.

Although during the period 2007-10 there was an important increase in government guarantees and in the loans guaranteed, the average coverage decreased from 71% (2007) to 64% (2010), probably due to an increase in the amount of the loans.

SME government direct lending

Government direct lending for SMEs is provided through INDAP (*Institute for the Development of Agriculture and Livestock*) and is focused on micro and small enterprises in the agricultural sector. Most of the loans are short-term loans, and the share of the long-term loans in total loans decreased between 2007-10 from 34% to 29%.

Figure 4.4. **Value of direct government loans from INDAP, 2007-10**

In CLP millions

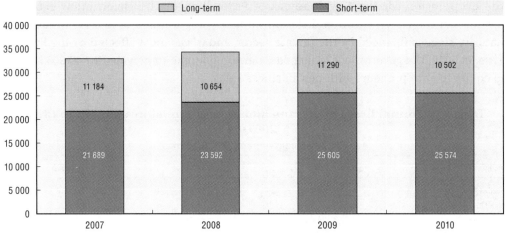

Source: Innova Chile, CORFO, SVS. Extracted from Echecopar and Rogers (2011).

StatLink ᔕᔕᔕ http://dx.doi.org/10.1787/888932578714

However, the number of new loans decreased during this period, from 47 720 (2007) to 43 807 (2010), which means that the average amount of the loans increased.

Finally, it is interesting to note that the average interest rates of these direct government loans were lower than the average interest rates in the financial market. In 2010, the average annual interest rate for short-term loans of INDAP was 5.87% *vs.* 7.5%; and for long-term loans INDAP's average interest rate was 6.99% *vs.* 13.1%.[5]

Table 4.7. **Number of new direct government loans in Chile, 2007-10**

	Short-term	Long-term	Total
2007	32 809	14 911	47 720
2008	30 566	12 583	43 149
2009	33 775	12 449	46 224
2010	31 741	12 066	43 807

Source: INDAP.

StatLink ᔕᔕᔕ http://dx.doi.org/10.1787/888932579531

Box 4.2. **Definition of SMEs used in Chile's SME and entrepreneurship finance Scoreboard**

Country definition

In Chile, the Law No. 20.416 establishes the criteria to define the size of a firm. These refer to the annual sales of the firm:

Size	Annual Sales (in UF)[1]
Micro-enterprise	Less than UF 2 400
Small	From UF 2 400 to UF 25 000
Medium	From UF 25 000 to UF 100 000
Large	More than UF 100 000

1. UF (*Unidad de Fomento*) is a unit of account that is adjusted to inflation. Thus, its real value remains constant. The UF of 31 July 2011 is CLP 21 947.23. SMEs in Chile are firms with annual sales up to UF 100 000.

Definition of SMEs used by financial institutions

Financial institutions define SMEs by the loan size. This definition is related to the debt that the firm has in the financial system. The amount of the loan (debt) used for this categorization is the maximum historic value available for each firm.

Size	Loan (Debt) Size (in UF)[1]
Micro loan	Less than UF 500
Small loan	From UF 500 to UF 4 000
Medium loan	From UF 4 000 to UF 18 000
Large loan	From UF 18 000 to UF 200 000
Mega loan	More than UF 200 000

1. UF (*Unidad de Fomento*) is a unit of account that is adjusted to inflation so its real value remains constant. The UF of 31 July 2011 is CLP 21 947.23. For financial institutions SMEs are firms with loans up to UF 18 000.

Source: Superintendency of Banks and Financial Institutions (SBIF).

Table 4.8. **Financing SMEs and entrepreneurs: Scoreboard for Chile, 2007-10**

Indicator	Units	2007	2008	2009	2010
Debt					
Business loans, SMEs	CLP millions	6 811 534	7 578 831	8 101 937	8 817 987
Business loans, total	CLP millions	40 905 328	49 889 809	46 293 290	48 379 040
Business loans, SMEs	% of total business loans	16.7	15.2	17.5	18.2
Short-term loans, SMEs	CLP millions	..	..	..	1 675 690
Long-term loans, SMEs	CLP millions	..	..	..	1 115 611
Total short and long-term loans, SMEs	CLP millions	..	..	..	2 791 301
Short-term loans, SMEs	% of total short and long-term SME loans	..	..	..	60
Government loan guarantees, SMEs	CLP millions	202 780	300 411	732 629	985 930
Government guaranteed loans, SMEs	CLP millions	284 405	490 267	1 182 495	1 531 928
Direct government loans, SMEs	CLP millions	32 873	34 246	36 896	36 077
Loans authorised, SMEs	Number of firms	..	147 655	..	..
Loans requested, SMEs	Number of firms	..	241 733	..	..
Ratio of loans authorised to requested, SMEs	%	..	61.1	..	..
Loans authorised, large firms	Number of firms	..	4 204	..	..
Loans requested, large firms	Number of firms	..	4 256	..	..
Ratio of loans authorised to requested, large firms	%	..	98.8	..	..
Non-performing loans, total	CLP millions	..	..	1 145 259	1 051 228
Non-performing loans, SMEs	CLP millions	..	..	576 629	583 289
Share of non-performing loans in total business loans	%	..	..	2.5	2.2
Share of non-performing SME loans in total SME business loans	%	..	..	7.1	6.6
Short-term interest rate, SMEs	%	..	..	..	7.5
Short-term interest rate, large firms	%	..	..	..	2.1
Short-term interest rate spread	%	..	..	..	5.4
Long-term interest rate, SMEs	%	..	..	..	13.1
Long-term interest rate, large firms	%	..	..	..	4.7
Long-term interest rate spread	%	..	..	..	8.3
Equity					
Venture and growth capital	CLP billions	29.8	29.4	25.5	..
Venture and growth capital	Year on year growth rate, %	n.a.	−1.3	−13.3	..
Other					
Payment delays, total enterprises	Weighted average number of days	..	..	1.9	1.5
Payment delays, SMEs	Weighted average number of days	..	..	5.0	4.4
Payment delays, large enterprises	Weighted average number of days	..	..	1.2	0.8

Sources: Refer to Table 4.9 "Definitions and sources of indicators for Chile's Scoreboard".

StatLink 🔗 http://dx.doi.org/10.1787/888932579550

Figure 4.5. **Trends in SME and entrepreneurship finance in Chile**

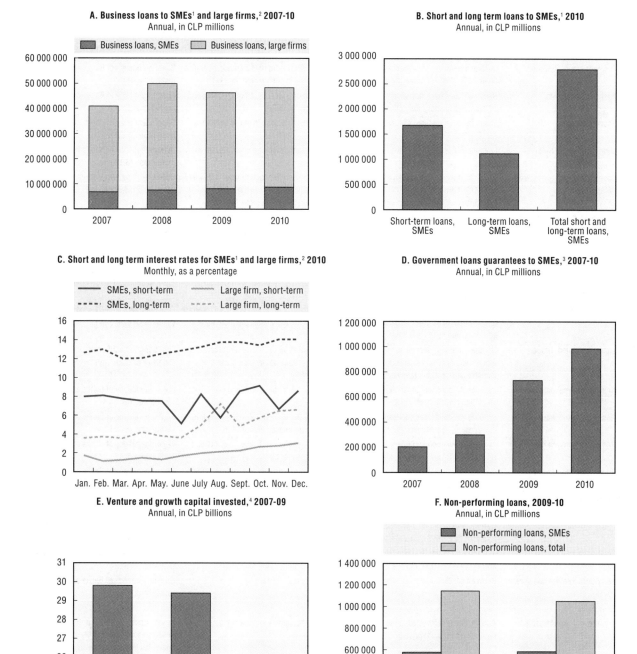

1. Loans up to UF 18 000.
2. For loans over UF 18 000.
3. Loans to micro and small agribusinesses.
4. Includes seed capital, angel financing and expansion capital.

Sources: Charts A, B, C and F: Superintendency of Banks and Financial Institutions (SBIF). Chart D: CORFO (Corporación de Fomento Productivo) and Banco Estado. Chart E: Innova Chile, CORFO and Superintendencia de Valores y Seguros-SVS.

StatLink ᵐˢᵖ http://dx.doi.org/10.1787/888932578733

Table 4.9. **Financing SMEs and entrepreneurs: Definitions and sources of indicators for Chile's Scoreboard**

Indicator	Definition	Source
Debt		
Business loans, SMEs	Business loans to SMEs (defined as loans up to UF 18 000) from banks and co-operative financial institutions under the supervision of SBIF (amount outstanding, stocks).[1]	Superintendency of Banks and Financial Institutions (SBIF)
Business loans, total	Business loans to all non-financial enterprises, amount outstanding, stocks. (Banks and co-operative financial institutions under the supervision of SBIF).	Superintendency of Banks and Financial Institutions (SBIF)
Short-term loans, SMEs	Loans to SMEs (defined as loans up to UF 18 000) equal to or less than one year (new loans).	Superintendency of Banks and Financial Institutions (SBIF)
Long-term loans, SMEs	Loans to SMEs (defined as loans up to UF 18 000) for more than one year (new loans).	Superintendency of Banks and Financial Institutions (SBIF)
Government loan guarantees, SMEs	Guarantees available to banks and financial institutions (new loan guarantees). FOGAIN and COBEX are provided by CORFO and FOGAPE by Banco Estado. SMEs are defined as enterprises with annual sales up to UF 100 000 or annual exports up to UF 400 000.	CORFO (Production Promotion Corporation) and Banco Estado
Government guaranteed loans, SMEs	Loans guaranteed by government (flows). These loans are guaranteed by different types of guarantees, provided by CORFO (Production Promotion Corporation) and Banco Estado. SMEs are defined as enterprises with annual sales up to UF 100 000 or annual exports up to UF 400 000.	CORFO (Corporación de Fomento Productivo) and Banco Estado
Direct government loans, SMEs	Direct loans from the Institute of Agricultural Development (INDAP), to micro and small agribusinesses (flows). INDAP's definition of SME loans is enterprises with less than 12 hectares and capital up to UF 3 500.	INDAP (Instituto de Desarrollo Agropecuario), Ministry of Agriculture.
Loans authorised, SMEs	Number of SMEs (defined as enterprises with annual sales up to UF 100 000) that received one or more loans during the years 2006-08. Does not include the fishing industry and education and health and social work sectors.	First Longitudinal Survey of Enterprises (Ministry of Economy)
Loans requested, SMEs	Number of SMEs (defined as enterprises with annual sales up to UF 100 000) that requested one or more loans during the years 2006-08. Does not include the fishing industry and education and health and social work sectors.	First Longitudinal Survey of Enterprises (Ministry of Economy)
Non-performing loans, total	Includes all loans that are in default (one day or more), from banks and financial institutions under supervision of SBIF.	Superintendency of Banks and Financial Institutions (SBIF)
Non-performing loans, SMEs	Includes all SMEs loans (defined as loan amounts up to UF 18 000) that are in default (one day or more), from banks and financial institutions under supervision of SBIF.	Superintendency of Banks and Financial Institutions (SBIF)
Short-term interest rate, SMEs	Average annual nominal rate for new loans, for maturity up to 1 year and amounts up to UF 18 000. (This is a weighted average by amount of the loan).	Superintendency of Banks and Financial Institutions (SBIF)
Short-term interest rate, large firms	Average annual nominal rate for new loans, for maturity up to 1 year and amounts more than UF 18 000. (This is a weighted average by amount of the loan).	Superintendency of Banks and Financial Institutions (SBIF)
Short-term interest rate spread	Between small and large enterprises; for maturity up to 1 year.	Superintendency of Banks and Financial Institutions (SBIF)
Long-term interest rate, SMEs	Average annual nominal rate for new loans, for maturity more than 1 year and amounts less than UF 18 000. (This is a weighted average by amount of the loan).	Superintendency of Banks and Financial Institutions (SBIF)
Long-term interest rate, large firms	Average annual nominal rate for new loans, for maturity more than 1 year and amounts more than UF 18 000. (This is a weighted average by amount of the loan).	Superintendency of Banks and Financial Institutions (SBIF)
Long-term interest rate spread	Between small and large enterprises; for maturity more than 1 year.	Superintendency of Banks and Financial Institutions (SBIF)
Equity		
Venture and growth capital	Annual amounts invested in the country (includes seed capital, angel financing, expansion). All enterprises.	Innova Chile, CORFO and Superintendencia de Valores y Seguros-SVS (the Chilean securities and insurance supervisor)
Other		
Payment delays, total enterprises	Weighted average of the unpaid amount of the loan and the number of days of delay. Three ranges of delay are considered: 1) Less than 30 days, 2) 30 days and less than 90 days, and 3) 90 days and more; the final result, for each year, is the sum of the weighted average of each range. Σ Xi*NDD, where i = range: 1, 2, and 3; X = share of the unpaid amount in total loans, and NDD = number of days of delay	Superintendency of Banks and Financial Institutions (SBIF)

Table 4.9. **Financing SMEs and entrepreneurs: Definitions and sources of indicators for Chile's Scoreboard** (cont.)

Indicator	Definition	Source
Payment delays, SMEs	Weighted average of the unpaid amount of the loan and the number of days of delay. SME loans are defined as loan amounts up to UF 18 000. Three ranges of delay are considered: 1) Less than 30 days, 2) 30 days and less than 90 days, and 3) 90 days and more; the final result, for each year, is the sum of the weighted average of each range. $\Sigma\, Xi^*NDD$, where i = range: 1, 2, and 3; X = share of the unpaid amount in total loans, and NDD = number of days of delay	Superintendency of Banks and Financial Institutions (SBIF)
Payment delays, large enterprises	Weighted average of the unpaid amount of the loan and the number of days of delay. Large enterprise loans are defined as loan amounts over UF 18 000. Three ranges of delay are considered: 1) Less than 30 days, 2) 30 days and less than 90 days, and 3) 90 days and more; the final result, for each year, is the sum of the weighted average of each range. $\Sigma\, Xi^*NDD$, where i = range: 1, 2, and 3; X = share of the unpaid amount in total loans, and NDD = number of days of delay	Superintendency of Banks and Financial Institutions (SBIF)

1. UF (Unidad de Fomento) is a unit of account that is adjusted to inflation so its real value remains constant. The UF of 31 July 2011 is CLP21 947.23. See Box 4.2 for the definition of SMEs used by financial institutions.

Notes

1. The data does not include the fishing industry and the education and health and social work sectors (ISIC Rev. 3: B M, and N).

2. It is important to note that the information is for the whole period and not only for one year.

3. This is for nominal interest rates. The spread for real interest rates is: 1.6% for short-term loans and 0.8% for long-term loans.

4. In 2011 CORFO introduced some changes in their guarantee programs: FOGAIN, which was oriented to guarantee loans for investment, now includes guarantees for working capital; COBEX, which was oriented to exports, now includes imports.

5. Nominal interest rates.

References

Banco Central de Chile (2011), "Encuesta sobre Condiciones Generales y Estándares en el Mercado de Crédito Bancario", June, Santiago, Chile.

Banco Central de Chile (2010), "Informe de Estabilidad Financiera". December, Santiago, Chile.

Cowan, K. and M. Marfán (2011), "The Evolution of Credit in Chile", BIS Papers, No. 54, December.

Echecopar, G. and A. Rogers (2011), Capital de Riesgo en Chile, Editorial Andrés Bello, Santiago, Chile.

Ministerio de Economía de Chile (2010), "Primera Encuesta Longitudinal de Empresas", December, Santiago, Chile.

Denmark

SME lending

In 2007, SMEs comprised almost all enterprises in Denmark (99.7%). Monetary financial institutions' (MFI) lending to SMEs, approximated by loans which amount to less than EUR 1 million, declined by around 30% between 2007 and 2009. SME lending recovered in 2010, registering a 23% increase. However, the total volume of lending was still well below pre-crisis levels. Total business loans declined in both 2009 and 2010. The share of SME loans in total business loans was small (12%) in Denmark, and it declined even further during the recession. As could be expected, the share of SME short-term loans in total SME loans increased over the crisis as SMEs sought financing to remedy liquidity problems. Short-term interest rates declined relative to longer-term interest rates.

Table 4.10. **Distribution of enterprises in Denmark, 2007**
By size of enterprise

Enterprise size (employees)	Number	%
All enterprises	212 129	100.0
SMEs (1-249)	211 406	99.7
Micro (1-9)	184 556	87.0
Small (10-49)	22 823	10.8
Medium (50-249)	4 027	1.9
Large (250+)	723	0.3

Note: Data include total industry and market services including NACE Categories C, D, E, F, G, H, I and K. Non-employer enterprises are not included.
Source: OECD Structural and Demographic Business Statistics Database.

StatLink ᴬᴵᴸᴾ http://dx.doi.org/10.1787/888932579569

Statistics Denmark undertook a survey of SMEs' access to financing as part of a Eurostat survey. It indicated that the smallest businesses applied for financing to a larger extent in 2010 than in 2007, but that significantly fewer obtained the full loan amount requested. Other surveys by the Confederation of Danish Industry and the Danish Federation of Small and Medium-Sized Enterprises indicated that SMEs still considered it difficult to obtain financing in 2010, and that this restrained output. For example, in December 2010, the Confederation of Danish Industry stated that 37% of SMEs reported that the financing situation had become more difficult or much more difficult compared with the pre-crisis period. This difficult situation is expected to continue. According to the bank lending survey conducted by the Danish Central Bank, credit institutions have maintained the tight credit policies introduced at the end of 2008 and the beginning of 2009. Banks also stated that they reduced their exposures in 2010 compared with 2009, and that they wished to reduce them further. Looking forward, international financial reforms and increased capital requirements for credit institutions are expected to be

Table 4.11. **Share of enterprises that applied for financing in Denmark according to growth record, 2007 and 2010**

As a percentage of total in each category

	SMEs	High-growth start ups	High-growth	Other enterprises
2007	35	47	44	34
2010	44	57	54	42

Source: Statistics Denmark.

StatLink 🔝 http://dx.doi.org/10.1787/888932579588

passed on to enterprises, which will have to comply with strict solvency requirements in order to obtain financing.

The per cent of SMEs applying for finance increased from 35% to 44% between 2007 and 2010. Of the 44% of SMEs that applied for finance in 2010, 23% were rejected. The chances of rejection were higher for smaller businesses. The Ministry of Economic and Business Affairs has analysed the relation between SMEs' ability to obtain a loan and a number of financial ratios derived from their financial statements. It found that SMEs that obtain loans have higher EBIT margins, a higher return on equity and lower gearing than SMEs that only partly obtained loans or were rejected.

Table 4.12. **Result of loan applications by size of firm in Denmark, 2010**

As a percentage

Result	% of SMEs that applied	5-9 workers	10-49 workers	50-99 workers	100-249 workers
Fully obtained	69	63	69	69	75
Partly obtained	24	25	23	28	22
Rejected	23	21	24	24	13

Source: Statistics Denmark.

StatLink 🔝 http://dx.doi.org/10.1787/888932579607

Credit conditions

Although existing rates are very low, interest rate spreads between loans to small enterprises and large enterprises increased from around 1 percentage point to 3 percentage points, because interest rates on loans larger than EUR 1 million declined more compared with interest rates on smaller loans. Credit institutions introduced stricter collateral and documentation requirements for all enterprises (OECD, 2010). According to the Danish Central Bank's bank lending survey, MFIs imposed higher prices and increased collateral requirements in late 2008 and the beginning of 2009. This is also reflected in MFI reports from 2009 and 2010, which state that in performing a credit assessment of enterprises, focus on the security provided for the loans and the development in the value of the security has been enhanced. They also stated they have increased their monitoring of SMEs' financial statements and their ability to generate the cash required to continue their operations. In addition, SMEs' clients demanded extended credit during the year. Thus, SMEs' liquidity was squeezed, on the one hand by their clients, and on the other hand by the MFIs, which offered poorer loan terms on renegotiation of loans.

Equity financing

According to the European Venture Capital Association data base, early-stage venture capital financing fell by more than half in 2009 and continued to decline in 2010.

Other indicators

The fact that SMEs were under stress is shown in the statistics for payment delays and bankruptcies. Payment delays increased from a low of 6.1 days to a high of 12 days. At the same time, bankruptcies increased two and a half times between 2007 and 2010.

Government policy response

In September 2009, the government introduced a package which improved SME financing and export opportunities by strengthening loan guarantees, get-started loans, export guarantees and improving access to risk capital for new businesses.

The scheme for loan guarantees to small and medium-sized enterprises was increased by DKK 1.5 billion until the end of 2010. In April 2010, the loan guarantee scheme was extended to the primary sector businesses and investments in commercial construction. It has been agreed to extend the scheme until the end of 2011. In 2009, utilised guarantee commitments totalled DKK 113.5 million, triggering total lending to 46 businesses of just over DKK 151 million. The demand increased significantly in 2010 and, at 31 December 2010, 492 applications for a total loan amount of DKK 1.2 billion had been received. Commitments for DKK 873 million were provided to 336 businesses, and 235 businesses utilised their guarantees for a total amount of DKK 512 million in 2010. This increase was due, in part, to the fact that since April 2010, it has been possible to grant loan guarantees for assets against which mortgage credit loans may be obtained and for the primary sector. A similarly high level of commitments for new loan guarantees is expected for 2011.

The "Get started loans" combine loan guarantees and consultancy schemes for new businesses. Loans of up to DKK 1 million may be granted with 75% guaranteed by the government. The scheme is intended to provide entrepreneurs with easier access to loans and credits with banks. At the same time, entrepreneurs are offered consultancy services before and after financing has been granted to make them better equipped to run their business. By 2010, "Get Started Loans" totalling DKK 87 million had been granted.

The Danish official export credit agency, EKF, offers a range of products aimed at SME and export businesses. Export guarantees are a temporary guarantee scheme for working credits and development loans for Danish export businesses. EKF may issue guarantees of DKK 2 billion. The scheme implies that EKF will be able to guarantee up to 80% in connection with export businesses' and their subcontractors' working credits and development loans raised with banks. By 2010, the liability under the scheme was DKK 650 million of the total guarantee of DKK 2 billion. A reinsurance scheme supports export transactions with short credit periods. The reinsurance solves the problems enterprises face when trying to obtain payment insurance for export transactions with private credit insurers. The demand for government reinsurance has been high. Almost 450 export businesses have signed up for the scheme. The guarantee liability totalled DKK 1.6 billion at 31 December 2010. EKF estimates that this scheme covers exports worth DKK 4-5 billion annually.

Finally, in January 2011, the government concluded an agreement with the pension sector to provide risk capital in the amount of DKK 5 billion to SMEs with growth potential. Together with this, the government has established three loan and guarantee schemes. This will strengthen the market for risk capital with up to DKK 10 billion over the coming years.

Table 4.13. **Financing SMEs and entrepreneurs: Scoreboard for Denmark, 2007-10**

Indicators	Units	2007	2008	2009	2010
Debt					
Business loans, SMEs	DKK millions	40 847	35 235	28 458	34 981
Business loans, total	DKK millions	332 336	385 286	317 460	312 638
Business loans, SMEs	% of total business loans	12.3	9.1	9.0	11.2
Short-term loans, SMEs	DKK millions	26 426	26 274	22 423	22 668
Long-term loans, SMEs	DKK millions	14 421	8 961	6 035	12 313
Total short and long-term loans, SMEs	DKK millions	40 847	35 235	28 458	34 981
Short-term loans, SMEs	% of total short and long-term SME loans	64.7	74.6	78.8	64.8
Government loan guarantees, SMEs	DKK millions	130.5	93.8	117.8	515.6
Interest rate, SMEs	%	6.57	7.59	5.77	5.22
Interest rate spread	%	0.89	1.93	3.33	2.65
Equity					
Early-stage venture capital	EUR millions	199.8	186.0	88.0	69.4
Early-stage venture capital	Year-on-year growth rate, %	n.a.	−6.9	−52.7	−21.1
Other					
Payment delays	Average number of days	7.2	6.1	12.0	12.0
Bankruptcies, total	Number	2 401	3 709	5 710	6 461
Bankruptcies	Year-on-year growth rate, %	n.a.	54.5	53.9	13.2
Bankruptcies	Per 10 000 firms	24	46	55	n.a.

Sources: Refer to Table 4.14 "Definitions and sources of indicators for Denmark's Scoreboard".

StatLink ⟶ http://dx.doi.org/10.1787/888932579626

Figure 4.6. **Trends in SME and entrepreneurship finance in Denmark**

A. Business loans to SMEs[1] and large firms,[2] 2007-10
Annual, in DKK millions

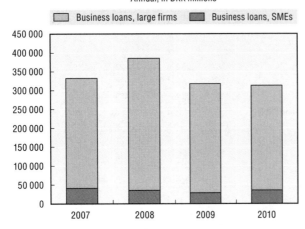

B. Short and long-term loans to SMEs,[1] 2007-10
Annual, as a percentage

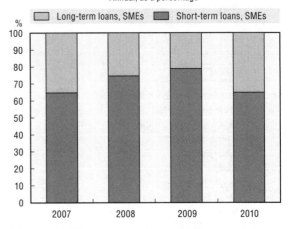

C. Interest rates for SMEs,[1] and interest rate spread, 2007-10
Quarterly, as a percentage

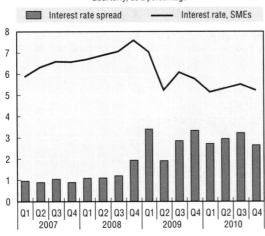

D. Government loan guarantees to SMEs, 2007-10
Annual, in DKK millions

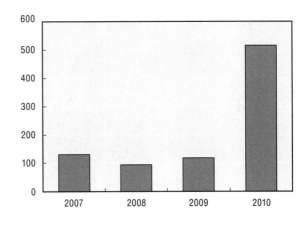

E. Early-stage venture capital invested, 2007-10
Annual, in DKK millions

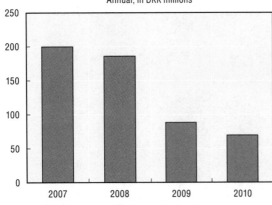

F. Bankruptcies, 2007-10
Quarterly, number of enterprises ruled bankrupt

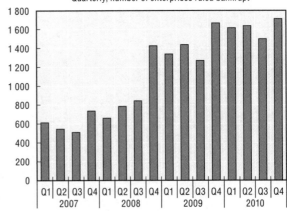

1. For loans up to EUR 1 million.
2. For loans over EUR 1 million.

Sources: Charts A, B and C: Nationalbanken. Chart D: Vækstfonden. Chart E: EVCA. Chart F: Statistics Denmark.

StatLink http://dx.doi.org/10.1787/888932578752

Table 4.14. **Financing SMEs and entrepreneurs: Definitions and sources of indicators for Denmark's Scoreboard**

Indicator	Definition	Source
Debt		
Business loans, SMEs	New loans (flows), loan amounts up to EUR 1 million.	Nationalbanken
Business loans, total	New loans (flows).	Nationalbanken
Short-term loans, SMEs	New lending amount up to EUR 1 million, interest rate fixation up to and including 1 year.	Nationalbanken
Long-term loans, SMEs	New lending amount up to EUR 1 million, interest rate fixation above 1 year.	Nationalbanken
Government loan guarantees, SMEs	Loans guaranteed by government, stocks or flows for firms with up to 250 employees.	Vækstfonden
Interest rate, SMEs	Average annual rates for new loans, base rate plus risk premium; for maturity less than 1 year; and amounts up to EUR 1 million.	Nationalbanken
Interest rate spread	Between small and large enterprises; for maturity less than 1 year; amounts up to EUR 1 million and equal to or greater than EUR 1 million.	Nationalbanken
Equity		
Early-stage venture capital	Actual amounts invested in Denmark in early stage development.	EVCA
Other		
Payment delays	Average number of days for business-to-business in 2008, 2009 and 2010. For 2007, average number of days for business-to-business, business-to-customer and public entities. All enterprises.	Intrum Justitia, European Payment Index 2008, 2009 and 2010
Bankruptcies, total	Number of enterprises ruled bankrupt.	Statistics Denmark
Bankruptcies (per 10 000 enterprises)	Number of bankrupt enterprises per 10 000 enterprises.	Statistics Denmark

References

OECD (2010), "Assessment of government support programmes for SMEs' and entrepreneurs' access to finance in the global crisis", OECD, Paris.

Ministry of Economy and Business Affairs (2011), "Developments in credit availability in Denmark in the second half of 2010", 29 June.

Ministry of Economy and Business Affairs (2011), "Developments in credit availability in Denmark in the first half of 2010", 11 January.

Finland

SME lending

In 2010, 99.4% of all firms in Finland were SMEs (107 934 SMEs), and they employed approximately 60% of the labour force. More than 83% were micro-enterprises with less than 1-9 employees. Total business loans decreased over three years (2007-09) but rebounded in 2010. SME loans declined even faster between 2007 and 2009 and experienced no rebound in 2010. Thus, their share of business loans plummeted from 27.1% (2007) to 14.4% (2010).[1] This indicates that SMEs faced tougher credit conditions than larger enterprises causing some of these SMEs to seek government assistance. As would be expected during a recession, there was a larger drop-off in SME long-term loans than in short-term loans. Their share in SME loans declined from 78.9% (2007) to 74% (2010).

Table 4.15. **Distribution of firms in Finland, 2010**
By size of firm

Firm size (employees)	Number	%
All firms	**108 548**	**100.0**
SMEs (1-249)	**107 934**	**99.4**
Micro (1-9)	91 099	83.9
Small (10-49)	14 514	13.4
Medium (50-249)	2 321	2.1
Large (250+)	**614**	**0.6**

Notes: Data include all industries (exluding primary production sectors) and exclude non-employer firms.
Source: Statistics Finland (Finnish enterprises [e-publication] and Labour force survey [e-publication]).

StatLink 🔗 http://dx.doi.org/10.1787/888932579645

SME authorised loans compared to requested loans

The amount of SME loans authorised declined over the 2007-10 period. The total amount of new SME loans authorised was EUR 9.9 billion in 2009 and EUR 7.8 billion in 2010. At the same time, the percentage of SMEs requesting loans moved in the opposite direction and increased from an average of 23% to 29%-30% depending on the sector. While the supply of SME loans declined, the percentage of SMEs seeking loans increased. Therefore, the decline in loan supply cannot be attributed to lack of demand. The comparison of loans authorised to loans requested is thought to be a good indicator of credit rationing. If this indicator is combined with the declining SME loan share, it is clear that SMEs were being denied financing while larger firms had easier access.

SME credit conditions

In reviewing interest rates, the base rate on small loans of up to EUR 1 million declined as a result of monetary policy. At the same time, the interest rate spreads between small and large loans increased. It appears that the collateral requirement was one of the biggest obstacles SMEs faced when seeking new loans. The percentage of SMEs reporting less favourable terms in accessing new loans increased from 5% to a high of 28% in 2009 but declined to 24% in 2010.

Equity financing

There was a drastic decline in venture and growth capital investment in 2008-09 which started to reverse in 2010, but has not yet regained its pre-crisis level.

Table 4.16. **Venture and growth capital investment in Finland, 2007-10**

By stage of investment, EUR millions

Type	2007	2008	2009	2010
Seed	19	11	11	5
Start-up	20	51	46	54
Other early stage	33	52	27	37
Expansion/growth	168	69	30	87
Total	**240**	**183**	**114**	**183**

Note: Total excludes buyout, turnaround and replacement capital.
Source: Finnish Venture Capital Association.

StatLink http://dx.doi.org/10.1787/888932579664

Other indicators

The average payment delays in Finland were historically low compared to some other countries before the crisis. Finnish firms have a strong payment discipline, which they maintained during the crisis. Their behaviour was reinforced by a law which requires late paying companies or public institutions to pay a debtor fee and interest on the unpaid amount. Bankruptcy proceedings for all enterprises increased from 0.9% to 1.2% in 2009, revealing the impact of the credit crunch and lack of liquidity. However, this impact was also seen in the results of a survey on solvency undertaken by the Confederation of Finnish Industries. The overall credit crunch contributed to SME cash flow problems, which resulted in increasing solvency problems for the SMEs. Short-term solvency problems normally involve 5-8% of SMEs. However, during the height of the crisis, 21% of SMEs on average reported problems and 15% reported difficulties during the recovery period (January 2011), which significantly exceeded what could be expected. Solvency problems in

Table 4.17. **Incidence of solvency problems in Finland, June 2009-May 2011**

By size of firm, as a percentage of firms within size class

Size of firm, employees	2009		2010			2011	
	June	September	January	May	August	January	May
1-4	33	39	31	30	36	27	n.a.
5-9	23	21	16	20	16	14	28[1]
10-49	19	19	20	18	17	14	13
50-249	13	12	10	10	8	10	11
Average	21	21	20	18	17	15	17

1. Including all firms with less than 10 employees.
Source: Confederation of Finnish Industries.

StatLink http://dx.doi.org/10.1787/888932579683

the case of Finnish SMEs declined as firm size grew. This is another indication that larger firms experienced fewer liquidity problems. For firms of all sizes, solvency problems abated thanks to the government response described below. However, in the 5-9 employees category, solvency problems rose dramatically in mid-2011.

Government policy responses

SME counter-cyclical loans and guarantees

Finnvera is a financing company owned by the government of Finland and it is the official export credit agency of Finland. Finnvera provides financing for the start up, growth and internationalisation of enterprises and guarantees against risks arising from exports. The company acquires its funds mainly from the capital market. Total government loan guarantees increased from EUR 1 491 million (2007) to over EUR 4 000 million annually (2008-10). The financial crisis increased the SME demand for public financing, and the number of SMEs applying to Finnvera grew by 12% in 2009. SME loans and guarantees granted by Finnvera increased from EUR 801 million (2007) to EUR 1 067 million (2009). As part of its recovery strategy, Finnvera introduced counter-cyclical loans and guarantees. The greatest use for such loans and guarantees was to finance working capital. Counter-cyclical loans were intended for enterprises with less than 2 000 employees whose profitability or liquidity declined because of the crisis. These loans will continue until the end of 2011. Despite this, the level of Finnvera's assistance declined in 2010 to almost pre-crisis levels (EUR 844 million), of which EUR 105 million was in counter-cyclical financing for 303 enterprises. Without such public financing, the number of job losses would have been twice as high as actual job losses (23 700) in 2009 and 2010.

Table 4.18. **SME loans and guarantees granted by Finnvera, 2007-10**

In EUR millions

Instrument	2007	2008	2009	2010
Loans	385	468	593	397
Guarantees	416	438	474	447
Subtotal	*801*	*906*	*1 067*	*844*
Export guarantees	96	122	127	71
Total	**897**	**1 027**	**1 195**	**914**

Note: SMEs refer to firms with less than 250 employees.
Source: Finnvera, *Annual Reports* 2009 and 2010.

StatLink ⟶ http://dx.doi.org/10.1787/888932579702

Finnvera offers both export guarantees and export credit guarantees. An export guarantee allows exporters to acquire pre- or post-delivery financing from a bank for working capital. An export credit guarantee covers the risks related to buyers' defaults. Finnvera's export credit guarantee programme dwarfs its other forms of assistance to enterprises. Export credit guarantees offered amounted to 72% (EUR 2 380 million) of total assistance compared to 28% (EUR 914 million) for loans, domestic guarantees and export guarantees offered. Export credit guarantees cover 6% of Finland's total exports. Of the total export credit guarantees offered (EUR 2 380 million), SMEs accounted for EUR 100.3 million.

Table 4.19. **SME export credit guarantees in Finland, 2007-10**

In EUR millions

	2007	2008	2009	2010
Offered	38.3	76.8	79.6	100.3
In effect	43.3	43.0	73.8	79.7

Source: Finnvera, *Annual Report* 2010.

StatLink http://dx.doi.org/10.1787/888932579721

Finnvera's subsidiary, Veraventure LTD, invests in regional venture capital funds. Finnvera also makes direct investments in early stage innovative enterprises via Seed Fund Vera Ltd. At the end of 2010, the Seed Fund Vera Ltd. had investments in 127 enterprises.

Experience during the recovery period

The fact that the recovery was weak in 2010 was confirmed in that the most pressing problems for many SMEs were competition and finding customers, rather than access to finance, according to the demand survey of 485 Finnish SMEs undertaken by the European Central Bank/European Commission. Nevertheless, a large percentage of those surveyed had made use of external finance in the last six months.

Table 4.20. **Use of external finance by SMEs in Finland in the last six months, 2H 2010**

Type of finance	% of firms using finance	No. of firms using finance	No. of firms applying for finance
Trade credit	44	213	19
Leasing	37	179	–
Bank loan	27	131	63
Bank overdraft	17	82	10
Equity	5	24	–

Source: European Central Bank and European Commission.

StatLink http://dx.doi.org/10.1787/888932579740

Of the SMEs interviewed by the ECB/EC, 27% had used bank loans during the 2H2010, and 12% of SMEs had access to subsidised loans. Table 4.20 gives a breakdown of the type of finance sought and used. 21% of SMEs thought the willingness of banks to provide a loan had improved, while only 7% thought it had deteriorated. This is in contrast to the finding of the Confederation of Finnish Industries survey issued in May 2011, where 14% of SMEs surveyed encountered difficulties to access finance. In the ECB/EC survey, 50% of SMEs seeking finance encountered higher interest rates and 31% increased collateral requirements. It is probable that in the long run, the share of SMEs having major financing difficulties will remain higher than before the crisis (around 4-6%).

> ## Box 4.3. **Definition of SMEs used in Finland's SME and entrepreneurship finance Scoreboard**
>
> **Country definition**
>
> SMEs in Finland are firms with less than 250 employees. In 2010, there were 107 934 SMEs in Finland (excluding non-employer firms). This is 99.4% of all firms.
>
> **The SME definition used by financial institutions**
>
> Bank of Finland statistics report SME loans by the size of loan up to EUR 1 million. However, when dividing SME loans to short-term and long-term loans, the size of firm is used for the estimations made based on the annual joint survey undertaken by the Confederation of Finnish Industries, the Bank of Finland and the Ministry of Employment and the Economy. The table below shows for each indicator whether the size of firm or size of loan was used.
>
> | Indicator | SME definitions |
> | --- | --- |
> | Business loans, SMEs | Size of loan (up to EUR 1 million) |
> | Short-term loans, SMEs | Size of firm (with less than 250 employees) |
> | Long-term loans, SMEs | Size of firm (with less than 250 employees) |
> | Value of government guaranteed loans, SMEs | Size of firm (with less than 250 employees) |
> | Loans authorised, SMEs | Size of loan (up to EUR 1 million) |
> | Loans requested, SMEs | Size of firm (with less than 250 employees) |
> | Interest rate, loans < EUR 1 million | Size of loan (up to EUR 1 million) |
> | Interest rate spread | Size of loan (up to EUR 1 million *vs.* EUR > 1 million) |
> | Collateral, SMEs | Size of firm (with less than 250 employees) |

Table 4.21. **Financing SMEs and entrepreneurs: Scoreboard for Finland, 2007-10**

Indicators	Units	2007	2008	2009	2010
Debt					
Business loans, SMEs	EUR millions	11 576	11 881	9 944	7 761
Business loans, total	EUR millions	42 698	54 368	50 850	53 724
Business loans, SMEs	% of total business loans	27.1	21.9	19.6	14.4
Short-term loans, SMEs	EUR millions	1 500	2 000	2 100	1 612
Long-term loans, SMEs	EUR millions	5 600	5 100	5 000	4 588
Total short and long-term loans, SMEs	EUR millions	7 100	7 100	7 100	6 200
Short-term loans, SMEs	% of total loans	21.1	28.2	29.6	26.0
Value of government guarantees, total	EUR millions	1 491	4 507	4 490	4 048
Value of government guarantees, SMEs	EUR millions	416	438	474	447
SME government guarantees	% of SME business loans	3.6	3.7	4.8	5.8
Direct government loans, SMEs	EUR millions	385	468	593	397
Loans authorised, SMEs	EUR millions	11 576	11 881	9 944	7 761
Loans requested, SMEs	% of SMEs requesting loans during last 12 months	23	26-31	29-30	29
Non-performing loans, total	EUR millions	132	210	341	339
Interest rate, loans < 1 million	%	5.39	5.58	3.02	2.70
Interest rate, loans > 1 million	%	4.83	5.08	2.24	1.86
Interest rate spread (between loans < 1 million and > 1 million)	%	0.56	0.50	0.78	0.84
Collateral, SMEs	% of SMEs required to provide increased collateral	5	16	28	24
Equity					
Venture and growth capital	EUR millions	240	183	114	183
Venture and growth capital	% annual growth rate	. .	−59.0	0.6	60.5
Other					
Payment delays	Average number of days	6	5	7	7
Bankruptcies, total	% of firms in bankruptcy proceedings	0.9	1.0	1.2	1.0

Sources: Refer to Table 4.22 "Definitions and sources of indicators for Finland's Scoreboard".

StatLink ▰ﯮ▱ http://dx.doi.org/10.1787/888932579759

Figure 4.7. **Trends in SME and entrepreneurship finance in Finland**

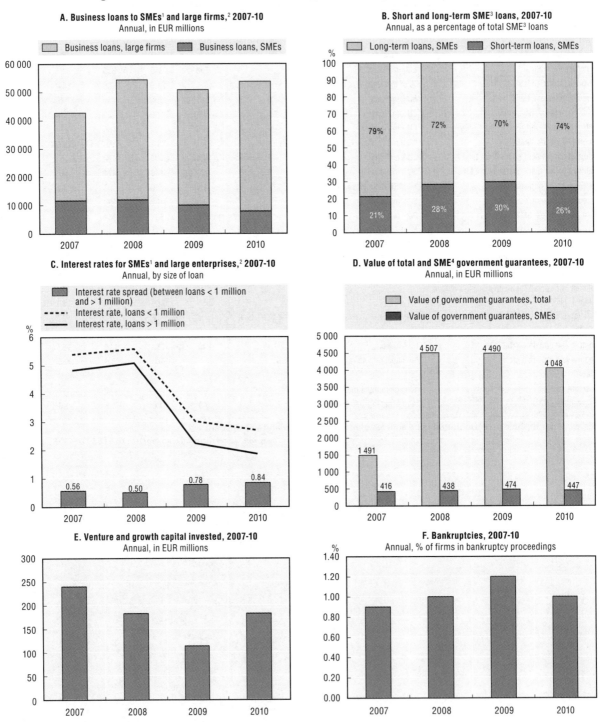

1. For loans up to EUR 1 million.
2. For loans over EUR 1 million.
3. Based on estimates for firms with less than 250 employees.
4. Value of guarantees granted by Finnvera to firms with less than 250 employees.

Sources: Charts A and C: Bank of Finland. Chart B: Estimate by Confederation of Finnish Industries EK based on the joint survey undertaken by EK, Bank of Finland and Ministry of Employment and the Economy, Annual Business Financing Survey. Chart D: Statistics Finland and Finnvera. Chart E: The Finnish Venture Capital Association. Chart F: Statistics Finland.

StatLink ᴍᴤᴘ http://dx.doi.org/10.1787/888932578771

Table 4.22. **Financing SMEs and entrepreneurs: Definitions and sources of indicators for Finland's Scoreboard**

Indicators	Definition	Source
Debt		
Business loans, SMEs	New business loans up to EUR 1 million; including renegotiated loans and loans to housing corporations. Lines of credit are excluded.	Bank of Finland (demand and supply-side surveys)
Business loans, total	New business loans from all financial institutions.	Bank of Finland (supply-side survey)
Short-term loans, SMEs	Working capital loans for up to one year. Estimate of SME loans, which are defined as loans to firms with less than 250 employees. Excludes loans to housing corporations.	Estimate by Confederation of Finnish Industries EK based on the joint survey undertaken by EK, Bank of Finland and Ministry of Employment and the Economy, Annual Business Financing Survey
Long-term loans, SMEs	Loans for over one year. Estimate of SME loans, which are defined as loans to firms with less than 250 employees. Excludes loans to housing corporations.	Estimate by Confederation of Finnish Industries (see above)
Value of government guarantees, total	All new guarantees to SMEs and large firms for which the state is ultimately liable. Includes guarantees granted by Finnvera.	Statistics Finland
Value of government guarantees, SMEs	Value of guarantees granted to SMEs (defined as firms with less than 250 employees) by Finnvera.	Finnvera
Direct government loans, SMEs	Loans granted to SMEs (defined as firms with less than 250 employees) by Finnvera.	Finnvera
Loans authorised, SMEs	New loans granted to SMEs (defined as loans up to EUR 1 million).	Bank of Finland, Finnish MFI new business on euro-denominated loans to euro area non-financial corporations by loan amount
Loans requested, SMEs	Percentage of SMEs (defined as firms with less than 250 employees) that requested loans during the last 12 months.	Confederation of Finnish Industries, Bank of Finland and Ministry of Employment and the Economy; SME-Barometer by Federation of Finnish Enterprises and Finnvera
Non-performing loans, total	All non-performing business loans, including housing corporations. A loan is non-performing if principal and/or interest have remained unpaid for 3 months or longer.	The Financial Supervisory Authority
Interest rate, loans < 1 million	Average interest rates for SMEs (defined as loans up to EUR 1 million), initial rate fixation of up to and over 1 year, base rate plus risk premium.	Bank of Finland.
Interest rate, loans > 1 million	Average interest rates on loans over EUR 1 million, initial rate fixation of up to and over 1 year, base rate plus risk premium	Bank of Finland.
Interest rate spread (between loans < 1 million and > 1 million)	Interest rate spread between new, euro-denominated business loans less than and more than EUR 1 million to euro area non-financial corporations by Finnish MFIs with an initial fixation rate up to and over one year.	Bank of Finland.
Collateral, SMEs	Percentage of SMEs (defined as firms with less than 250 employees) which reported increased collateral requirements.	Confederation of Finnish Industries, Bank of Finland and Ministry of Employment and the Economy
Equity		
Venture and growth capital	Invested capital; seed, start-up, other early stage, expansion by private investment companies. All enterprises.	The Finnish Venture Capital Association
Other		
Payment delays	Average number of days for business-to-business in 2008, 2009 and 2010. For 2007, average number of days for business-to-business, business-to-customer and public entities. All enterprises.	Intrum Justitia, European Payment Index 2008, 2009 and 2010
Bankruptcies, total	Percentage of firms which are in bankruptcy proceedings.	Statistics Finland

Notes

1. According to the Bank of Finland, "the MFI data collection scheme was revised as of June 2010, and hence the figures published are not totally comparable with earlier observations. The differences may be due to improved data collection accuracy, revised statistical definitions (*e.g.* extending the definition of overdrafts and credit card credit to include revolving credits) and the collection of detailed data from all MFIs." (Bank of Finland, *www.suomenpankki.fi*, November 2011)

France

SME lending

There are roughly 2.5 million SMEs in France. They account for 99.8% of all enterprises and employ 60.5% of the labour force. Both total business loans and SME loans increased over the period 2007-10. This includes both drawn (utilised) and undrawn (not utilised) loans. However, the year-on-year growth rates declined during the recession. The share of SME loans in total business loans stood at 26.2%, the same level as in 2010. The share of SME drawn short-term loans in total SME drawn loans decreased from 21.7% (2007) to 17.7% (2010).

Table 4.23. **Distribution of enterprises in France, 2007**

By size of enterprise

Enterprise size (employees)	Number	%
All enterprises	**2 566 290**	**100.0**
SMEs (1-249)	**2 561 180**	**99.8**
Micro (1-9)	2 386 241	93.0
Small (10-49)	151 826	5.9
Medium (50-249)	23 113	0.9
Large (250+)	**5 110**	**0.2**

Note: Data include total industry and market services including NACE Categories D, E, F, G, H, I and K. Non-employer enterprises are not included.
Source: OECD Structural and Demographic Business Statistic Database.

StatLink ᵐˢᵖ http://dx.doi.org/10.1787/888932579778

Figure 4.8. **Growth rates of bank loans to all firms in France, 2007-11**

Year-on-year growth rate, as a percentage

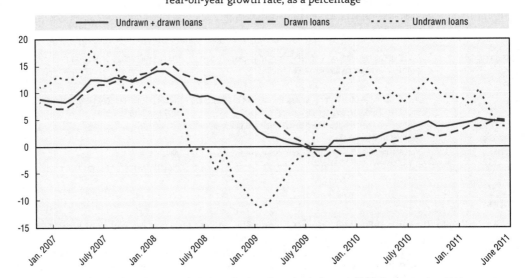

Source: Bank of France, Companies Directorate, Central credit register, data available in September 2011.

StatLink ᵐˢᵖ http://dx.doi.org/10.1787/888932578790

The Bank of France has broken business loans into various categories including: microenterprises and independent SMEs, SMEs belonging to a group, large enterprises and holdings. When analysing SME lending by type of SME, lending to independent SMEs and to SMEs in a group showed positive growth between 2007 and 2010.

SME loans utilised compared to authorised

SME loans drawn compared to authorised declined slightly to about 88% over the period 2007-10. Nevertheless, this figure of 88% indicated a high degree of utilisation and a tight credit market. Other supplementary information can be gathered from periodic supply-side surveys such as the *Enquête trimestrielle auprès des banques sur la distribution du crédit en France* from the Banque de France. The majority of the respondents (77.6%) thought there was a more severe tightening in the credit criteria for all enterprises and an even larger balance of respondents (82.6%) thought it more severe for SMEs than for large enterprises in 3Q08. By 2Q09 a smaller balance of respondents (16.4%) still felt there was a severe tightening for SMEs. In terms of the demand for credit in 2Q09, the balance of respondents felt that it was decreasing more for large enterprises than for SMEs. By 4Q09 a minority of respondents (3.4%) felt that the demand for credit by SMEs and large firms had begun to rise and 28.9% felt that credit conditions were easing.

SME credit conditions

The above opinions were borne out by the comparison of interest rates charged for large loans *vs.* small. Not only did small borrowers pay more, but Figure 4.11 shows that the spread increased between July 2008 and July 2009, even as rates were declining. The spread diminished between July 2009 and April 2011, though it still remains considerably higher than pre-2008 levels.

Figure 4.9. **Credit conditions for SMEs in France and the euro area (supply side survey), 2007-11**

Change in credit conditions to SMEs (balance of opinion), as a percentage

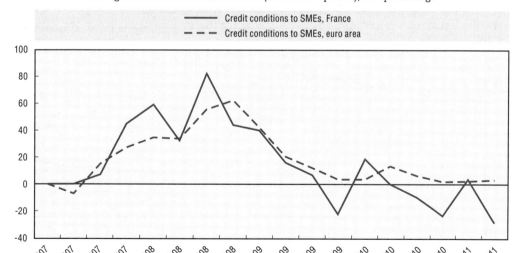

Sources: Bank of France (DGS-DSMF) and ECB (BLS survey).

StatLink ⟰ *http://dx.doi.org/10.1787/888932578809*

The European Central Bank/European Commission demand-side survey on SME credit conditions revealed that bank rejection rates in France declined from 12% in the first half of 2009 to 10% in the second half of 2010. This could be evidence that the French credit mediation scheme was bearing positive results.

Figure 4.10. **Credit demand for SMEs in France and the euro area (supply side survey), 2007-11**

Change in demand for credit from SMEs (balance of opinion), as a percentage

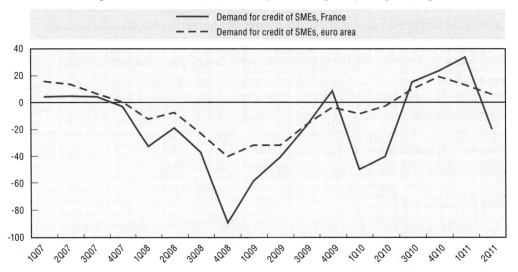

Sources: Bank of France (DGS-DSMF) and ECB (BLS survey).

StatLink ᵐᵉ http://dx.doi.org/10.1787/888932578828

Figure 4.11. **Interest rates in France, 2007-11**

By size of firm, as a percentage

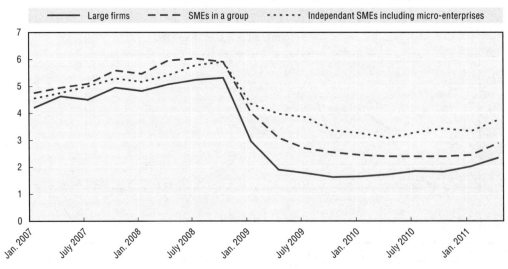

Source: Bank of France, Companies Directorate.

StatLink ᵐᵉ http://dx.doi.org/10.1787/888932578847

Equity financing

The value of venture and expansion capital invested appears to have recovered from its low in 2002 and reached EUR 2 915 million in 2010. However, this was a mere fraction of SME debt financing.

Table 4.24. **Private equity investment in France, 2005-10**

By stage of investment, in EUR millions

Stage	2005	2006	2007	2008[1]	2009	2010
Venture capital	481	536	677	758	587	605
Expansion capital	895	1 057	1 310	1 653	1 798	2 310
Sub-total	*1 376*	*1 593*	*1 987*	*2 411*	*2 385*	*2 915*
LBO	6 287	8 075	10 340	7 399	1 605	3 512
Turnaround capital	59	95	84	99	84	90
Others	349	401	143	100	26	80
Total investment	**4 253**	**3 796**	**5 660**	**3 164**	**2 782**	**3 967**

1. Investment in the enterprises of the CAC40 since 2008.

Source: Association française des investisseurs en capital (AFIC)/Grant Thornton.

StatLink ᕫᑭ *http://dx.doi.org/10.1787/888932579797*

Other indicators

Payment delays measured in terms of the duration of the suppliers' payment period decreased by 6.1% between 2007 and 2009. It appears that the *Modernization of the Economy Act of 2008*, which required the reduction of payment periods, was having an effect.

Insolvencies for SMEs *other than microenterprises* grew by 13.1% in 2009. While SMEs represented 94% of all bankruptcies in 2010, they declined by 3.5%.

Figure 4.12. **Changes to supplier and client payment delays for SMEs in France, 1999-2009**

Average delay, client delays expressed in days of sales and supplier delays expressed in days of purchasing

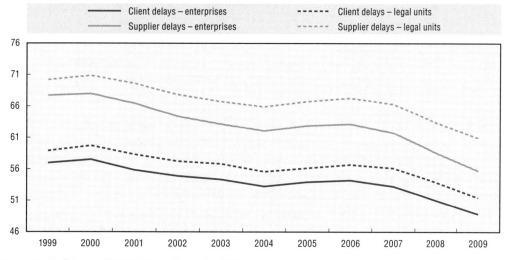

Source: Bank of France, *FIBEN Database*, December 2010.

StatLink ᕫᑭ *http://dx.doi.org/10.1787/888932578866*

Government policy response

As bankruptcies for all enterprises were on the rise in 2008 and 2009, the government adopted specific measures to finance SMEs and created a credit mediation service to promote SMEs' access to credit.

The most significant measure by far was the injection of funds into OSEO Garantie, which is funded by the government (58.3%) and the private sector (41.3%). It provides guarantees, co-financing, direct loans, and support for innovation and services. It also guarantees risk capital funds. Among OSEO's traditional beneficiaries were micro-businesses (46.5%), small (31%) and medium-sized (17.5%) enterprises. OSEO is known for its tough selection procedures and technical support, which underpin its financing activities. Between October and December 2009, the government strengthened OSEO by:

- increasing its lending capacity to banks;
- increasing guarantee volumes;
- opening a credit line for short term funds by guaranteeing SMEs short term loans;
- increasing eligibility for firms with up to 5 000 employees;
- increasing the coverage of the guarantee to 90%; and
- providing equity financing loans for a period of 5-7 years but with no guarantee.

As a result, OSEO's capacity for intervention increased by EUR 10 billion and guaranteed loans increased 64%. OSEO estimated that 50% of the enterprises they had supported were saved from bankruptcy and 30 000 jobs had been saved throughout France (OSEO, 2009a, 2009b). The OSEO guarantees allowed more than 73 000 enterprises to obtain EUR 11.5 billion in financing in 2010 (Observatoire du financement des enterprises, 2011).

Table 4.25. **Measures to finance SMEs in France**

Measure	Amount
Reimbursement of the tax to finance research	EUR 3.8 billion
Reimbursements of fines or overpayments	EUR 1.8 billion
Monthly reimbursement of VAT	EUR 3.6 billion
Accelerated depreciation	EUR 0.7 billion
Faster payment for public procurement	EUR 1 billion
Payment of debts to suppliers of Min. of Defence	EUR 0.5 billion
Injection of funds to OSEO for supplementary loans and guarantees to SMEs	EUR 10 billion for co-financing, guarantees, conversion of short term loans to long term, equity financing

Credit mediation was set up in November 2008 to assist SMEs to resolve their liquidity problems by maintaining or obtaining bank credit. To start the process, the enterprise must establish a "mediation file" on the website of the Credit Mediator who has been appointed at the national level to coordinate and act as a final "referee". He is assisted by departmental mediators from the Bank of France. After the file is received, the banks are notified by mail and they have five business days to reply to the enterprise. After this, the departmental mediator has five business days to review the file and indicate how the file should be treated. When the mediator has identified solutions, the enterprise is notified by mail. If the enterprise is not satisfied, it may appeal to the national mediator. As of June 2011:

- 31 86 enterprises had sought mediation (there might be some double counting as some firms opened more than one file);
- 25 624 enterprises had been accepted for mediation; and
- the rate of successful mediation was 63%.

The credit mediation scheme has reinforced 14 290 firms of all sizes; unblocked EUR 3.5 billion in credit; and preserved 247 139 jobs (Médiateur de Crédit, 2011).

Box 4.4. **Definition of SMEs in the EU and France**

Definition of SMEs used in the EU

The EU definition of the size of a firm is based on four associated criteria:

- number of employees;
- turnover;
- total assets of legal units;
- independence (the firm is delimited according to the financial links between legal units).

Definition of SMEs used in France

In France, the implementing decree of the Law on the Modernization of the Economy (LME) of 4 August 2008 established categories of companies consistent with the European Commission's definition of size.

To define the firms' size, and thus SMEs, the Bank of France complies as much as possible with the LME definition.

Indeed, when calculating structural ratios with balances sheet data, it already follows the LME definition.

When calculating the firms' size for which private banks declare "credit risks" to the French Central Credit Register, the independence criteria is not yet taken into account. Therefore, the classification currently applies to legal units.

As for classifying business failures by firm size, the relevant level remains the legal unit because it is the reference for judging bankruptcy.

Furthermore, when both the profit and loss account and the balance sheet are unavailable, the magnitude of the risks declared to the Central Credit Register is taken as a proxy to estimate the total assets.

Note: For methodological details, see the article: "The Position of Firms in 2009: A Decline in Business and a Reluctance to invest during the crisis", Bank of France, Quarterly selection of articles, Winter 2010-11, *http:// bdfbs-ws01.heb3.fr.colt.net/gb/publications/telechar/bulletin/qsa/qsa20/quarterly-selection-of-articles-winter-2010-20- etude_1.pdf.*

Table 4.26. **Financing SMEs and entrepreneurs: Scoreboard for France, 2007-10**

Indicator	Units	2007	2008	2009	2010
Debt					
Business loans, SMEs (drawn + undrawn)	EUR millions	248 793	259 469	262 189	277 162
Business loans, total (drawn + undrawn)	EUR millions	946 135	1 006 049	1 015 917	1 053 800
Share of SME business loans in total business loans	%	26.3	25.8	25.8	26.3
Share of SMEs drawn business loans in total SMEs business loans	% of total drawn and undrawn SMEs business loans	89.4	89.6	89.2	88.3
Short-term loans, SMEs (drawn)	EUR millions	48 253	47 831	42 907	43 407
Medium and long-term loans, finance leases and securitised loans, SMEs (drawn)	EUR millions	174 158	184 616	190 961	201 449
Total loans, SMEs (drawn)	EUR millions	222 412	232 447	233 868	244 856
Share of SMEs short-term loans in total drawn loans	% of total short and long-term drawn loans	21.7	20.6	18.3	17.7
OSEO guaranteed loans	EUR millions	5 850	6 861	11 267	..
Value of OSEO loan guarantees	EUR millions	2 707	3 219	5 752	..
Share of the outstanding loans of failing companies, SMEs without micro-enterprises	% of the total outstanding amounts of loans drawn	1.0	1.3	1.7	1.4
Interest rate, loans < 1 million (new loans)	%	5.28	5.34	3.45	3.34
Interest rate, loans > 1 million (new loans)	%	4.16	4.15	2.11	2.31
Interest rate spread (between loans < 1 million and > 1 million)	%	1.12	1.19	1.34	1.03
Equity					
Venture and expansion capital	EUR millions	1 987	2 411	2 385	2 915
Venture and expansion capital	Year-on-year growth rate, %	24.9	21.2	−1.1	22.2
Other					
Payment delays	Average number of days past due date	14.3	16.0	18.0	18.0
Bankruptcies, total	Number	51 343	55 562	63 219	60 585
Bankruptcies, total	Year-on-year growth rate, %	7.1	8.2	13.8	−4.2
Bankruptcies, SMEs	Number	48 111	52 104	58 930	56 883
Bankruptcies, SMEs	Year-on-year growth rate, %	6.6	8.3	13.1	−3.5

Sources: Refer to Table 4.27 "Definitions and sources of indicators for France's Scoreboard".

StatLink 🔗 *http://dx.doi.org/10.1787/888932579816*

Figure 4.13. **Trends in SME and entrepreneurship finance in France**

A. Business loans (drawn + undrawn) to SMEs, 2007-10
Annual, in EUR millions

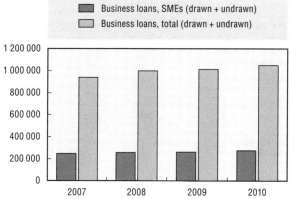

B. Year-on year growth rate of drawn and undrawn credit, 2007-11
Monthly, as a percentage

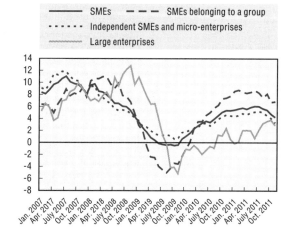

**C. Interest rates and interest rate spread
for SMEs, 2007-10**
Annual, as a percentage

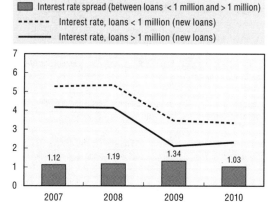

**D. Share of the outstanding loans of failing companies,
SMEs (without micro-enterprises),
2007-10**
Annual, as a percentage of the total outstanding
amounts of loans drawn

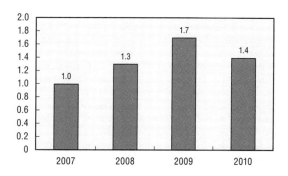

E. Venture and expansion capital invested, 2007-10
Annual, in EUR millions

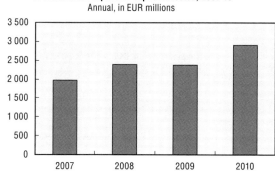

F. Bankruptcies of SMEs, 2007-11
Monthly, number (cumulative over 12 months)

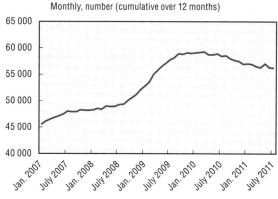

Sources: Charts A, B, C, D and F: Bank of France. Chart E: Association française des investisseurs en capital.

StatLink ⸻ http://dx.doi.org/10.1787/888932578885

Table 4.27. **Financing SMEs and entrepreneurs: Definitions and sources of indicators for France's Scoreboard**

Indicator	Definition	Source
Debt		
Business loans, SMEs (drawn + undrawn)	Total drawn and undrawn credit (crédits mobilisés et mobilisables) for SMEs (both independent and belonging to a group), comprised of short-term, medium-term, long-term, finance leases and securitised loans. A bank must inform the Banque de France Central credit register whenever one of its branch offices has granted more than EUR 25 000 to a firm (total outstanding loan).	Banque de France, les encours de crédits aux entreprises résidentes par catégorie et taille
Business loans, total (drawn + undrawn)	Total drawn and undrawn credit (crédits mobilisés et mobilisables) comprised of short-term, medium-term, long-term, finance leases and securitised loans. A bank must inform the Banque de France Central credit register whenever one of its branch offices has granted more than EUR 25 000 to a firm (total outstanding loan).	Banque de France, les encours de crédits aux entreprises résidentes par catégorie et taille
Short-term loans, SMEs (drawn)	Short-term credit drawn by SMEs, *i.e.* loans with a maturity less than or equal to one year. A bank must inform the Banque de France Central credit register whenever one of its branch offices has granted more than EUR 25 000 to a firm (total outstanding loan).	Banque de France, le financement des PME en France
Medium and long-term loans, finance leases and securitised loans SMEs (drawn)	Medium and long-term loans, finance leases and securitised loans drawn by SMEs. 'Medium and long-term' refers to loans with a maturity of more than one year.	Banque de France, le financement des PME en France
OSEO guaranteed loans	Government guaranteed loans to SMEs are proxied by the amount of loans guaranteed by OSEO.	OSEO, Annual Report 2008 and 2009
Value of OSEO loan guarantees	Value of government loan guarantees to SMEs are the net amount of risk covered by OSEO for guarantees to all firms.	OSEO, Annual Report 2008 and 2009
Share of the outstanding loans of failing companies, SMEs except micro-enterprises	Outstanding loans of failing SMEs (except microenterprises), expressed as a percentage of total outstanding amounts of SMEs drawn loans (except microenterprises).	Banque de France, le financement des PME en France
Interest rate, loans < 1 million (new loans)	Interest rate for new loans to SMEs (defined as loans of up to EUR 1 million). Interest rate prevailing in December of each relevant year, all PFIT's.	Banque de France, Montant des crédits nouveaux à la clientèle résidente – France
Interest rate, loans > 1 million (new loans)	Interest rate for new loans to large firms (defined as new loans over EUR 1 million). Interest rate prevailing in December of each relevant year, all PFIT's.	Banque de France, Montant des crédits nouveaux à la clientèle résidente – France
Interest rate spread (between loans < 1 million and > 1 million)	Interest rate spread between interest rate for new loans less than EUR 1 million and interest rate for new loans more than EUR 1 million (all PFIT's). Interest rate prevailing in December of each relevant year.	Banque de France, Montant des crédits nouveaux à la clientèle résidente – France
Equity		
Venture and expansion capital	Amount of funds invested in venture capital and expansion capital stages in France. All enterprises.	Association française des investisseurs en capital (AFIC)
Other		
Payment delays	Average number of days beyond the agreed date for business-to-business in 2008, 2009 and 2010. For 2007, average number of days beyond the agreed date for business-to-business, business-to-customer and public entities. All enterprises.	Intrum Justitia, European Payment Index 2008, 2009 and 2010
Bankruptcies, total	Total bankruptcies of all enterprises. Bankruptcies of legal units over the year. The statistics are established on the date of judgement.	Banque de France, Les défaillances d'entreprises
Bankruptcies, SMEs	Bankruptcies of SMEs. Bankruptcies of legal units over the year. The statistics are established on the date of judgment.	Banque de France, Les défaillances d'entreprises

References

Banque de France (2011), " En 2010, les PME bénéficient de la reprise mais diffèrent leurs investissements ", *http://bdfbs-ws01.heb3.fr.colt.net/gb/publications/telechar/bulletin/qsa/qsa20/quarterly-selection-of-articles-winter-2010-20-etude_1.pdf.*

Banque de France (2011), Stat info "Le financement des PME", *www.banque-france.fr/economie-et-statistiques/entreprises/credits-par-type-dentreprise.html.*

Médiateur de Crédit (2011), Rapport d'activité de la Médiation du crédit aux entreprises au 30 juin 2011, available at : *www.mediateurducredit.fr/site/Actualites/Rapport-d-activite-de-la-Mediation-du-credit-aux-entreprises-au-30-juin-2011* (accessed 4/10/2011).

Observatoire du financement des entreprises (2011), *Rapport sur le financement des PME-PMI et ETI en France*, April 2011, Ministère de l'Économie, des Finances et de l'Industrie, Paris.

OSEO (2009a), *Rapport annuel 2009*, Paris.

OSEO (2009b), *Bilan 2009 des mesures OSEO du plan de relance : 23 500 entreprises accompagnées*, Communiqué de presse, 22 December, Paris.

Hungary

SME lending

Hungary defines SMEs using the standard criteria provided by the European Union. An SME is an enterprise with fewer than 250 employees and which has an annual turnover not exceeding EUR 50 million. The total number of active, employer enterprises in Hungary was 547 440 at the end of 2010, almost all of which were SMEs. This included those which were legal entities as well as non-legal (informal) entities. It also includes self-employed persons, which is in keeping with the EU definition of an SME but departs from the OECD practice of reporting only on "employer" enterprises.

Table 4.28. **Distribution of enterprises in Hungary, 2007**
By size of enterprise

Enterprise size (employees)	Number	%
All enterprises	547 440	100.0
SMEs (1-249)	546 641	99.9
Micro (1-9)	516 334	94.3
Small (10-49)	26 017	4.8
Medium (50-249)	4 290	0.8
Large (250+)	799	0.1

Note: Data include total industry and market services including NACE Categories D, E, F, G, H, I and K. Non-employer enterprises are not included.
Source: OECD Structural and Demographic Business Statistic Database.

StatLink ᴍᴦᴾ http://dx.doi.org/10.1787/888932579835

The proportion of loans to enterprises granted in foreign currencies is between 50-60%, which could impose additional burdens on SMEs if exchange rate changes are unfavourable. There was a moderate decrease in both total business loans and SME loans over the period. The SME loan share in total business loans was stable at 56% over the period. The share of overdrafts in SME loans (overdrafts and investment loans) was 34%. The share of non-performing loans was extremely high about 15.4%. It increased significantly in 2010. However, the definition is wider and goes beyond loans in default (bad loans) and includes loans at risk that are classified as substandard or doubtful.

SME credit conditions

The average annual interest rate for short-term SME loans to non-financial enterprises was high in Hungary. It rose to 12.3% in 2009 before declining to 8.99% in 2010. Information on collateral requirements was not available.

Equity financing

Venture and growth capital financing declined between 2007 and 2009 and then recovered in 2010 to almost double its 2007 level.

Table 4.29. **Venture and growth capital financing in Hungary, 2007-10**

In HUF millions

	Seed, start-up, early stage	Later stage expansion	Total[1]
2007	494	3 455	3 949
2008	479	13 303	13 782
2009	420	300	720
2010	5 013	1 969	6 982

1. The total excludes buy outs, which were very large in Hungary between 2007 and 2009.
Source: Hungarian Venture Capital Association.

StatLink ᴀ🖳 http://dx.doi.org/10.1787/888932579854

Other indicators

Bankruptcies in Hungary increased 142% between 2007 and 2010.

Government policy responses

Hungary has a loan guarantee programme, as well as direct loans for SMEs. The guarantee programme is run by partly-owned state institutions (Garantiga Hitelgarancia, Agrár-vállalkozási Hitelgarancia Alapítvány). They provide guarantees for 50-80% of the loan. Their guarantees are counter-guaranteed by the State budget. The amount of guaranteed loans increased between 2009 and 2010. Approximately 12.6% of SME loans had a government guarantee. The Hungarian Development Bank provides direct loans and loans to refinance banks. Direct loans increased 168% over the 2007 and 2010 period. There are also micro-loans disbursed by microcredit institutions financed from State or EU Budget.

Table 4.30. **Financing SMEs and entrepreneurs: Scoreboard for Hungary, 2007-10**

Indicator	Units	2007	2008	2009	2010
Debt					
Business loans, SMEs	HUF millions	4 100 178	4 302 384	4 009 766	4 063 063
Business loans, total	HUF millions	7 162 846	7 737 543	7 218 483	7 019 145
Business loans, SMEs	% of total business loans	..	..	..	..
Overdraft loans, SMEs	HUF millions	..	..	678 358	688 369
Investment loans, SMEs	HUF millions	..	..	1 284 869	1 345 103
Total overdraft and investment loans, SMEs	HUF millions	..	..	1 963 227	2 033 472
Government guaranteed loans, SMEs	HUF millions	..	..	466 101	512 383
Share of SME government guaranteed loans in SME business loans	%	..	..	11.6	12.6
Direct government loans, SMEs	HUF millions	131 726	172 870	209 597	222 063
Non-performing loans, SMEs	Number	..	..	494 674	616 977
Average interest rate, SMEs	%	10.19	11.25	12.31	8.99
Equity					
Venture and growth capital	HUF millions	3 949	13 782	720	6 982
Venture and growth capital	Year-on-year growth rate, %	n.a.	249.0	−94.8	869.7
Other					
Bankruptcies, total	Per 10 000 firms	566	624	726	805

Sources: Refer to Table 4.31 "Definitions and sources of indicators for Hungary's Scoreboard".

StatLink ⟐ http://dx.doi.org/10.1787/888932579873

Figure 4.14. **Trends in SME and entrepreneurship finance in Hungary**

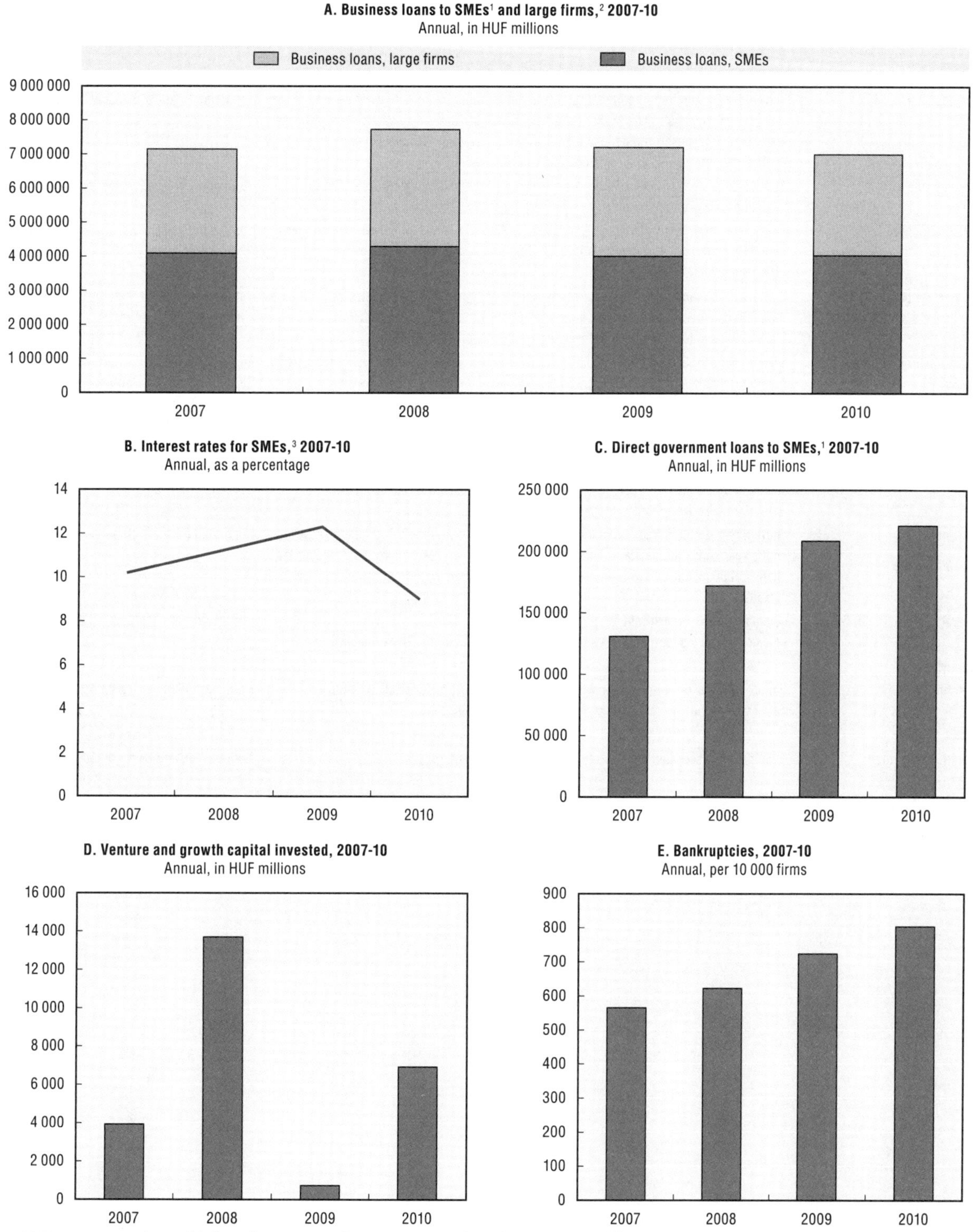
A. Business loans to SMEs[1] and large firms,[2] 2007-10
Annual, in HUF millions
Business loans, large firms
Business loans, SMEs
9 000 000
8 000 000
7 000 000
6 000 000
5 000 000
4 000 000
3 000 000
2 000 000
1 000 000
0
2007
2008
2009
2010
B. Interest rates for SMEs,[3] 2007-10
Annual, as a percentage
14
12
10
8
6
4
2
0
C. Direct government loans to SMEs,[1] 2007-10
Annual, in HUF millions
250 000
200 000
150 000
100 000
50 000
D. Venture and growth capital invested, 2007-10
Annual, in HUF millions
16 000
14 000
12 000
10 000
8 000
6 000
4 000
2 000
E. Bankruptcies, 2007-10
Annual, per 10 000 firms
900
800
700
600
500
400
300
200
100

1. SMEs are enterprises with less than 250 employees, turnover less than EUR 50 million and total assets below EUR 10 million.
2. Large firms have more than 250 employees, turnover more than EUR 50 million and total assets over EUR 10 million.
3. For loans over EUR 1 million.

Sources: Chart A: Hungarian Financial Supervisory Authority. Chart B: Hungarian National Bank. Chart C: Administrative data from Hungarian Development Bank and the Economic Development Programme. Chart D: Hungarian Venture Capital Association. Chart E: National Tax and Customs Administration.

StatLink http://dx.doi.org/10.1787/888932578904

Table 4.31. **Financing SMEs and entrepreneurs: Definitions and sources of indicators for Hungary's Scoreboard**

Indicator	Definition	Source
Debt		
Business loans, SMEs	Sum of SME loans from credit institutions and microfinance institutions at the end of the year (including loans to financial enterprises). SMEs are defined as enterprises with less than 250 employees, turnover less than EUR 50 million and total assets below EUR 10 million. Non-employer enterprises are included.	Hungarian Financial Supervisory Authority
Business loans, total	Sum of loans from credit institutions and microfinance institutions at the end of the year to all non-financial enterprises.	Hungarian Financial Supervisory Authority
Overdraft loans, SMEs	Sum of overdraft loans at the end of the year. SMEs are defined as enterprises with less than 250 employees, turnover less than EUR 50 million and total assets below EUR 10 million. Non-employer enterprises are included.	Hungarian Financial Supervisory Authority
Investment loans, SMEs	Sum of investment loans at the end of the year. SMEs are defined as enterprises with less than 250 employees, turnover less than EUR 50 million and total assets below EUR 10 million. Non-employer enterprises are included.	Hungarian Financial Supervisory Authority
Government guaranteed loans, SMEs	Sum of loans for SMEs at the end of the year guaranteed by state owned institutions, partly counter-guaranteed by the state. SMEs are defined as enterprises with less than 250 employees, turnover less than EUR 50 million and total assets below EUR 10 million. Non-employer enterprises are included.	Administrative data from Hungarian Development Bank, Garantiqa Hitelgarancia Zrt, AFGHA, and the Economic Development Programme
Direct government loans, SMEs	Sum of direct loans to SMEs from Hungarian Development Bank, microfinance programmes financed from state resources. SMEs are defined as enterprises with less than 250 employees, turnover less than EUR 50 million and total assets below EUR 10 million. Non-employer enterprises are included.	Administrative data from Hungarian Development Bank and the Economic Development Programme
Non-performing loans, SMEs	Sum of non-problem free (substandard, doubtful, bad) classifiable SME loans at the end of the year. SMEs are defined as enterprises with less than 250 employees, turnover less than EUR 50 million and total assets below EUR 10 million. Non-employer enterprises are included.	Hungarian Financial Supervisory Authority
Average interest rate, SMEs	Average annual interest rate for all new SME loans. (Non overdraft loans, maturity less than 1 year, amounts up to EUR 1 million).	Hungarian National Bank
Equity		
Venture and growth capital	Actual amounts of venture and growth capital invested. Includes seed, start-up, early- and late-stage expansion capital. Excludes buy-outs. All enterprises.	Hungarian Venture Capital Association
Other		
Bankruptcies, total	Liquidation proceeding and dissolution procedure. All enterprises.	National Tax and Customs Administration

Italy

SME lending

SMEs comprise 99.9% of enterprises in Italy and account for 80% of the industrial and service labour force. The sector has a relatively small-scale structure: the share of micro-enterprises is higher than the EU average, while the percentage of small and medium-sized firms is below average (Eurostat, 2011). Data collected from the debt side were mainly available for most of the firms with less than 20 employees, which represent nearly the entire universe.

Table 4.32. **Distribution of firms in Italy, 2009**

By size of firm

Firm size (employees)	Total active enterprises		Of which: according to the SBS Regulation (No. 295/2008)[1]	
	Number	%	Number	%
All firms	**4 470 748**	**100.0**	**3 860 241**	**100.0**
SMEs (up to 249)	4 467 058	99.9	3 857 033	99.9
Micro (up to 9)	4 284 400	95.8	3 687 395	95.5
Small (10-49)	160 993	3.6	150 280	3.9
Medium (50-249)	21 665	0.5	19 358	0.5
Large (250+)	**3 690**	**0.1**	**3 208**	0.1

1. Data include all market activities in Sections B, C, D, E, F, G, H, I, J, L, M, N of the common statistical classification of economic activities in the European Community as established by Regulation (EC) No 1893/2006 (Nace Rev. 2). Data include firms with and without employees.
Source: Istat, *Statistical Business Register*.

StatLink ᵃⁱˢᵖ *http://dx.doi.org/10.1787/888932579892*

In Italy, the impact of the crisis on the national banking system was cushioned by a sound model of intermediation, more oriented towards direct lending than to transactions on capital markets. This meant that there was less exposure to toxic assets arising from collateralised debt obligations. The consequences of the crisis were felt particularly by the largest banking groups, more reliant on wholesale funding. Although their capital ratios were lower than those of other large international financial institutions, owing to stringent regulation major Italian banks could rely on better quality tier one capital, which is more able to absorb losses. Also, Italian banks had a lower level of leverage compared to non-Italian ones.

Total business loans grew through 2008, but at a slower rate than in 2007, and then declined in absolute terms in 2009. They started to recover in 2010. SME loan growth held steady till mid-2008 and then decelerated sharply during the crisis; it showed a positive trend in 2010 (Figure 4.15). The share of SME loans in total business loans declined through 2008 but recovered over the following two years. SME short-term loans showed a marked slowdown as the financial crisis intensified, lending conditions tightened and credit demand from firms shrank. They continued to decline in 2009 and 2010.

Figure 4.15. **Lending to firms in Italy, 2005-11**

Monthly data, 12 month percentage changes

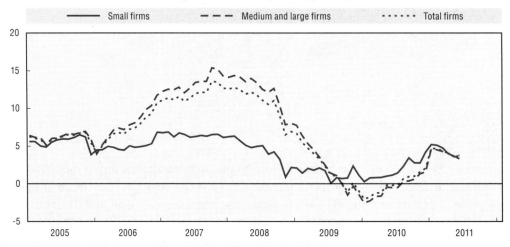

Note: The percentage changes are adjusted for the effects of reclassifications.

Source: Bank of Italy.

StatLink ᵃᵍ⋆ http://dx.doi.org/10.1787/888932578923

Figure 4.16 shows the distribution of bank lending among the institutional sectors. In 2010 half of the total stock was absorbed by firms; the SME share reached 10%. The remainder went to consumer households (26%), government (14%) and financial institutions (9.6%).

Figure 4.16. **Bank lending to various sectors in Italy, 2010**

As a percentage

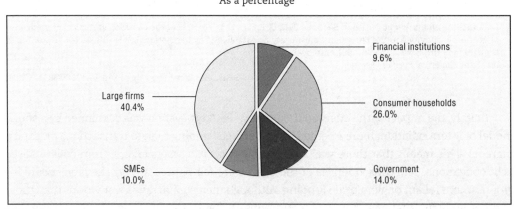

Note: SMEs include producer households; consumer households include non-profit institutions serving households; financial institutions other than banks (i.e. it does not include interbank lending).

Source: Bank of Italy.

StatLink ᵃᵍ⋆ http://dx.doi.org/10.1787/888932578942

SME loans used *vs.* authorised

The ratio of loans used to authorised rose from 80% in 2007 to 83% in 2010, revealing the presence of strains in the credit market. A more in-depth analysis – disaggregating data by type of loan – showed that the used/granted ratio declined for matched loans (such as advances backed by discounted invoices), mirroring the general economic downturn. In contrast, credit use intensified significantly for overdrafts; the upward trend was confirmed in 2010, suggesting that firms met their liquidity needs through greater recourse to short-term credit lines. Since 2009 the increased use of overdrafts partly reflected a change in the banks' pricing policies established by law.

SME credit conditions

Following the turmoil in the financial markets in mid-2007, the results of the Bank Lending Survey, carried out by the euro area, highlighted a tightening of the criteria applied by the largest Italian banks for loan approvals and the opening of credit lines to enterprises. In 2008, this greater strictness, which mirrored the perception of heightened risk in connection with the worsening economic outlook, continued and gradually increased in the autumn as the crisis intensified after the failure of Lehman Brothers. The tightening involved amounts, margins, maturities and specific covenants aimed at limiting risk. Lending standards, which kept tightening, were broadly unchanged during 2010, although they became slightly more restrictive, implying larger margins and increased collateral requirements on riskier loans.

By autumn 2008, reductions in official interest rates were gradually being passed on to bank customers. SME interest rates (including fees and commissions) rose during 2007 and 2008; they peaked at 6.6% in 3Q08 before declining to 3.6% in 4Q09 due to monetary easing and remained in this range during 2010. The spread between interest rates paid by the small vs. large enterprises continued to grow from 0.6% in 4Q07 to 1.5% in 4Q10, indicating that SMEs were facing tougher credit conditions.

The decrease in collateral requirements between 2008 and 2009 followed the lowering of the Central Credit Register reporting threshold and the inclusion of small, less secured loans. However, by the end of 2010, they were on the rise. Surveys conducted by Institute for Studies and Economic Analysis (ISAE) showed a gradual worsening of conditions for enterprises to access credit. The share of manufacturing firms indicating a tightening increased from more than 20% in the first half of 2008 to 27.2% in September; in November the percentage rose sharply to 43.5% (ISAE, 2008). According to the Bank of Italy's Survey on Industrial and Service Firms with at least 20 workers, in 2010 the difficulty of accessing credit also involved, more than in 2009, medium-sized and large firms.

Equity financing

Total venture and growth capital fell drastically between 2008 and 2009. It rose in 2010, but not for SMEs. Targeted anti-crisis provisions introduced by the government included the establishment of a private equity fund with an initial endowment of EUR 1 billion to boost the capitalisation of SMEs. It became operational in 2010 with the involvement of the Ministry of Economy.

Table 4.33. **Early stage and expansion capital in Italy, 2006-10**

EUR thousands

Number of employees	2006	2007	2008	2009	2010
0-9	36 445	110 472	111 349	98 746	141 424
10-19	8 310	39 433	120 667	29 592	23 626
20-99	82 048	79 615	243 437	136 044	113 223
100-199	49 173	113 513	56 684	65 459	72 644
200-249	6 466	17 554	23 602	28 089	1 500
SMEs sub-total	**182 442**	**360 587**	**555 739**	**357 930**	**352 417**
250-499	16 525	52 353	98 015	18 524	26 960
500-999	62 260	113 900	65 411	25 787	11 533
1 000-4 999	283 488	180 468	27 050	66 419	267 710
> 5 000	496 866	0	164 853	0	13 600
Total	**1 041 581**	**707 308**	**911 068**	**468 660**	**672 220**

Source: AIFI-PwC.

StatLink ⫸ http://dx.doi.org/10.1787/888932579911

Payment delays, non-performing loans and bankruptcies

The slump in sales and the tightening of credit conditions contributed to SME cash flow problems, which in turn were partly reflected in the increase in payment delays. Moreover, after the outbreak of the crisis, suppliers began to claim faster payments: for SMEs, payment delays rose from 15 days in 2008 to 17 days in 2009. They dropped to 14.8 days in 2010, mainly as a consequence of the extension of agreed payment terms between suppliers and customers at the first signs of economic recovery. This trend was common to all firm sizes; however, compared to SMEs, large firms alleviated their liquidity constraints by delaying payments to a larger extent, exploiting their stronger bargaining power.

Another indicator of the ability of SMEs to repay debts is non-performing loans. There was a noticeable increase in the proportion of SME bad debts in SME business loans from 6.8% (2007) to 9.4% (2010).

Figure 4.17. **Payment delays in Italy, 2008-11**

Average number of days

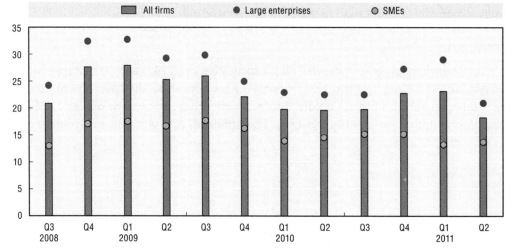

Source: Cerved Group, *Payline Database.*

StatLink ⫸ http://dx.doi.org/10.1787/888932578961

Bankruptcies rose from 11.2 per 10 000 enterprises in 2007 to 17.1 in 2009. The weak economic recovery in 2010 did not allow a significant improvement in the conditions of firms, as witnessed by the still rapid increase of the indicator (20.3 per 10 000 enterprises).

Government policy response

Besides the general measures to increase bank capitalisation, such as underwriting bank bonds, which are subordinated to commitments by the issuing banks to provide credit to SMEs, the government has undertaken several other measures to ensure SME access to finance particularly in the area of loan guarantees.

The Central Guarantee Fund (CGF) facilitates SME access to credit by providing public guarantees and counter-guarantees. The guarantee can be requested by banks or financial companies entered in a special register. The "counter guarantee" and "joint guarantee" can be requested by Confidi (mutual guarantee institutions – MGIs) and other guarantee funds. Stringent scoring procedures applied to guarantee applications contained default losses in the past but the system has been seen as skimming the best credit risks among SMEs. Some studies have shown that medium-sized firms were the largest beneficiaries (Zecchini and Ventura, 2006).

In response to the financial crisis, the government has refinanced the Central Guarantee Fund. The CGF provides, in its own right, loan guarantees for SMEs with less than 250 employees. From 2000 to 2007, it provided EUR 4.2 billion in guarantees for EUR 8.7 billion worth of loans. During the financial crisis, the government announced further allocations to the CGF. In 2010, the CGF exhibited an unprecedented growth. It helped 50 000 firms to cope with the general economic downturn, providing more than EUR 5.2 billion in guarantees for EUR 9.1 billion worth of loans; micro and small enterprises received 70% of the amount.

The financial crisis underlined the important role of MGIs in easing access to credit by SMEs. In 2009, in spite of the contraction in SME lending, the guarantees provided by the MGIs to SMEs increased by nearly 16%. In pre-crisis years, Confidi helped affiliated firms to obtain better conditions, when applying for a loan. In the current crisis conditions, their activity has been aimed primarily at facilitating access to bank loans.

Further actions undertaken to overcome liquidity problems included the one-year debt moratorium for SMEs that allowed firms (with no bad debts, restructured loans or ongoing foreclosures) to suspend repayment of the bank loan principal and to obtain an extension of the duration of loans for credit advances. The measure applied to enterprises which employed fewer than 250 persons, with an annual turnover not exceeding EUR 50 million and/or an annual balance sheet total not exceeding EUR 43 million. By December 2010, 200 000 applications had been accepted, and EUR 13 billion worth of debts rolled over.

Another measure enhancing SMEs' access to credit was the use of the Deposits and Loans Fund (Cassa Depositi e Prestiti, CDP). The agreement, signed by the Italian Banking Association and CDP, made available EUR 8 billion – drawn from the postal deposits – to the banking system, which was committed to lend to SMEs. By the end of 2010 banks had allocated EUR 2.8 billion to SMEs.

Overall, the impact of these initiatives was not negligible: it has been estimated that the additional resources available to SMEs accounted for more than 10% of the loans (other than overdrafts) up to EUR 1 million granted by banks in 2009 and 2010. The government also attempted to boost liquidity by providing for tax exemptions, tax deductions and delayed payment of VAT. However, the effect of these tax measures would only be felt to the extent that sales and profits are realised.

Box 4.5. **Definition of SMEs used in Italy's SME and entrepreneurship finance Scoreboard**

Country definition

In accordance with Eurostat standards, the Italian National Institute of Statistics defines small and medium enterprises as firms with fewer than 250 employees. In detail, micro-enterprises and small firms have, respectively, less than 10 and 10-49 employees, while medium-sized enterprises are defined as those with 50-249 employees.

The SME definition used by financial institutions

The Bank of Italy classifies data on business lending by firm size: small firms are defined as limited partnerships, general partnerships, informal partnerships, *de facto* companies and sole proprietorships with fewer than 20 workers. This data disaggregation has been used for most indicators on the debt side.

Table 4.34. **Financing SMEs and entrepreneurs: Scoreboard for Italy, 2007-10**

Indicators	Units	2007	2008	2009	2010
Debt					
Business loans, SMEs	EUR millions	186 699	190 628	192 856	205 637
Business loans, total	EUR millions	994 469	1 063 053	1 052 639	1 083 758
Business loans, SMEs	% of total business loans	18.8	17.9	18.3	19.0
Short-term loans, SMEs	EUR millions	59 026	56 335	51 607	49 984
Long-term loans, SMEs	EUR millions	114 912	120 437	124 801	136 284
Short-term loans, SMEs	% of total short and long-term SME loans	33.9	31.9	29.3	26.8
Government guaranteed loans, CGF	EUR billions	2.3	2.3	4.9	9.1
Direct government loans, SMEs	EUR millions	354	373	255	276
Ratio of loans used to authorised, SMEs	%	79.7	80.7	80.7	82.8
Non-performing loans, total	EUR millions	44 546	50 122	65 744	80 238
Non-performing loans, SMEs	EUR millions	12 760	13 857	16 449	19 368
Non-performing loans, large firms	EUR millions	31 786	36 265	49 295	60 870
Interest rate, average SME rate	%	6.3	6.3	3.6	3.7
Interest rate spread (between average SME and large firm rate)	%	0.6	1.4	1.4	1.5
Collateral, SMEs	% of collateralised loans	54.4	54.3	51.9	53.0
Equity					
Venture and expansion capital, total	EUR millions	707	911	469	672
Venture and expansion capital, SMEs	EUR millions	361	556	358	352
Venture and expansion capital, SMEs	Year-on-year growth rate, %	97.6	54.1	−35.6	−1.5
Other					
Payment delays, all firms	Average number of days	..	24.4	25.2	20.6
Payment delays, SMEs	Average number of days	..	15	17	14.8
Payment delays, large firms	Average number of days	..	28.3	29.2	23.9
Bankruptcies, total	Number	6 165	7 521	9 429	11 289
Incidence of insolvency, total	Per 10 000 enterprises	11.2	13.8	17.1	20.3

Sources: Refer to Table 4.35 "Definitions and sources of indicators for Italy's Scoreboard".

StatLink http://dx.doi.org/10.1787/888932579930

Figure 4.18. **Trends in SME and entrepreneurship finance in Italy**

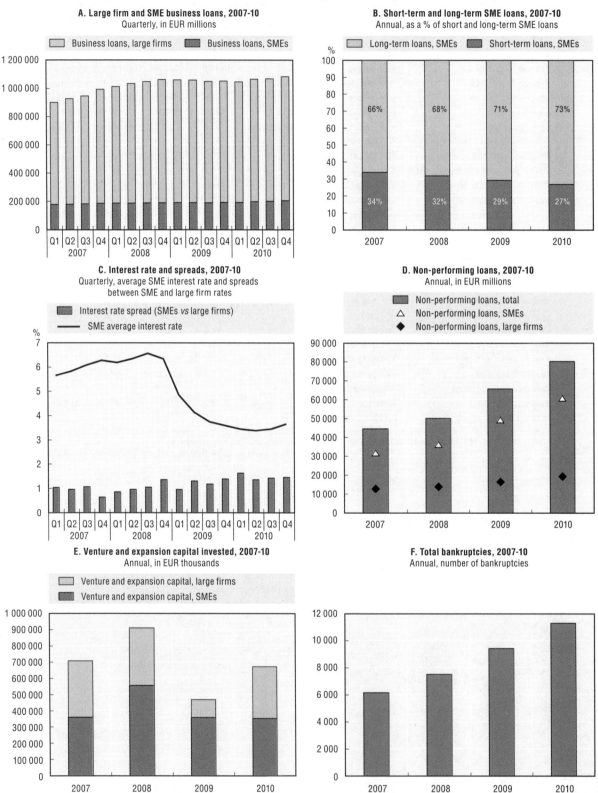

Sources: Charts A, B, C and D: Bank of Italy. Chart E: A I F I – Italian Private Equity and Venture Capital Association. Chart F: Cerved Group.

StatLink http://dx.doi.org/10.1787/888932578980

Table 4.35. **Financing SMEs and entrepreneurs: Definitions and sources of indicators for Italy's Scoreboard**

Indicators	Definition	Source
Debt		
Business loans, SMEs	Performing and non-performing loans (bad debts) outstanding (stocks) by banks and other financial institutions. For bank loans: performing loans (including repos) and excluding factoring; bad debts excluding factoring from Q408 only. For other financial intermediaries loans: performing loans (including repos) excluding factoring; bad debts including factoring. As of June 2010, loans include securitized, or otherwise transferred, loans which do not satisfy the criteria for derecognition as established in the international accounting standard IAS 39.	Bank of Italy, *Supervisory returns* (for bank loans) and Central Credit Register (for other financial intermediaries loans; subject to reporting threshold: as of January 2009, the reporting threshold for loans and guarantees, which was previously set to EUR 75 000, has been lowered to EUR 30 000; no threshold applies for reporting bad debts); supply side data sets
Business loans, total	Performing and non-performing loans (bad debts) outstanding (stocks) by banks and other financial institutions. For bank loans: performing loans (including repos) and excluding factoring; bad debts excluding factoring from Q408 only. For other financial intermediaries loans: performing loans (including repos) excluding factoring; bad debts including factoring. As of June 2010, loans include securitized, or otherwise transferred, loans which do not satisfy the criteria for derecognition as established in the international accounting standard IAS 39.	Bank of Italy, *Supervisory returns* (for bank loans) and Central Credit Register (for other financial intermediaries loans; subject to reporting threshold)
Short-term loans, SMEs	Performing loans (including repos) excluding factoring; maturity up to 12 months (up to 18 months until Q308 for data drawn from supervisory returns and until Q109 for data drawn from the Central Credit Register).	Bank of Italy, *Supervisory returns* (for bank loans) and Central Credit Register (for other financial intermediaries loans; subject to reporting threshold)
Long-term loans, SMEs	Performing loans (including repos) excluding factoring; maturity more than 12 months (more than 18 months until Q308 for data drawn from supervisory returns and until Q109 for data drawn from the Central Credit Register).	Bank of Italy, *Supervisory returns* (for bank loans) and Central Credit Register (for other financial intermediaries loans; subject to reporting threshold)
Government guaranteed loans, CGF	Government guaranteed loans to SMEs (firms with less than 250 employees) by the Central Guarantee Fund.	Central Guarantee Fund – MedioCredito Centrale (MCC)
Direct government loans, SMEs	Sum of direct loans granted to SMEs (firms with less than 250 employees) by the Italian government.	Ministry of Economic Development
Loans authorised, SMEs	Sum of the loan facilities granted to each borrower by all the intermediaries reporting to the Central Credit Register.	Bank of Italy, Central Credit Register (subject to reporting threshold)
Loans used, SMEs	Sum of the loan facilities disbursed to each borrower by all the intermediaries reporting to the Central Credit Register.	Bank of Italy, Central Credit Register (subject to reporting threshold)
Non-performing loans, total	Bank and other intermediaries' bad debts. For bank bad debts: including factoring up to Q308; excluding factoring from Q408. For other financial intermediaries bad debts including factoring. Bad debts are defined as the total loans outstanding to borrowers who have been declared insolvent or who are in a basically comparable situation.	Bank of Italy, *Supervisory returns* (for bank bad debts) and Central Credit Register (for other financial intermediaries bad debts)
Non-performing loans, SMEs	Bank and other intermediaries' bad debts. For bank bad debts: including factoring up to Q308; excluding factoring from Q408. For other financial intermediaries bad debts including factoring.	Bank of Italy, *Supervisory returns* (for bank bad debts) and Central Credit Register (for other financial intermediaries bad debts)
Non-performing loans, large firms	Bank and other intermediaries' bad debts. For bank bad debts: including factoring up to Q308, excluding factoring from Q408. For other financial intermediaries bad debts including factoring.	Bank of Italy, *Supervisory returns* (for bank bad debts) and Central Credit Register (for other financial intermediaries bad debts)
Interest rate, average SME rate	Annual Percentage Rate of Charge (*i.e.* including fees and commissions) on new business.	Bank of Italy, *Survey of lending rates*. The survey refers to the rates charged to non-bank customers for the following transactions: matched loans, term loans and revocable loans, provided the sum of the amounts of the above forms of financing granted or used reported to the Central Credit Register equals or exceeds EUR 75 000
Interest rate spread (between average SME and large firm rate)	Spread between average interest rate charged to SMEs and large firms. Annual figures taken from fourth quarter of the respective year.	Bank of Italy, *Survey of lending rates*
Collateral, SMEs	Percentage of SME bank and other financial intermediaries loans backed by real guarantees.	Central Credit Register, subject to reporting threshold

Table 4.35. **Financing SMEs and entrepreneurs: Definitions and sources of indicators for Italy's Scoreboard** (cont.)

Indicators	Definition	Source
Equity		
Venture and expansion capital, total	Investment in all enterprises. Data include early stage and expansion phases, not turnaround or buyout/replacement stages.	A I F I – Italian Private Equity and Venture Capital Association; (supply-side survey)
Venture and expansion capital, SMEs	Amounts invested in SMEs (defined as firms with less than 250 employees). Data include early stage and expansion phases, not turnaround or buyout/replacement stages.	A I F I – Italian Private Equity and Venture Capital Association; (supply-side survey)
Other		
Payment delays, all firms	Average payment delay in days for business-to-business, all firms	Cerved Group, *Payline database*
Payment delays, SMEs	Average payment delay in days for business-to-business, SMEs (defined as firms with turnover of up to EUR 50 million)	Cerved Group, *Payline database*
Payment delays, large firms	Average payment delays in days for business-to-business, large firms (with turnover exceeding EUR 50 million)	Cerved Group, *Payline database*
Bankruptcies, total	The judicial procedure through which the property of an insolvent entrepreneur is removed and destined to the equal satisfaction of the creditors. The bankruptcy closing is declared by the court with a justified decree, on the request of the trustee, the creditor or also officially. The closing decree could be claimed within 15 days, in front of the Court of Appeal, from every admitted creditor. All enterprises.	Cerved Group

References

Bank of Italy (2009), *Annual Report for 2008*, Ordinary Meeting of Shareholders, Rome.

Bank of Italy (2010), *Annual Report for 2009*, Ordinary Meeting of Shareholders, Rome.

Bank of Italy (2011), *Annual Report for 2010*, Ordinary Meeting of Shareholders, Rome.

Bank of Italy, *Economic Bulletin*, various issues, Rome.

Bank of Italy (2011), "Survey on Industrial and Service Firms 2010", Rome.

Bartiloro, L., L. Carpinelli, P. Finaldi Russo and S. Pastorelli (2012), *Access to credit in times of crisis: measures to support firms and households*, Bank of Italy, *Occasional Papers*, No. 111, January.

Eurostat (2011), *Key figures on European Business 2011*, European Union.

ISAE (2008), "Inchiesta mensile sulle imprese manifatturiere ed estrattive", ISAE, November.

Zecchini, S. and M. Ventura (2006), "The Role of State-Funded Credit Guarantee Schemes for SMEs: Italy's Experience", *The SME Financing Gap Volume II: Proceedings of the Brasilia Conference*, OECD Publishing.

Korea

SME lending

SMEs constitute 98.9% of industrial enterprises and employ 71% of the industrial labour force in Korea. SME and total business loans increased over the period under study. SME loan shares were calculated on the basis of total business loans outstanding (*i.e.* stocks). SME loans increased between 2007 and 2009, but in 2010 they declined by 0.6%. The decline was due to the restructuring of junk bonds and the banks' conservative management. The SME share of business loans declined from 86.8% (2007) to 81.5% (2010) and most of this decline occurred between 2007 and 2008 when larger firm loans were experiencing faster loan growth. The share of short-term loans in total SME loans increased over the period, as the need for working capital took precedence over investments. SMEs continued to have access to credit despite the alarming rates of increase in non-performing SME loans: 124% between 2007 and 2008 and 44.5% between 2008 and 2009. Data for non-performing loans include domestic *and* foreign currency loans.

Table 4.36. **Distribution of establishments in Korea, 2006**

By size of establishment

Establishment size (employees)	Number	%
All establishments	**119 798**	**100.0**
SMEs (5-199)	118 518	98.9
Micro (5-9)	*59 223*	*49.4*
Small (10-49)	*51 674*	*43.1*
Medium (50-199)	*7 621*	*6.4*
Large (200+)	**1 280**	1.1

Note: Data only include ISIC Rev. 3 Categories C and D. Non-employer establishments are not included.
Source: OECD *Structural and Demographic Business Statistics Database*.

StatLink ᴍᴎ☜ http://dx.doi.org/10.1787/888932579949

SME credit conditions

The average interest rates charged on new SME loans rose between 2007 and 2008, and they were lower in 2009 and 2010. Nevertheless, they were high compared to those in western economies which had assumed loose monetary stances. Interest rate spreads between large and small enterprises declined to almost zero in 2009, but increased in 2010. It appears that banks were easing conditions for small enterprises compared to large enterprises. Banks eased lending conditions for SMEs not because of their willingness to absorb SMEs' credit risks, which were high, but because of the government's advice to banks to automatically roll over loans to SMEs. Roll-over rates reached 90%. The government justified this approach on the grounds that banks were not capable of making an accurate assessment of the viability of borrowers during the crisis. Additionally, government guarantee programmes, discussed below, contributed to the banks' lending behaviour to SMEs despite their own liquidity shortage and difficulty in meeting regulatory standards. By the end of 2010, domestic banks carried KRW 443 billion in SME loans or an increase of 5% over 2008.

After the Korean currency crisis in 1997, the large corporations accessed financing in the form of corporate bonds and equity. Meanwhile, the banking sector focused on SME loans, which had government guarantees. Therefore, SME loans increased dramatically over 15 years.

Figure 4.19. **Large enterprise and SME loans in Korea, 1995-2010**
KRW trillions

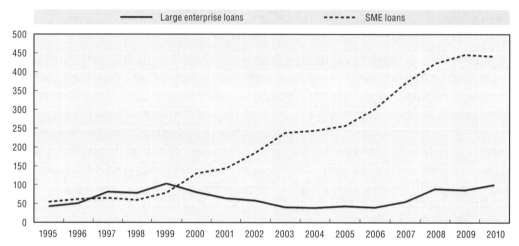

Source: Financial Supervisory Service (FSS), Small and Medium Business Administration (SMBA).
StatLink http://dx.doi.org/10.1787/888932578999

Equity financing

Venture and growth capital declined between 2007 and 2009 as in other countries but rebounded in 2010, though not to its 2007 level.

Table 4.37. **Venture and growth capital in Korea, 2007-10**
KRW billions

Stage	2007	2008	2009	2010
Early stage	365.0	290.8	247.6	319.2
Expansion	377.4	255.3	260.1	290.4
Total	**742.4**	**546.1**	**507.7**	**609.6**

Source: Small and Medium Business Administration (SMBA).
StatLink http://dx.doi.org/10.1787/888932579968

Payment delays and insolvency

Data available on payment delays were for loans overdue rather than for the average payment delays of customers, suppliers or government. Overdue loans declined in 2009 as well as insolvencies despite the earlier evidence from the Financial Supervisory Service that non performing loans in the economy increased dramatically. This was because the firms missing payments were not declared insolvent. The government bail-out programmes also prevented SME business failures. Although many SMEs in Korea were financially pinched after the outbreak of the global financial crisis, they avoided bankruptcy, thanks to the financial support from the government. Although enterprises were financially distressed, bankruptcies decreased both in 2009 and 2010 because of the credit easing policies of the central and regional governments.

Government policy response

SME government guaranteed loans and direct lending

There was a massive increase in the amount of government loan guarantees during the crisis. Also, the guarantee coverage ratio was raised temporarily from 85% to 95%, or even 100% in the case of export credit guarantees. Loan guarantees provided by the central government increased 8% between 2007 and 2008, and by a record 31% in 2009, and remained at that level in 2010. While the Small Business Corporation (SBC) increased its direct lending by only 6.2% between 2007 and 2008; there was a dramatic jump in 2009 (83% increase between 2008 and 2009). At the same time, the SBC loan authorisation rate rose from 58.5% to 59.3%. Loan applications in 1Q09 alone reached KRW 5.3 trillion, while they were KRW 6.0 trillion for all of 2008. During the recovery, direct loans, as well as authorisation rates, declined, indicating that government assistance was easing off.

Box 4.6. **Definition of SMEs used in Korea's SME and entrepreneurship finance Scoreboard**

BOK (Bank of Korea) and FSS (Financial Supervisory Service) have the same definition of small and medium-sized enterprises (SMEs).

SMEs denotes an establishment that has less than 300 regular employees or paid-in-capital less than or equal to KRW 8 billion (about USD 8 million). This definition of SMEs is based on the Article 2 of the Framework Act on Small and Medium Enterprises and Article 3 of its enforcement decree. SMEs can also be defined as follows:

Definition of SMEs used by BOK and FSS

Sector[1]	SMEs		Small Business	Micro-enterprises
	No. of workers	Capital and sales	No. of workers	
Manufacturing	Less than 300	Capital worth USD 8 m or less	Less than 50	Less than 10
Mining, construction and transportation	Less than 300	Capital worth USD 3 m or less	Less than 50	Less than 10
Large general retail stores, hotel, recreational condominium operation, communications, information processing and other computer-related industries, engineering service, hospital and broadcasting	Less than 300	Sales worth USD 30 m or less	Less than 10	Less than 5
Seed and seedling production, fishing, electrical, gas and waterworks, medical and orthopaedic products, wholesales, fuel and related products wholesales, mail order sale, door-to-door sale, tour agency, warehouses and transportation-related service, professional, science and technology service, business support service, movie, amusement and theme park operation	Less than 200	Sales worth USD 20 m or less	Less than 10	Less than 5
Wholesale and product intermediation, machinery equipment rent for industrial use, R&D for natural science, public performance, news provision, botanical garden, zoo and natural parks, waste water treatment, waste disposal and cleaning related service	Less than 100	Sales worth USD 10 m or less	Less than 10	Less than 5
Other sectors	Less than 50	Sales worth USD 5 m or less	Less than 10	Less than 5

1. General Criteria (Article 2 of Framework Act on SMEs and Article 3 of Enforcement Decree of the Act). For micro-enterprises, Article 2 of the Act of Special Measures on Assisting Small Business and Micro-enterprises shall apply.

Table 4.38. **Financing SMEs and entrepreneurs: Scoreboard for Korea, 2007-10**

Indicators	Units	2007	2008	2009	2010
Debt					
Business loans, SMEs	KRW millions	368 865 630	422 438 638	443 474 111	441 024 211
Business loans, total	KRW millions	424 795 812	511 201 319	531 071 696	541 069 424
Business loans, SMEs	% of total business loans	86.8	82.6	83.5	81.5
Short-term loans, SMEs	KRW trillions	253	287	304	..
Long-term loans, SMEs	KRW trillions	116	135	134	..
Total short and long-term loans, SMEs	KRW trillions	369	422	438	441
Short-term loans, SMEs	% of total SME loans	68.56	68.01	69.41	..
Government loan guarantees, SMEs	KRW millions	39 729 666	42 961 344	56 381 030	56 207 100
Government guaranteed loans, SMEs	% of SME business loans	10.8	10.2	12.7	12.7
Direct government loans, SMEs	KRW millions	2 480 319	2 634 900	4 811 597	3 098 350
Loans authorised, SMEs	KRW millions	2 721 365	3 201 214	5 821 329	3 415 856
Loans requested, SMEs	KRW millions	4 653 212	6 057 369	9 819 052	6 657 082
Ratio of loans authorised to requested, SMEs	%	58.5	52.8	59.3	51.3
Non-performing loans, SMEs	KRW millions	3 445 872	7 711 192	11 146 424	..
Non-performing loans, SMEs	% of SME business loans	0.93	1.83	2.51	..
Average interest rate	%	6.72	7.31	5.65	5.68
Interest rate spread (between average rate for SMEs and large firms)	%	0.74	0.73	0.61	0.55
Equity					
Venture and growth capital	KRW billions	742	545	507	609
Venture and growth capital	Year-on-year growth rate, %	n.a.	−26.5	−7.0	20.1
Other					
Payment delays, SMEs	Number of days loans past due date	11.0	12.1	9.9	12.1
Bankruptcies, total	Number	2 294	2 735	1 998	1 570
Bankruptcies, total	Year-on-year growth rate, %	n.a.	19.2	−26.9	−21.4

Sources: Refer to Table 4.39 "Definitions and sources of indicators for Korea's Scoreboard".

StatLink http://dx.doi.org/10.1787/888932579987

Figure 4.20. **Trends in SME and entrepreneurship finance in Korea**

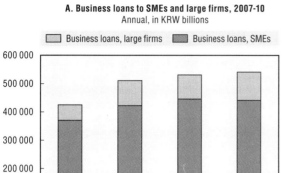

A. Business loans to SMEs and large firms, 2007-10
Annual, in KRW billions

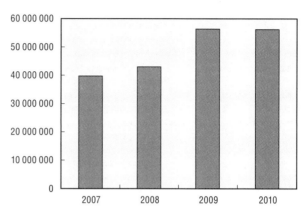

B. Government loan guarantees to SMEs, 2007-10
Annual, in KRW millions

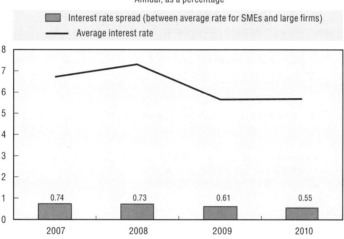

C. Interest rate and spread, 2007-10
Annual, as a percentage

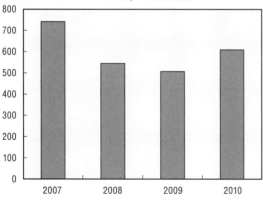

D. Venture and growth capital invested, 2007-10
Annual, in KRW billions

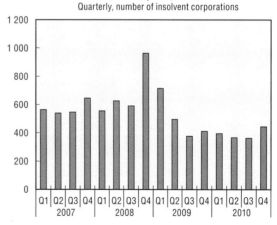

E. Bankruptcies, 2007-10
Quarterly, number of insolvent corporations

Sources: Chart A: Financial Supervisory Service (FSS). Chart B: Financial Supervisory Service (FSS) and Small and Medium Business Administration (SMBA). Chart C: Bank of Korea (BOK). Chart D: Small and Medium Business Administration (SMBA). Chart E: Small Business Corporation (SBC).

StatLink http://dx.doi.org/10.1787/888932579018

Table 4.39. **Financing SMEs and entrepreneurs: Definitions and sources of indicators for Korea's Scoreboard**

Indicators	Definitions	Source
Debt		
Business loans, SMEs	Bank loans to non-financial SMEs, amount outstanding, stocks. The definition of SMEs differs according to sector. Refer to Box 4.6 for details.	Financial Supervisory Service (FSS)
Business loans, total	Business bank loans to all non-financial enterprises, amount outstanding, stocks.	Financial Supervisory Service (FSS)
Short-term loans, SMEs	Outstanding amounts, loans of less than one year. The definition of SMEs differs according to sector. Refer to Box 4.6 for details.	Financial Supervisory Service (FSS)
Long-term loans, SMEs	Outstanding amounts, loans of greater than one year. The definition of SMEs differs according to sector. Refer to Box 4.6 for details.	Financial Supervisory Service (FSS)
Government loan guarantees, SMEs	Value of loans guaranteed by KODIT, KIBO; stocks. The definition of SMEs differs according to sector. Refer to Box 4.6 for details.	Financial Supervisory Service (FSS) and SMBA
Direct government loans, SMEs	Direct government loans supplied by SBC only. The definition of SMEs differs according to sector. Refer to Box 4.6 for details.	Small Business Corporation (SBC)
Loans authorised, SMEs	Direct government loans from the SBC database (not from commercial banks). The definition of SMEs differs according to sector. Refer to Box 4.6 for details.	Small Business Corporation (SBC)
Loans requested, SMEs	Direct government loans from the SBC database (not from commercial banks). The definition of SMEs differs according to sector. Refer to Box 4.6 for details.	Small Business Corporation (SBC)
Non-performing loans, SMEs	Domestic Banks' SME non-performing loans out of total credit including Won-denominated loans, foreign currency-denominated loans, credit card receivables and others (outstanding amount). The definition of SMEs differs according to sector. Refer to Box 4.6 for details.	Financial Supervisory Service (FSS)
Average interest rate	Average interest rates charged on new loans during the period.	Bank of Korea (BOK)
Interest rate spread (between average rate for SMEs and large firms)	SME loan rate – large corporation loan rate.	Bank of Korea (BOK)
Equity		
Venture and growth capital	Annual amounts invested including early and expansion stages.	Small and Medium Business Administration (SMBA)
Other		
Payment delays, SMEs	Average days of delay past loan contract date. The definition of SMEs differs according to sector. Refer to Box 4.6 for details.	Small Business Corporation (SBC)
Bankruptcies, total	Bankrupt firms in Small Business Corporation's portfolio.	Small Business Corporation (SBC)

The Netherlands

SME lending

SMEs comprise 99.6% of enterprises in the Netherlands and employ 68% of the labour force. The Netherlands does not have a definition of SMEs that is applicable to all situations. The national definition conforms to the EU definition of less than 250 employees. However, the Central Bank of the Netherlands uses loan size of less than EUR 1 million to define an SME loan. Furthermore, each bank uses its own reporting system, constituting a challenge to the aggregation of loan data of importance to policy makers.

The Netherlands is one of the most open economies in Europe. The slump in exports in 2008 caused economic growth to stagnate, and in 2009 the economy contracted by 4%. SMEs that were internationally active were the most affected. New SME loans decreased between 2007 and 2009 and increased slightly in 2010. Total business loans increased over the entire period. The SME share in business loans cannot be calculated because the figures for SME loans are flows and those for business loans, stocks. The share of SME short-term loans in total SME loans declined significantly from 55% in 2007 to 48% in 2010.

Table 4.40. **Distribution of enterprises in the Netherlands, 2010**

By size of enterprise

Enterprise size (full time employees)	Number	%
All enterprises	**863 840**	**100.0**
SMEs (0-250)	860 735	99.6
Micro (0-10)	791 630	91.6
Small (10-49)	57 340	6.6
Medium (50-250)	11 765	1.4
Large (250+)	3 100	0.4

Note: Number of employees refers to full-time employees. All industries are included, as are non-employer enterprises.
Source: Centraal Bureau voor de Statistiek (Statistics Netherlands).

StatLink http://dx.doi.org/10.1787/888932580006

SME loans authorised vs. requested

The growth in credit authorised for all enterprises peaked in 1Q08 and declined thereafter. Loan amounts authorised vs. requested declined between 2008 and 2009; only 45% of the SMEs that sought loans in 2009 had them fully authorised as compared with 72% in 2008. The number of SMEs seeking loans fluctuated (19% in 2008, 29% in 2009, 13.5% in 2010 and 22% in 2011).

SME credit conditions

Interest rates declined over the period, but not as fast as expected given the decreases in euribor rates, rose in 2010 and again sharply declined in 2011. 47% of SMEs were required to provide more collateral on their last bank loan in 2009, and 50% in 2010.

Equity financing

Investments by Dutch private equity investors fell from EUR 3 billion in 2007 to EUR 651 million in 2009, but rebounded to EUR 1.1 billion in 2010.

Other indicators

Payment delays increased from 13.2 (2007) to 17 days (2010). With declining access to debt and equity, bankruptcies almost doubled from 4 602 in 2007 to 8 040 in 2009. The majority of these were SMEs.

Government policy response

Government guaranteed loans increased from EUR 634 million (2007) to over EUR 1 billion (2009) and continued at that level in 2010. The government increased the size of the SME target group to include larger enterprises and it increased the loan amount that could be guaranteed.

The Guarantee Scheme for SMEs (BMKB) assists SMEs that have a shortage of collateral to obtain credit from banks. The State guarantees the loan segment for which collateral is lacking and in that way lowers the risk for banks. In November 2008, to facilitate access to finance the government expanded the guarantee scheme to include up to 250 employees instead of just 100 employees. The guaranteed loan amount was increased from EUR 1 million to EUR 1.5 million per enterprise. The maximum guarantee was expanded from 50% to 80% for start ups. It was later extended to existing enterprises. Participants in the guarantee scheme were offered the opportunity to postpone the repayment of their loans up to two additional years. In 2012 the maximum guarantee for small non-start-ups again reduced from 80% to 50% and the maximum for start-ups reduced from 80% to 75%.

The Growth Facility (GFAC) offers banks and private equity enterprises a 50% guarantee on newly issued equity or mezzanine loans up to EUR 5 million. The GFAC has been extended during the crisis and now up to EUR 25 million in equity per enterprise can be guaranteed.

The Guarantee for Entrepreneurial Finance (GO) was launched in March 2009. It provides banks with a 50% guarantee on new bank loans ranging from EUR 1.5 million to EUR 150 million. This substantially lowers the bank risk when issuing credit to entrepreneurs applying for new bank loans.

In 2009, a successful microcredit institution, Qredits, was launched, supported by the government and the banks. For a pilot period of one year, the maximum loan amount increased to EUR 50 000. A programme to support coaching and advice for micro-entrepreneurs was also recently funded by the government.

These programmes have no doubt played a role in increasing bank lending to all enterprises, including SMEs. Before 2009, only SMEs were eligible. In 2009, large enterprises received 20% of the loan guarantees.

In 2011, the Ministry of Economic Affairs, Agriculture and Innovation set up a Business Financing Expert Group to determine if business finance was and would remain available in light of the recent financial and economic crisis. They noted in their report that SME financing problems, particularly for small businesses and innovative businesses, predated the crisis but were becoming more evident. The OECD Scoreboard on SME and entrepreneurship finance confirms this as SME loans grew at a slower rate. Sustainable growers (*i.e.* traditional SMEs) could continue to experience financing problems because of losses incurred in 2007-10. Banks might not be able to meet the growing demand for credit, especially long-term loans, due to additional capital and liquidity requirements. More than in the past, Dutch banks will concentrate on large and medium-sized companies. Thus, the financing of SMEs is not automatically assured. This applies, in particular, to the smaller businesses and the innovative "gazelles".

The report from this expert group recommended:

- better and more standardised loan information and creation of a centralised information register;
- diversification of SME financing sources including credit unions, crowd funding and micro-lending;
- promoting private placements for medium-sized enterprises;
- improve financing knowledge of SMEs and their advisors;
- support the availability of (quasi) equity of SMEs by promoting informal stock exchange, fiscal incentives and a fund of fund for later stage venture capital;
- keep currently existing support measures in place.

Table 4.41. **Financing SMEs and entrepreneurs: Scoreboard for the Netherlands, 2007-10**

Indicators	Units	2007	2008	2009	2010
Debt					
Business loans, SMEs (new loans)	EUR billions	21.8	20.7	15.7	16.5
Business loans, total (outstanding amounts)	EUR billions	258.5	304.8	313.5	325.7
Business loans, SMEs	% of total business loans	..	..	..	..
Short-term loans, SMEs	EUR billions	12.1	11.3	9.0	8.0
Long-term loans, SMEs	EUR billions	9.7	9.4	6.7	8.6
Short-term loans, SMEs	% of total SME business loans	55.5	54.6	57.4	48.1
Government loan guarantees, total	EUR millions	634	647	1 060	1 318
Government loan guarantees, SMEs	EUR millions	409	400	370	945
Loans authorised, SMEs	% of SMEs which requested a bank loan and received it in full	..	72.0	45.0	39.5
Loans requested, SMEs	% of SMEs requesting a bank loan	..	19.0	29.0	13.5
Interest rate	%	5.4	5.7	4.5	6.0
Collateral, SMEs	% of SMEs required to provide collateral for last bank loan	..	..	47	45
Equity					
Private equity	EUR millions	3 000	1 250	651	1 106
Private equity	Year-on-year growth rate, %	..	−58.33	−47.92	69.90
Other					
Payment delays	Average number of days	13.2	13.9	16.0	17.0
Bankruptcies, total	Number	4 602	4 635	8 040	7 211
Bankruptcies, total	Year-on-year growth rate, %	..	0.72	65.03	−10.30
Bankruptcies, total	Per 10 000 firms	58.0	56.0	87.0	83.5

Sources: Refer to Table 4.42 "Definitions and sources of indicators for the Netherlands' Scoreboard".

StatLink 🔗 http://dx.doi.org/10.1787/888932580025

Figure 4.21. **Trends in SME and entrepreneurship finance in the Netherlands**

A. Business loans to SMEs,[1] 2007-10
Annual, in EUR billions

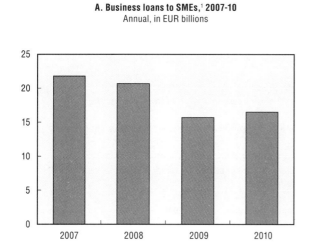

B. Short and long-term business loans to SMEs,[1] 2007-10
Annual, in EUR billions

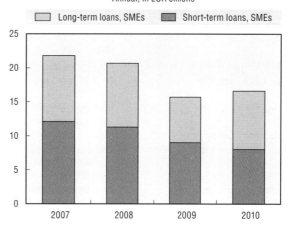

C. Credit authorised by Dutch MFIs to firms, 2006-11
Annual and monthly, growth rate as a percentage

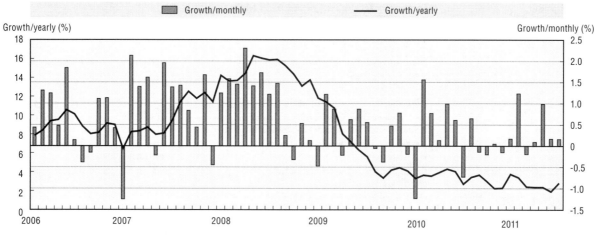

D. Private equity invested, 2007-10
Annual, in EUR millions

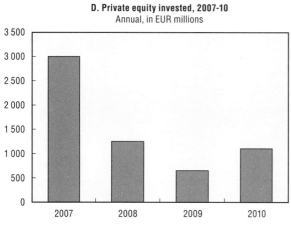

E. Bankruptcies, 2007-10
Annual, number of firms

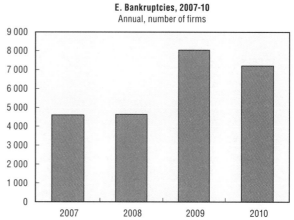

1. For loans up to EUR 1 million.

Sources: Charts A and C: De Nederlansche Bank. Chart B: Ministry of Economic Affairs. Chart D: European Venture Capital Association/NVP. Chart E: Centraal Bureau voor de Statistiek (Statistics Netherlands).

StatLink ᎷᏚᏢ http://dx.doi.org/10.1787/888932579037

Table 4.42. **Financing SMEs and entrepreneurs: Definitions and sources of indicators for the Netherlands' Scoreboard**

Indicators	Definitions	Sources
Debt		
Business loans, SMEs (new loans)	Loans to "SMEs" are defined as the total amount of new loans of up to EUR 1 million.	De Nederlansche Bank
Business loans, total (outstanding amounts)	Total business loan amount outstanding for all firms.	De Nederlansche Bank
Short-term loans, SMEs	New loans to SMEs (loans up to EUR 1 million) with a duration of up to one year.	Ministry of Economic Affairs
Long-term loans, SMEs	New loans to SMEs (loans up to EUR 1 million) with a duration of more than one year.	Ministry of Economic Affairs
Government loan guarantees, total	Government loan guarantees to all firms by BMKB and GFAC and GO.	Ministry of Economic Affairs
Government loan guarantees, SMEs	Government loan guarantees to SMEs (defined as loans guaranteed under BMKB, GFAC and part of GO: companies under 250 employees).	Ministry of Economic Affairs
Loans authorised, SMEs	Loans authorised to SMEs (defined as firms with less than 250 employees).	EIM
Loans requested, SMEs	Loans requested by SMEs (defined as firms with less than 250 employees).	EIM
Interest rate	Interest rate for loans to non-financial corporations for a duration of up to one year.	De Nederlansche Bank
Collateral, SMEs	The proportion of SMEs which were required to provide collateral on last bank loan. SMEs are defined as enterprises with less than 250 employees.	EIM
Equity		
Private equity	Investments made by Dutch private equity investors in the private sector. All enterprises.	European Venture Capital Association/NVP
Other		
Payment delays	Average number of days for business-to-business in 2008 and 2009. For 2007, average number of days for business-to-business, business-to-customer and public entities. All enterprises.	Intrum Justitia European Payment Index 2008, 2009 and 2010
Bankruptcies, total (number)	Number of organisations (pronounced bankrupt).	Centraal Bureau voor de Statistiek (Statistics Netherlands)
Bankruptcies (per 10 000 firms)	Number of organisations (pronounced bankrupt) per 10 000 organisations.	Centraal Bureau voor de Statistiek (Statistics Netherlands)

New Zealand

SME lending

As of February 2010, 99.6% of New Zealand firms were classified as SMEs, defined as enterprises with 0-99 employees. This proportion has stayed relatively stable since 2001. The loan data includes all enterprises, the majority of which are SMEs.

Table 4.43. **Distribution of enterprises in New Zealand, 2010**
By size of enterprise

Enterprise size (employees)	Number	%
All enterprises	**249 140**	**100.0**
SMEs (0-99)	**248 076**	**99.6**
Micro (0-9)	233 236	93.6
Small (10-49)	13 605	5.5
Medium (50-99)	1 235	0.5
Large (100+)	**1 064**	**0.4**

Source: Statistics New Zealand.

StatLink ⟲ http://dx.doi.org/10.1787/888932580044

Prior to the credit crunch, New Zealand's SMEs had access to a range of both debt and equity finance options, including banks and bank overdrafts, finance companies, angel investors and venture capital. Bank lending to businesses grew by 14% in 2008 but declined by 1.5% in 2009 and 2010. Throughout the recession, banks tightened their lending standards while firms scaled back investment plans. During 2009 and 2010 firms reported a deterioration in their perceptions of the ease in accessing finance. The Reserve Bank of New Zealand's Financial Stability Report commented that firms had little appetite for borrowing and had generally reduced their expenditure plans. This may indicate some structural change with firms wanting to maintain lower levels of debt over the longer term.

SME loans authorised *vs.* requested

Among SMEs with six or more employees, 28% requested debt finance in the years 2007-09. Of those requesting finance in 2007, 94% obtained it. In subsequent years there was a continuous decline, indicating the increasing reluctance of banks to lend. The percentage of those requesting financing and obtaining it declined from 87% in 2008, to 82% in 2009. In 2010, the percentage of those requesting debt finance (26%) and obtaining it (78%) also declined.

The decline from recent years is likely to reflect a change in lenders' appetite for risk and the terms they offered.

Table 4.44. **SMEs requesting and obtaining finance in New Zealand, 2007-10**

As a percentage

SMEs	2007	2008	2009	2010
Requesting debt finance	28	28	28	26
Obtaining debt finance	94	87	82	78

Source: Statistics New Zealand, Business Operations Survey.

StatLink ⬛️🛢🖰 *http://dx.doi.org/10.1787/888932580063*

SME credit conditions

Since the beginning of the economic downturn, banks have become increasingly risk-averse. Banks were perceived in November 2008 to be rationing credit and putting pressure on SMEs by increasing interest rates to reflect higher risk levels. The Small Business Advisory Group was established in 2003 to advise government on issues affecting SMEs and to help government agencies communicate more effectively with SMEs. The Small Business Advisory Group reported that SMEs were finding that investment capital was more difficult to secure, that credit was not being renewed and that cash flow was their biggest concern. By December 2010, the banks' average base lending rate for SMEs had declined from 12.15% in December 2007 to 10.22% in 2010. The Reserve Bank of New Zealand conducted quarterly surveys of major banks on credit conditions throughout 2009. The November 2009 report indicated that credit conditions for SMEs were relatively tight compared to the past three years. The majority of banks experienced a further increase in demand for working capital which they believe was driven by payment delays. Most banks continued to tighten their lending policies and credit terms for SMEs in 2009. This tightening was focused on margins and non-interest fees. Over half of respondent banks reported increased delinquency rates across the SME sector.

Growth in non-property lending began to turn positive in 2010, reversing 18 months of negative growth. With some stabilisation in the economy, there are signs that a few more firms were willing to invest and able to meet current bank criteria which banks report have eased slightly.

Equity financing

The global financial crisis has had an adverse effect on New Zealand's venture capital market, although there are signs that access to capital for early stage, high-growth firms has started to improve. The NZ Venture Capital Monitor reports that venture capital and early stage investment activity grew from NZD 34 million in 2009 to NZD 94 million in 2010, including two international deals totaling NZD 45 million.

In August 2010, the government provided the Venture Capital Fund with NZD 40 million in capital for underwriting. The Fund was established in 2001 to co-invest NZD 160 million with the private sector in innovative young New Zealand firms and catalyse the evolution of a viable venture capital market in New Zealand. The underwriting will enable the operator of the Fund to continue to engage with prospective co-investment partners. A NZD 40 million Seed Co-Investment Fund for early stage ventures was launched in 2006.

Payment delays

The per cent of respondents waiting more than 60 days for payment increased from just 5.3% to 22.9% during the recession. According to Dun and Bradstreet, the number of late payers (business to business) increased during the recovery (2Q2010 to 2Q2011), as natural disasters and the after-effects of the global financial crisis have strained the finances of many New Zealand firms. In 2010-11, there were 2 718 cumulative bankruptcies. It was not possible to see the impact of cash flow problems on SME survival.

Government policy response

The government has no general loan guarantee facility or direct loan programme, although there is one for guaranteeing exporters' working capital. On 4 February 2009, the Prime Minister announced a small business relief package that included five major provisions:

- a series of tax reduction and tax payment deferments;
- an expansion of the working capital guarantee scheme for exporters with a turnover of up to NZD 50 million;
- an extended jurisdiction for the Disputes Tribunal, allowing businesses to settle more claims without the recourse to the courts;
- expansion of business advice services such as a hotline, health check, seminars, and mentors; and
- prompt payment requirement for government agencies.

In 2011, these measures were still in force. The Short Term-Trade Credit Guarantee was extended in May 2009, bringing the total available to NZD 150 million.

Table 4.45. **Financing SMEs and entrepreneurs: Scoreboard for New Zealand, 2007-10**

Indicator	Units	2007	2008	2009	2010
Debt					
Business loans, SMEs		..	..	..	..
Business loans, total	NZD billions	111.0	126.5	122.7	120.9
Business loans, SMEs (% of total business loans)		..	..	..	..
Short-term loans, SMEs		..	..	..	..
Long-term loans, SMEs		..	..	..	..
Total short and long-term loans, SMEs		..	..	..	..
Loans authorised, SMEs	%	94	87	82	78
Loans requested, SMEs	%	28	28	28	26
Non-performing loans, total		..	..	..	..
Non-performing loans, SMEs		..	..	..	..
Interest rate, loans < NZD 1 million	%	12.15	11.23	10.05	10.22
Interest rate, loans > NZD 1 million		..	..	..	..
Interest rate spread (between loans < 1 million and > 1 million)		..	..	..	..
Collateral, SMEs		..	..	..	..
Equity					
Venture capital	NZD millions	..	66	34	94
Venture capital	Year-on-year growth rate, %	..	..	−51.5	276.0
Other					
Payment delays	% of respondents waiting more than 60 days	..	5.3	22.8	..

Sources: Refer to Table 4.46 "Definitions and sources of indicators for New Zealand's Scoreboard".

StatLink ᴍ⟨ᴛ⟩ http://dx.doi.org/10.1787/888932580082

Figure 4.22. **Trends in SME and entrepreneurship finance in New Zealand**

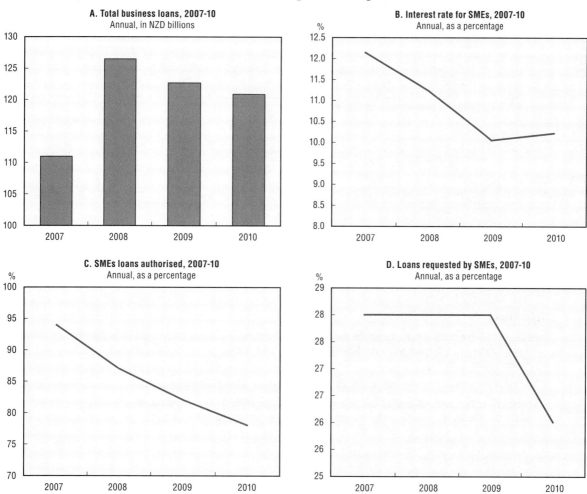

Sources: Charts A and B: Reserve Bank of New Zealand. Charts C and D: Statistics New Zealand.

StatLink ᓂᔑ᠍᠍᠍ http://dx.doi.org/10.1787/888932579056

Table 4.46. **Financing SMEs and entrepreneurs: Definitions and sources of indicators for New Zealand's Scoreboard**

Indicators	Definitions	Source
Debt		
Business loans, total	Corporate firms (including financial firms, government administration and defence).	Reserve Bank of New Zealand
Loans authorised, SMEs	Percentage of SMEs (firms with 6-19 employees) requesting debt finance that received it on reasonable terms.	Statistics New Zealand, Business Operations Survey
Loans requested, SMEs	Percentage of SMEs (firms with 6-19 employees) requesting debt finance.	Statistics New Zealand, Business Operations Survey
Interest rate, loans < NZD 1 million	Base interest rate for new overdraft loans for SMEs (loan amounts less than NZD 1 million), non-farm enterprises.	Reserve Bank of New Zealand, Survey of Registered Banks
Equity		
Venture capital	Amount invested in early stage only (excludes buy outs). All enterprises.	NZ Private Equity and Venture Capital Association and Ernst and Young
Other		
Payment delays	Percentage of respondents waiting for more than 60 days for payment.	Survey of 659 firms, February 2009

References

Dun and Bradstreet, "Longer Payments for New Zealand Businesses", 28 July 2011 available at: *http://dnb.co.nz/Header/News/News_Archive/2011/Longer_payment_terms_for_New_Zealand_businesses/indexdl_7585.aspx.*

Ministry of Economic Development, "SMEs in New Zealand: Structure and Dynamics".

Statistics New Zealand, "Business Operations Survey", available at: *www.stats.govt.nz/browse_for_stats/businesses/business_growth_and_innovation/business-op-survey-2010-tables.aspx.*

Portugal

SME lending

In 2008, SMEs comprised 99.7% of enterprises in Portugal and employed 72.5% of the business sector labour force. Portugal complies with the EU definition for SMEs. The vast majority of enterprises are SMEs, 86% are micro-enterprises, 12% are small and 2% are medium-sized. The share of SME loans in total business loans was nearly 78% during the years 2007-10. The proportion of SME short-term loans in total SME loans ranged between 31%-33%, indicating that SME loans were mainly used to finance investment. In 2010, the global stock of business loans decreased by around EUR 2.3 billion. 83%, or EUR 1.9 billion, was related to SME loans. The share of government guaranteed loans in total SME loans grew significantly from 1% in 2007 to 7% in 2011, demonstrating the sustained public efforts to maintain SME access to finance.

Table 4.47. **Distribution of enterprises in Portugal, 2008**
By size of enterprise

Enterprise size (employees)	Number	%
All enterprises	**350 871**	**100.0**
SMEs (2-249)	349 756	99.7
Micro (2-9)	300 228	85.6
Small (10-49)	42 960	12.2
Medium (50-249)	6 568	1.9
Large (250+)	**1 115**	**0.3**

Note: Companies with up to one employee were excluded (there were 431 092 companies with up to one employee). Includes the non-financial business economy (NACE Ver 2, B to J, L to N and 95).
Source: Statistics Portugal, IP.

StatLink ᵐˢ⁵ http://dx.doi.org/10.1787/888932580101

SME credit conditions

During 2009-10, banks tightened lending conditions to SMEs. The average interest rate increased 50 basis points, from 5.7% to 6.2%, and the interest rate spread between SMEs and large firms also increased from 1.7% in 2008 to 2.4% in 2010, indicating less favourable conditions for SMEs. 81% of collateralised loans were SME loans.

Equity financing

The global amount of venture capital invested in SMEs fell significantly in 2009 to EUR 43 million, 55% less than in 2008, due to investors' extreme risk aversion as a consequence of the financial crisis. After the government undertook measures, it recovered 49% during 2010, to a total amount of EUR 64 million. Nevertheless, it was one-third less than the 2008 global investment of EUR 96.8 million. Most of the investment was in early stage, and in particular in the start-up stage.

Table 4.48. **Equity capital invested by stage in Portugal, 2007-10**

EUR millions

Stage	2007	2008	2009	2010
Early stage	38.8	56.7	30.4	51.9
Seed	0.2	0	0.1	0
Start up	38.5	56.7	30.3	51.9
Later stage	71.6	40.1	12.7	12.2

Source: Portuguese Venture Capital Association.

StatLink http://dx.doi.org/10.1787/888932580120

Payment delays, non-performing loans and bankruptcies

The drop in sales and the difficulties in accessing finance had a negative impact on SME cash flow, causing an increase in payment delays, which rose from 33 days in 2008 to 37 days in 2010. The number of enterprise bankruptcies also increased from 24 917 (2009) to 26 990 (2010).

Government policy response

The global financial crisis has undoubtedly affected SME demand for credit. Financiers have adopted a more conservative position in credit decisions. Risk premiums have increased and credit maturities have been reduced.

In the framework of the Anti-Crisis Measures adopted by Portugal, SMEs' access to finance has been a major priority for the government. In this context, eight "SME Invest" credit lines to facilitate SME access to credit were launched. These credit lines, with a total stock of bank credit of EUR 9.7 billion, have long-term maturities (up to 7 years) and preferential conditions, namely, partially subsidised interest rates and risk-sharing public guarantees, which cover between 50% and 75% of the loan. These credit lines aim to support fixed investment and also SME working capital.

As of 30 September 2011, about 86 200 projects were eligible within the SME Invest credit lines amounting to EUR 8.1 billion in finance to about 55 000 SMEs (15% of SMEs), supporting more than 755 000 jobs. As part of the global package of the SME Invest credit lines, the government proceeded to recapitalise the Mutual Counter-Guarantee Fund.

The government has created the "Leaders Programme" to improve relations between banks and SMEs. The Leaders Programme identifies the "best" SMEs and even the "best of the best". Such identification builds trust between SMEs and banks.

Other alternative financing schemes were implemented to reinforce SMEs' permanent capital. An Autonomous Fund Supporting Company Concentration and Consolidation (FACCE) with a sum of EUR 175 million support restructuring, concentration, consolidation and acquisition of enterprises, especially SMEs. A Special Real Estate Company Support Fund (FIEAE), with a sum of EUR 150 million, facilitates the acquisition of real estate that is part of companies' assets in order to provide these same companies with immediate financial resources. Normally it is accompanied by the companies' right to use and the right or obligation to repurchase the said real estate. Another public intervention is the export credit insurance with guarantees, which reduces the impact of credit restrictions and clients' increased risk in the markets where those enterprises operate.

Table 4.49. **Financing SMEs and entrepreneurs: Scoreboard for Portugal, 2007-10**

Indicators	Units	2007	2008	2009	2010
Debt					
Business loans, SMEs	EUR millions	84 866	92 662	94 351	92 423
Business loans, total	EUR millions	108 317	119 188	121 679	119 359
Business loans, SMEs	% of total business loans	78.3	77.7	77.5	77.4
Short-term loans, SMEs	EUR millions	26 758	27 928	29 295	27 196
Long-term loans, SMEs	EUR millions	56 308	62 098	60 474	60 268
Total short and long-term loans, SMEs	EUR millions	83 066	90 026	89 770	87 464
Short-term loans, SMEs	% of total SME loans	32.2	31.0	32.6	31.1
Government guaranteed loans, CGF	EUR millions	740	1 552	4 961	6 825
Government guaranteed loans, CGF	% of SME business loans	1	2	5	7
Non-performing loans, total	EUR millions	1 888	2 806	5 003	5 261
Non-performing loans, SMEs	EUR millions	1 801	2 636	4 581	4 959
Non-performing loans, large	EUR millions	87	170	422	302
Interest rate, average SME rate[1]	%	7.0	7.6	5.7	6.2
Interest rate spread (between average SME rate and large firm rate)	%	1.8	1.7	1.9	2.4
Collateral, SMEs	% of collateralised loans granted to SMEs in total collateralised loans	..	..	0.82	0.81
Equity					
Venture capital	EUR millions	110.4	96.8	43.1	64.1
Venture capital	Year-on-year growth rate, %	53	149	−55	49
Other					
Payment delays	Days	39.9	33.0	35.0	37.0
Bankruptcies, total	Number	26 446	31 167	24 917	26 990
Bankruptcies, total	Year-on-year growth rate, %	−16.0	17.9	−20.1	8.3
Incidence of insolvency, total	Per 10 000 enterprises	757	891	709	764

1. No data on interest rates by size of firm are available. As a proxy, data on interest rates on new loans up to EUR 1 million (prior to 2010) and loans up to EUR 0.25 million (in 2010) are used. Data on interest rates cover only loans granted by banks.
Sources: Refer to Table 4.50 "Definitions and sources of indicators for Portugal's Scoreboard".

StatLink ᐧᓂᔅᐱ *http://dx.doi.org/10.1787/888932580139*

Figure 4.23. **Trends in SME and entrepreneurship finance in Portugal**

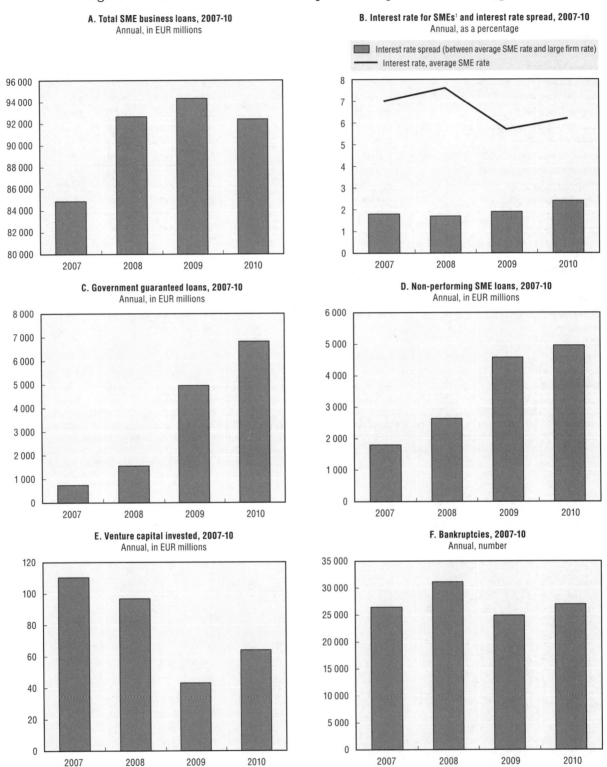

1. Concerning interest rates no data by firm size are available. As a proxy for SMEs, data on interest rates on new loans up to EUR 1 million (prior to 2010) and loans up to EUR 0.25 million (in 2010) are used. Data on interest rates cover only loans granted by banks.

Sources: Charts A, B and D: Bank of Portugal. Chart C: SPGM, SA. Chart E: Portuguese Venture Capital Association. Chart F: Statistics Portugal, IP and COSEC, SA.

StatLink ⟦⟧ http://dx.doi.org/10.1787/888932579075

Table 4.50. **Financing SMEs and entrepreneurs: Definitions and sources of indicators for Portugal's Scoreboard**

Indicators	Definition	Source
Debt		
Business loans, SMEs	Performing and non-performing loans outstanding granted by banks and other financial institutions. Performing loans do not include factoring without recourse. Companies with less than one employee are included as they cannot be distinguished from other micro companies. SMEs defined following the EU definition (less than 250 employees and annual turnover below EUR 50 million and/or balance sheet below EUR 43 million, Com Recommendation 2003/361/EC). Excluding holding companies and sole traders.	Bank of Portugal
Business loans, total	Performing and non-performing loans outstanding granted by banks and other financial institutions. Performing loans do not include factoring without recourse.	Bank of Portugal
Short-term loans, SMEs	Performing loans; maturity up to 12 months. SMEs defined following the EU definition (less than 250 employees and annual turnover below EUR 50 million and/or balance sheet below EUR 43 million, Com Recommendation 2003/361/EC). Excluding holding companies and sole traders.	Bank of Portugal
Long-term loans, SMEs	Performing loans; maturity more than 12 months. SMEs defined following the EU definition (less than 250 employees and annual turnover below EUR 50 million and/or balance sheet below EUR 43 million, Com Recommendation 2003/361/EC). Excluding holding companies and sole traders.	Bank of Portugal
Government guaranteed loans, CGF	Government guaranteed loans to SMEs by the public Mutual Counter-guarantee Fund.	SPGM, SA
Non-performing loans, total	Loans outstanding overdue for more than 30 days; in the case of factoring without recourse only amounts overdue for more than 90 days are included.	Bank of Portugal
Non-performing loans, SMEs	Loans outstanding overdue for more than 30 days; in the case of factoring without recourse only amounts overdue for more than 90 days are included. SMEs defined following the EU definition (less than 250 employees and annual turnover below EUR 50 million and/or balance sheet below EUR 43 million, Com Recommendation 2003/361/EC). Excluding holding companies and sole traders.	Bank of Portugal
Non-performing loans, large	Loans outstanding overdue for more than 30 days; in the case of factoring without recourse only amounts overdue for more than 90 days are included. Large companies include holding companies.	Bank of Portugal
Interest rate, average SME rate	No data on interest rates by firm size are available. As a proxy to SME, data on interest rate on new loans up to EUR 1 million (prior to 2010) and loans up to EUR 0.25 million (in 2010) are used. Data on interest rates only cover loans granted by banks.	Bank of Portugal
Interest rate spread (between average SME rate and large firm rate)	No data on interest rates by firm size are available. As a proxy for SMEs, data on interest rates on new loans up to EUR 1 million (prior to 2010) and loans up to EUR 0.25 million (in 2010) are used. For large firms, data on interest rates on new loans over EUR 1 million are used. Data on interest rates only cover loans granted by banks.	Bank of Portugal
Collateral, SMEs	The percentage of collateralised loans granted to SMEs in total collateralised loans. Information on collateral is only available from January 2009 onwards. SMEs defined following the EU definition (less than 250 employees and annual turnover below EUR 50 million and/or balance sheet below EUR 43 million, Com Recommendation 2003/361/EC). Excluding holding companies and sole traders.	Bank of Portugal
Equity		
Venture capital	Investment in all enterprises. Data include early stage and expansion phases, not turnaround or buyout/replacement.	Portuguese Venture Capital Association
Other		
Payment delays	Average payment delay in days for business-to-business in 2008, 2009 and 2010. For 2007, average delay in days for business-to-business, business-to-consumer and public entities. All enterprises.	Intrum Justitia, European Payment Index
Bankruptcies, total	Data include all dissolved companies.	Statistics Portugal, IP and COSEC, SA
Incidence of insolvency, total	Number of dissolved enterprises per 10 000 enterprises.	Statistics Portugal, IP and COSEC, SA

Slovak Republic

SME lending

The Slovak Republic joined the OECD Scoreboard on financing SMEs and entrepreneurs in 2010. It is in the process of amending its methodology to collect statistics on SME financing. Thus, the data in the current Scoreboard are likely to change as data collection improves. The current framework uses the EU definition for an SME which is an enterprise with less than 250 employees. However, not all banks use this definition. As Table 4.51 shows, SMEs dominate the Slovak economy.

Table 4.51. **Distribution of enterprises in the Slovak Republic, 2007**

By size of enterprise

Enterprise size (employees)	Number	%
All enterprises	**57 805**	**100.0**
SMEs (1-249)	**57 286**	**99.1**
Micro (1-9)	*42 281*	*73.1*
Small (10-49)	*12 964*	*22.4*
Medium (50-249)	*2 044*	*3.5*
Large (250+)	**519**	**0.9**

Note: Data include ISIC Rev. 3 Categories C, D, E, F, G, I and K. Non-employer enterprises are not included.
Source: OECD Structural and Demographic Business Statistics Database.

StatLink ᴍ⃞ᴼᵖ http://dx.doi.org/10.1787/888932580158

The data for SME sector are currently collected from the database of financial statements (balance sheets) available from the tax authorities. The data are aggregated into categories according to the size of the firm represented by number of employees. After a revision of the methodology used for collecting bank statistics, it will be possible to obtain more detailed and accurate data on SME financing from the banking sector.

Both SME and total business lending continued to increase in 2008. While they stagnated in 2009, they suffered no serious declines. The SME share in total business loans increased from 66% (2007) to 79% (2009). Surprisingly, the share of SME long term loans in total SME loans grew between 2007 and 2009 indicating that investment was still taking place. However, the rate of growth in long-term loans slowed in 2009 along with the rest of the economy.

Credit conditions

SME interest rates declined from 6% (2007) to 3.5% (2009) but rose again in 2010 to 4.45%. According to Slovak authorities SMEs were required to provide collateral for development and expansion loans. Operating loans do not usually require specific collateral as they are covered by the framework of the funding agreements which are collateralised.

Venture capital and other indicators

While at very low levels, venture capital grew between 2007 and 2009 and then declined in 2010. At the same time, bankruptcies doubled.

Table 4.52. **Breakdown of venture capital investments in SMEs in the Slovak Republic according to investment stages, 2007-10**

In EUR

	2007	2008	2009	2010
Seed	215 760	3 845 847	2 099 247	61 988
Start-up	46 471	451 437	3 895 833	10 896 510
Development	6 771 559	3 693 587	8 370 533	459 500
Total	**7 033 791**	**7 990 872**	**14 365 613**	**11 417 998**

Source: National Agency for Development of Small and Medium Enterprises.

StatLink ⬛🖘 *http://dx.doi.org/10.1787/888932580177*

Government policy response

There are special government SME loan programmes operated by specialised state banks and the National Agency for SME Development (NADSME). During the financial crisis, government guaranteed loans and SME government direct loans increased 36% to EUR 157 million (2008). Direct loans to SMEs by the government increased 37% between 2007 and 2008 up to EUR 160 million. This was a temporary anti-crisis measure in response to the decline in loans by commercial banks.

Table 4.53. **Financing SMEs and entrepreneurs: Scoreboard for the Slovak Republic, 2007-10**

Indicators	Units	2007	2008	2009	2010
Debt					
Business loans, SMEs	EUR millions	9 136	12 092	12 032	..
Business loans, total	EUR millions	13 906	15 679	15 156	15 174
Short-term loans, SMEs	EUR millions	4 609	4 797	4 981	..
Long-term loans, SMEs	EUR millions	4 528	7 295	7 050	..
Government loan guarantees, SMEs	EUR millions	82	99	81	70
Government guaranteed loans, SMEs	EUR millions	115	157	143	139
Direct government loans, SMEs	EUR millions	117	160	139	147
Interest rate[1]	%	6.07	4.92	3.51	4.45
Collateral, SMEs[2]	% of SMEs required to provide collateral on latest bank loan	100	100	100	100
Equity					
Venture capital, SMEs	EUR millions	7.0	8.0	14.4	11.4
Venture capital, SMEs	Year-on-year growth rate, %	n.a.	14	80	−11
Other					
Payment delays	B2B (days)	19.7	8	13	17
	B2C (days)	21.8	8	10	15
Bankrupcies, total	Number	169	251	276	344
Bankrupcies, total	Year-on-year growth rate, %	n.a.	48.5	10.0	24.6
Bankrupcies, total	Per 10 000 firms	16.75	21.05	21.78	24.15

1. Figures represent the general interest rate for all business. Specific rates for SMEs are not available at this time.
2. Figures relate to development loans, for working capital loans collateral is usually not requested.
Sources: Refer to Table 4.54 "Definitions and sources of indicators for the Slovak Republic's Scoreboard".

StatLink ⬛ http://dx.doi.org/10.1787/888932580196

Figure 4.24. **Trends in SME and entrepreneurship finance in the Slovak Republic**

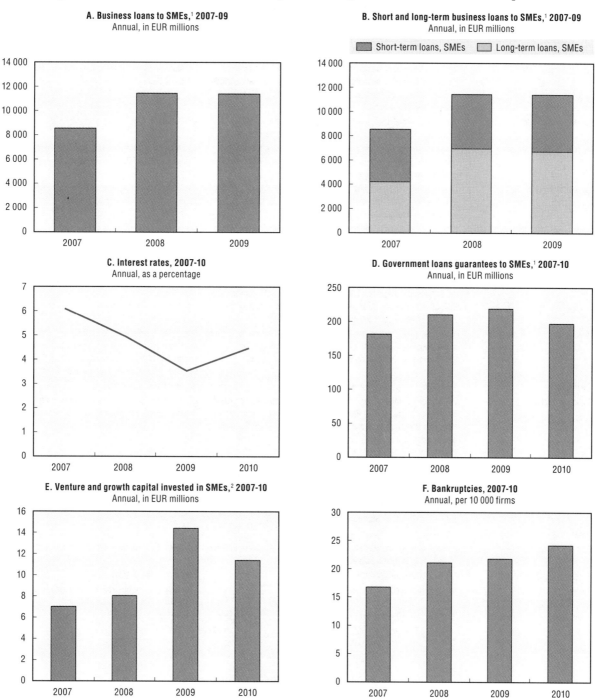

1. Enterprises with less than 250 employees, including natural persons – entrepreneurs.
2. SMEs defined following the EU definition (less than 250 employees and annual turnover below EUR 50 million and/or balance sheet below EUR 43 million, Com Recommendation 2003/361/EC).

Sources: Chart A: Tax Authority/financial statements (balance sheets) database. Chart B: Corporate financial statements (balance sheets) database, National Bank of Slovakia. Chart C: National Bank of Slovakia. Chart D: Annual reports on the state of SMEs in the Slovak Republic (National Agency for Development of Small and Medium Enterprises), Slovak Guarantee and Development Bank, Export-Import Bank. Chart E: National Agency for Development of Small and Medium Enterprises. Chart F: Conversion based on business database of the Statistical Office of the Slovak Republic.

StatLink 🔗 http://dx.doi.org/10.1787/888932579094

Table 4.54. **Financing SMEs and entrepreneurs: Definitions and sources of indicators for the Slovak Republic's Scoreboard**

Indicators	Definition	Source
Debt		
Business loans, SMEs	Bank and financial institution loans to SMEs, amount outstanding (stocks) at the end of period; by firm size using the national definition of SME (enterprises with less than 250 employees, including natural persons – entrepreneurs).	Tax Authority/financial statements (balance sheets) database
Business loans, total	Bank and financial institution business loans to all non-financial enterprises, including natural persons – entrepreneurs, stocks	National Bank of Slovakia
Short-term loans, SMEs	Loans equal to or less than one year by firm size using the national definition of SME (enterprises with less than 250 employees, including natural persons – entrepreneurs).	Corporate financial statements (balance sheets) database, National Bank of Slovakia
Long-term loans, SMEs	Loans for more than one year by firm size using the national definition of SME (enterprises with less than 250 employees, including natural persons – entrepreneurs).	Corporate financial statements (balance sheets) database, National Bank of Slovakia
Government loan guarantees, SMEs	Guarantees available to banks and financial institutions – new by firm size using the national definition of SME (enterprises with less than 250 employees, including natural persons – entrepreneurs).	Annual reports on the state of SMEs in the Slovak Republic (National Agency for Development of Small and Medium Enterprises), Slovak Guarantee and Development Bank, Export-Import Bank
Government guaranteed loans, SMEs	Loans guaranteed by government – new. SMEs defined following the EU definition (less than 250 employees and annual turnover below EUR 50 million and/or balance sheet below EUR 43 million, Com Recommendation 2003/361/EC)	Slovak Guarantee and Development Bank
Direct government loans, SMEs	New loans guaranteed by government, (state owned banks) by firm size using the national definition of SME (enterprises with less than 250 employees, including natural persons – entrepreneurs).	Annual reports on the state of SMEs in the Slovak Republic (National Agency for Development of Small and Medium Enterprises), Slovak Guarantee and Development Bank, Export-Import Bank
Interest rate	Interest rate for all businesses.	National Bank of Slovakia
Collateral, SMEs	Percentage of SMEs that were required to provide collateral on latest development bank loan. SMEs defined following the EU definition (less than 250 employees and annual turnover below EUR 50 million and/or balance sheet below EUR 43 million, Com Recommendation 2003/361/EC)	National Bank of Slovakia, National Agency for Development of Small and Medium Enterprises survey,
Equity		
Venture capital, SMEs	Actual amounts invested in SMEs: seed and start-up phase. SMEs defined following the EU definition (less than 250 employees and annual turnover below EUR 50 million and/ or balance sheet below EUR 43 million, Com Recommendation 2003/361/EC)	Annual reports on the state of SMEs in the Slovak Republic (National Agency for Development of Small and Medium Enterprises)
Other		
Payment delays	Average number of days delay beyond the contract period for Business to Business (B2B) and Business to Customer (B2C).	European Payment Index reports (Intrum Justitia)
Bankruptcies, total (number)	Number of enterprises ruled bankrupt.	Statistics of the Ministry of Justice
Bankruptcies, total (per 10 000 firms)	No. bankrupt per 10 000 enterprises.	Conversion based on business database of the Statistical Office of the Slovak Republic

Slovenia

SME lending

For the purpose of the OECD Scoreboard on SME and entrepreneurship finance, Slovenia defines SMEs as enterprises with less than 250 employees. This definition is also used by the Statistical Office of the Republic of Slovenia, although the official legal definition and the definition used by the Ministry of the Economy are wider and contain additional criteria, including asset value, revenue threshold and requirements from Commission Recommendation 2003/361/ES. The number of SMEs was 165 615 in 2010. Many SMEs were suppliers to large enterprises which were hit hard by the recession. Thus, many SME suppliers also failed.

Enterprises with more than EUR 2 million in assets have to report their debt, but sole proprietors are excluded. Data on business loans are collected by the Bank of Slovenia, but SME loans are not disaggregated. Information on SME loans comes from the balance sheets of enterprises (S11 enterprises) with assets between EUR 2 million and EUR 17.5 million. Thus, many smaller SMEs are omitted from the loan data. Total business loans increased over this period while SME loans decreased, as did the SME loan share, which declined from 57% (2007) to 50% (2010). SME short-term loans also declined from 43%-38%. It appears that large enterprises enjoyed better access to credit than SMEs.

Table 4.55. **Distribution of enterprises in Slovenia, 2009**

By size of enterprise

Enterprise size (employees)	Number	%
All enterprises	160 931	100.0
SMEs (0-249)	160 568	99.8
Micro (0-9)	150 916	93.8
Small (10-49)	7 500	4.7
Medium (50-249)	2 152	1.3
Large (250+)	363	0.2

Notes: Data include enterprises in all industries and non-employer enterprises.
Source: Statistical Office of the Republic of Slovenia.

StatLink ᴍᴤ▰ http://dx.doi.org/10.1787/888932580215

Credit conditions

SME interest rates declined from 6.7% (2008) to 6% (2010), but the spread between interest rates for SMEs and large enterprises grew. Large enterprises enjoyed better credit terms.

Government policy response

Government direct loans to SMEs declined by almost half between 2007 and 2010. These loans are mostly provided by public funds such as the Slovene Enterprise Fund (SEF), the Slovenian Regional Development Fund and the Housing Fund of the Republic of Slovenia. The Ministry of the Economy provides credit guarantees and interest rate subsidies through the Slovene Enterprise Fund. The programme for interest rate subsidies started in the beginning of 2009, but the guarantees for bank loans were provided prior to this by the SEF. Guarantees are also provided by SID Bank which is responsible for developing, providing and promoting innovative and long-term financial services which are designed to supplement financial markets for the sustainable development of Slovenia. SID Bank also provides direct loans to SMEs in case of market failure.

Table 4.56. **Financing SMEs and entrepreneurs: Scoreboard for Slovenia, 2007-10**

Indicators	Units	2007	2008	2009	2010
Debt					
Business loans, total	EUR millions	17 508	20 704	20 908	21 013
Short-term loans, SMEs	EUR millions	4 289	5 499	4 945	4 001
Long-term loans, SMEs	EUR millions	5 653	6 103	6 557	6 492
Total short and long-term loans, SMEs	EUR millions	9 942	11 602	11 502	10 493
SME share in business loans	%	56.7	56.0	55.0	49.9
Short-term loans, SMEs	% of total SME loans	43.1	47.4	43.0	38.1
Direct government loans, SMEs	EUR millions	242	241	110	126
Interest rate, SMEs (new loans < EUR 1 million)	%	5.99	6.76	6.23	6.07
Interest rate large firms (new loans > = EUR 1 million)	%	5.58	6.34	5.66	5.37
Interest rate spread (between SME and large firms)	%	0.41	0.42	0.57	0.70

Sources: Refer to Table 4.57 "Definitions and sources of indicators for Slovenia's Scoreboard".

StatLink ⟡ *http://dx.doi.org/10.1787/888932580234*

Figure 4.25. **Trends in SME and entrepreneurship finance in Slovenia**

A. Total business and SME loans, 2007-10
Annual, in EUR millions

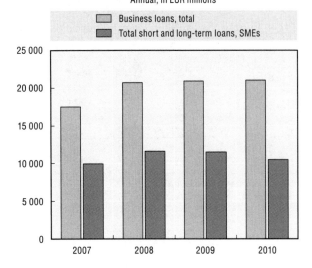

B. Short-term loans to SMEs, 2007-10
Annual, in EUR millions and as a % of total loans

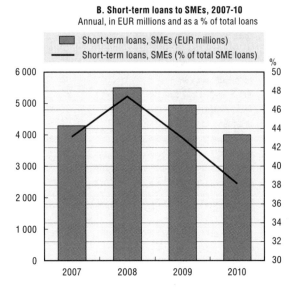

C. Direct government loans to SMEs, 2007-10
Annual, in EUR millions

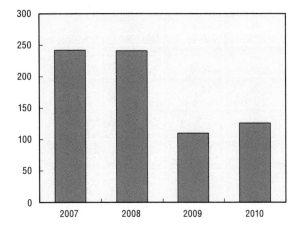

D. Interest rates for loans to SMEs and to large firms, 2007-10
Annual, as a percentage

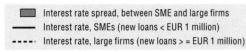

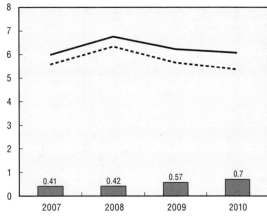

Source: Bank of Slovenia.

StatLink 🔗 http://dx.doi.org/10.1787/888932579113

Table 4.57. **Financing SMEs and entrepreneurs: Definitions and sources of indicators for Slovenia's Scoreboard**

Indicators	Definition	Source
Debt		
Business loans, total	Business loans, amount outstanding.	Bank of Slovenia
Short-term loans, SMEs	Estimated from the balance sheets, amount outstanding, with a due date less than 12 months includes financial firms. SMEs are defined enterprises with less than or equal to 250 employees and asset value less than or equal to EUR 17.5 million.	Bank of Slovenia
Long-term loans, SMEs	Estimated from the balance sheets, amount outstanding with a due date more than 12 months includes financial firms. SMEs are defined enterprises with less than or equal to 250 employees and asset value less than or equal to EUR 17.5 million.	Bank of Slovenia
Direct government loans, SMEs	Direct loans from government to SMEs, stocks. SMEs are defined enterprises with less than or equal to 250 employees and asset value less than or equal to EUR 17.5 million.	Bank of Slovenia
Interest rate, SMEs (new loans < EUR 1 million)	Weighted average annual interest rates for new loans to enterprises with less than 250 employees; for maturity less than 1 year; and amounts less than EUR 1 million.	Bank of Slovenia
Interest rate large firms (new loans > = EUR 1 million)	Weighted average annual interest rates for new loans to enterprises with more than or equal to 250 employees; for maturity less than 1 year; and amounts more than or equal to EUR 1 million.	Bank of Slovenia

Sweden

SME lending

SMEs constitute 99.9% of Swedish enterprises and employ 63.5% of the labour force. The majority of SMEs use the commercial banking sector when seeking external finance. Since no data were available through supply-side surveys, the loans were based on a proxy (enterprise liabilities) obtained from tax record information. Using tax information creates a lag of 18 months in terms of its availability. Both total business loans and SME loans increased between 2007 and 2009. The SME share in business loans was almost constant at 88% between 2007 and 2008 and increased to 92% in 2009. The high share of SME loans in business loans could possibly be explained by the fact that intercompany loans, an important component of the debt of large companies, have been excluded. If one firm raises capital from the market and is acting as the "bank" within the enterprise group, then these loans might not be included if the "bank" is classified as a financial company or if it is located abroad.

Table 4.58. **Distribution of firms and employment in Sweden, 2009**

By size of firm

Enterprise size (employees)	Enterprises		Employment	
	Number	%	Number	%
All enterprises	**927 917**	**100.0**	**2 441 926**	**100.0**
SMEs (0-249)	**926 973**	**99.9**	**1 550 062**	**63.5**
Micro (0-19)	*912 141*	*98.3*	*801 736*	*32.8*
Small (20-49)	*10 232*	*1.1*	*303 994*	*12.4*
Medium (50-249)	*4 600*	*0.5*	*444 332*	*18.2*
Large (250+)	**944**	**0.1**	**891 864**	**36.5**

Source: Statistics Sweden, *Structural Business Statistics 2009*.

StatLink ᴍ⑤🖳 http://dx.doi.org/10.1787/888932580253

SME credit conditions

As in most other euro area countries, interest rates peaked in 3Q08 and declined thereafter as a result of monetary easing. The average base interest rate for SME loans was 4.86% (2007), rising to 5.66% (2008) before declining in 2009 to 2.42%. In 2010, interest rates rose slightly to 2.58%. However, the interest rate spreads between small and large enterprises, while volatile, declined absolutely, whereas in some other euro area countries they continued to grow. Nevertheless, the relative difference between large and small enterprise interest rates increased between 2008 and 2010, indicating that SMEs' risk premium had increased. For example, in 2008, the average large enterprise interest rate was 85.5% of the SME rate, but in 2010, it was 62.8% of the SME rate. According to a survey in March 2009 by ALMI Business Partner, 30% of bank managers reported having tightened credit terms for enterprises compared to the previous quarter. In the quarterly surveys carried out since then (2Q2009 to 2Q2011), almost none have reported relaxed credit terms, and most reported unchanged or tightened terms.

Equity financing

There was also a significant deterioration in equity financing. In 2010, it was about half that for 2008. It should be pointed out that the decrease between 2009 and 2010 was modest – the significant deterioration of equity financing occurred earlier. In December 2010, the government established a new venture capital fund for northern Sweden, "Inlandsinnovation" with EUR 200 million.

Payment delays and bankruptcies

A survey of SME managers by the Swedish Federation of Business Owners indicated that payment delays on the part of customers had a negative impact on SME cash flow and, in turn, caused problems of payment ability for these enterprises. The share of enterprises having difficulties caused by payment delays increased from 19% (4Q08) to 24% (1Q09). Other reports, such as the Soliditet Betalnings index, showed a decline in 2010 compared to earlier years. However, while payment delays increased during the recession, they remained among the lowest in Europe. The combined drop in sales, increased payment delays and the credit crunch caused a jump in the number of enterprise bankruptcies, from 5 791 (2007) to 7 638 (2009). They continued at a high level (7 274) in 2010.

Box 4.7. **Situation of Swedish SMEs during the crisis**

The general picture indicates substantial negative effects on product demand, sales, employment and exports. There are also indications of an increased problem of payment delays, which have a negative effect on cash flows. Following this development, many enterprises experienced a need for working capital at the same time as credit terms got stricter, and an increased number of SMEs reported difficulties regarding access to finance.

Source: Ministry of Enterprise, Energy and Communications, 12 January 2010.

Government policy response

While the Swedish government undertook a number of measures, such as supporting the banking sector (through measures to strengthen the capital base and secure bank lending), tax credits, export credit facilitation and business development programmes, the most targeted government measure taken to increase access to finance for SMEs was to increase the support of the Swedish development bank, ALMI. A capital injection by the government increased lending capacity in 2009 compared to 2008, combined with allowing a higher share of co-financing. As the crisis subsided, the lending volume of ALMI returned to a more normal level in 2010 (about 65% of the 2009 level and 120% of the 2008 level). Most measures concerning SME financing continue to remain in place. No new measures have been undertaken, as SME loans continued to expand and credit conditions were largely unchanged. The recovery has been good in Sweden, and it has spilled over to the SMEs, whose profitability has generally recovered to the pre-crisis levels.

SME guaranteed loans and direct government loans

Government guaranteed lending in the traditional sense was quite marginal in Sweden. There were 14 regional guarantee funds (funded by the State and regions) associated with the Swedish Credit Guarantee Association (SKGF), which provided state guarantees for SME bank loans. In total, the value of the issued guarantees amounted to approximately EUR 3 million in 2008 and EUR 1.5 million in 2009. The SKGF guarantee funds were part of a government project running from 2003 to 2010. Since the end of the project, all funds have been or are currently in the process of being dissolved. The SKGF Association will continue to assist the phasing out of the individual funds. However, SKGF is and has not been the only provider of government guaranteed loans for SMEs. Government-owned ALMI issued guarantees for SMEs amounting to SEK 46.2 million during 2010, and EKN issued government backed loan guarantees for exporting businesses amounting to SEK 446 million.

The main government tool for strengthening SME access to loans and credit was through a supplementary financing actor, ALMI, the Swedish development bank. During the second half of 2008, the government took steps to support SME access to finance by enhancing the activities of ALMI. The main activity of ALMI is the provision of SME loans and credits, rather than providing guarantees for bank loans. To some extent, this can be seen as a type of guarantee, as ALMI loans are co-financed by private banks. Following the financial crisis, it was decided to increase the cap for the maximum ALMI share in a loan from 50% to 80%. ALMI financed 100% of micro-credits, and increased the loan size from SEK 100 000 to SEK 250 000. ALMI added a "new" client segment: the upper-tier SMEs.

There was also increased co-operation with private banks in terms of co-financing, as ALMI requires private banks' co-participation and involvement in every deal. But co-financing is not the same as the government guarantee systems that are in place in other countries in this report. SME direct government loans increased from SEK 1 422 million (2007) to SEK 3 231 million (2009) but declined to SEK 2 112 million in 2010.

SME authorised loans compared to loans requested

ALMI loans authorised continued to grow over the period. To avoid undesired competition with private banks, the interest rate offered by ALMI was higher than the rate offered by private banks. The first choice for enterprises seeking external finance would have been to get the full loan from a private bank. This meant that most of those approaching ALMI had already approached banks, which had turned down their application or required co-financing from ALMI. There was evidence that the percentage of non-performing loans in relation to total loans reported by the Swedish Riksbank increased from 0.5 (1Q07) to 1.7 (4Q09 and 4Q10). Thus, banks would have had an incentive to toughen the credit requirements for SME lending.

Given the openness of the Swedish economy, measures were undertaken to enhance access to finance for exporting enterprises. The Swedish Export Credit Corporation was granted a borrowing facility of a maximum of SEK 100 billion and the possibility to purchase state guarantees for its new borrowing, as well as SEK 3 billion in new equity. Furthermore, the limit for export credit guarantees from the Swedish Export Credit Guarantee Board was raised from SEK 200 billion to SEK 350 billion.

Other measures were also taken that did not target the financial system. To reduce the liquidity problems of enterprises during the financial crisis, the government introduced a temporary act to defer tax payments in March 2009. Employers were able to obtain a respite, for a maximum of one year, in paying employees' social security contributions and preliminary taxes for their employees for two months during 2009. This measure was later extended, and relief from tax payment was in effect until January 2011.

Table 4.59. **Financing SMEs and entrepreneurs: Scoreboard for Sweden, 2007-10**

Indicators	Units	2007	2008	2009	2010
Debt					
Business loans, SMEs	SEK millions	608 171	651 870	784 561	..
Business loans, total	SEK millions	683 817	736 448	849 157	..
Business loans, SMEs	% of total business loans	88.9	88.8	92.4	..
Short-term loans, SMEs	SEK millions	83 393	77 961	93 314	..
Long-term loans, SMEs	SEK millions	524 778	753 909	691 247	..
Total short and long-term loans, SMEs	SEK millions	608 171	351 870	784 651	..
Short-term loans, SMEs	% of total SME loans	13.7	12.0	11.9	..
Government guaranteed loans, SMEs[1]	SEK millions	157	131	107	0
Government loan guarantees, SMEs[2]	SEK millions	53	31	15	0
Direct government loans, SMEs	SEK millions	1 422	1 716	3 231	2 112
Loans authorised, SMEs	Number	3 338	3 579	5 100	3 836
Non-performing loans, total	% of non-performing loans to total business loans	0.5	0.8	1.7	1.7
Interest rate, loans < EUR 1 million	%	4.86	5.66	2.42	2.58
Interest rate, loans > EUR 1 million	%	3.99	4.84	1.69	1.62
Interest rate spread (between loans < 1 million and > 1 million)	%	0.87	0.82	0.73	0.96
Relation between large firm and SME interest rates	%	82.1	85.5	69.8	62.8
Equity					
Venture and growth capital	SEK millions	3 976	5 803	2 987	2 663
Venture and growth capital	Year-on-year growth rate, %	n.a.	43.3	−47.6	−10.8
Other					
Payment delays	Average number of days	6.9	7.0	8.0	8.0
Bankruptcies, total	Number	5 791	6 298	7 638	7 274
Bankruptcies, total	Year-on-year growth rate, %	n.a.	8.8	21.3	−4.8
Bankruptcies, total	Per 10 000 firms	61	65	79	77

1. No new government guaranteed loans for SMEs were issued during 2010 by SKGF (Swedish Credit Guarantee Association). However, SKGF is and has not been the only provider of government guaranteed loans for SMEs.
2. Government-owned ALMI issued guarantees for SME loans to a value of SEK 46.2 million during 2010, and EKN issued government-backed loan guarantees for exporting businesses to a value of SEK 446 million.

Sources: Refer to Table 4.60 "Definitions and sources of indicators for Sweden's Scoreboard".

StatLink http://dx.doi.org/10.1787/888932580272

Figure 4.26. **Trends in SME and entrepreneurship finance in Sweden**

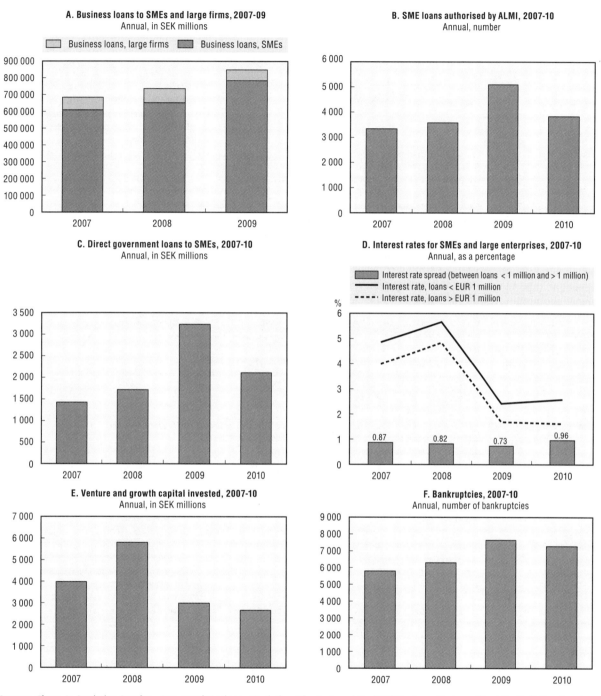

Sources: Chart A: Statistics Sweden, Structural Business Statistics. Charts B and C: ALMI Business Partner. Chart D: Statistics Sweden, Financial Market Statistics. Chart E: Swedish Venture Capital Association (SVCA). Chart F: The Swedish Agency for Growth Policy Analysis.

StatLink ⟡ http://dx.doi.org/10.1787/888932579132

Table 4.60. **Financing SMEs and entrepreneurs: Definitions and sources of indicators for Sweden's Scoreboard**

Indicators	Definitions	Sources
Debt		
Business loans, SMEs	Sum of SME short and long term liabilities from credit institutions, stocks. SMEs defined as enterprises with 1-249 employees, non-employer enterprises are not included.	Statistics Sweden, Structural Business Statistics. Based on administrative data on liabilities collected from the reports of the National Tax Agency; a proxy since supply side data broken down by SMEs not available
Business loans, total	Total sum of business liabilities from credit institutions.	Statistics Sweden, Structural Business Statistics. Based on administrative data on liabilities collected from the National Tax Agency. Supply side data broken down by SMEs not available
Short-term loans, SMEs	Sum of SME debts (liabilities) with a due date less than 12 months from closing day (includes overdraft facilities and other loans from credit institutions). SMEs defined as enterprises with 1-249 employees, non-employer enterprises are not included.	Statistics Sweden, Structural Business Statistics. Based on administrative data on liabilities collected from the National Tax Agency. Supply side data broken down by SMEs not available
Long-term loans, SMEs	Sum of SME debts (liabilities) with a due date 12 months or longer from closing day (includes bond loans, overdraft facilities and other loans from credit institutions). SMEs defined as enterprises with 1-249 employees, non-employer enterprises are not included.	Statistics Sweden, Structural Business Statistics. Based on administrative data on liabilities collected from the National Tax Agency. Supply side data broken down by SMEs not available
Government guaranteed loans, SMEs	Total value of guaranteed loans. No new government guaranteed loans for SMEs were issued during 2010 by SKGF (Swedish Credit Guarantee Association). However, SKGF is and has not been the only provider of government guaranteed loans for SMEs. SMEs defined as enterprises with 0-249 employees, non-employer enterprises are included.	Swedish Credit Guarantee Association (SKGF); reports on 14 regional and local associations. Supply side data
Government loan guarantees, SMEs	Value for all issued guarantees to SMEs by SKGF during the time period. No new government guaranteed loans for SMEs were issued during 2010 by SKGF (Swedish Credit Guarantee Association). However, SKGF is and has not been the only provider of government guaranteed loans for SMEs. Governmentally owned ALMI issued guarantees for SME loans to a value of SEK 46.2 million during 2010, and EKN issued governmentally backed loan guarantees for exporting businesses to a value of SEK 446 million. SMEs defined as enterprises with 0-249 employees, non-employer enterprises are included.	Swedish Credit Guarantee Association (SKGF). Supply side data
Direct government loans, SMEs	Total sum of new lending by ALMI. Total lending refers to the ALMI share of lending not including the bank share of the loan when co-investments are made. SMEs are defined as registered businesses with less than 250 employees.	ALMI Business Partner.
Loans authorised, SMEs	Number of new loan/credit applications approved by ALMI. SMEs defined as enterprises with 0-249 employees, non-employer enterprises are included.	ALMI Business Partner. Supply side data
Non-performing loans, total	Swedish data on loans outstanding to all firms. Percentages of non-performing loans in relation to total business loans (Definition: Economic claims on loans overdue for at least 60 days).	Swedish Riksbank. Based on information from the Swedish major bank groups: SEB, Handelsbanken, Nordea, and Swedbank
Interest rate, loans < EUR 1 million	Average annual rates for new loans to SMEs (defined as loans up to EUR 1 million), base rate plus risk premium; for maturity less than 1 year, enterprises only.	Statistics Sweden, Financial Market Statistics. Produced on behalf of the Riksbank. Supply side information reported by Swedish Monetary Financial Institutions.
Interest rate, loans > EUR 1 million	Describes average interest rate for short term (up to one year) loans up to and including EUR 1 million (as a proxy for SME loans).	Statistics Sweden, Financial Market Statistics. Produced on behalf of the Riksbank. Supply side information reported by Swedish Monetary Financial Institutions
Relation between large firm and SME interest rates	Calculated based on: interest rate for loans > EUR 1 million divided by interest rate for loans < EUR 1 million.	Statistics Sweden, Financial Market Statistics. Produced on behalf of the Riksbank. Supply side information reported by Swedish Monetary Financial Institutions.
Equity		
Venture and growth capital	Describes investment in Swedish companies from private equity companies. Includes early phases; seed, start-up and expansion – but not buyout. All enterprises.	Swedish Venture Capital Association (SVCA)
Other		
Payment delays	Average number of days beyond the agreed date for business-to-business in 2008, 2009 and 2010. For 2007, average number of days beyond the agreed date for business-to-business, business-to-customer and public entities. All enterprises.	Intrum Justitia, European Payment Index 2008, 2009 and 2010
Bankruptcies, total (number)	Number of court ruled bankruptcies. All enterprises.	The Swedish Agency for Growth Policy Analysis
Bankruptcies, total (per 10 000 firms)	Incidence of insolvency. All enterprises.	The Swedish Agency for Growth Policy Analysis

Switzerland

SME lending

SMEs, defined as firms with up to 250 employees, constitute 99.6% of Swiss enterprises and employ 66.6% of the labour force. Switzerland resisted the financial crisis better than other OECD countries for a number of reasons. Switzerland is known for its business-friendly policies and flexibility in working hours. It has benefited from an influx of highly educated workers and an early transition from traditional manufacturing to specialised growth areas. These factors contributed to low unemployment rates and a maintenance of domestic demand. This is not to say that Switzerland was entirely immune to the financial crisis, as one of its largest banks got caught up in the subprime crisis and had to be bailed out. Despite this, both SME and total business loans continued to grow during the crisis, albeit at a much slower pace. The share of SME loans in total business loans was over 81% in 2007. It was not possible to compare the 2007 ratio with 2010 because of definitional changes at the national level and reporting errors at a major bank.

Table 4.61. **Distribution of firms and employment in Switzerland, 2008**

By size of firm, as a percentage

Size by FTE	Enterprises	Employed persons
SMEs (up to 249)	**99.6**	**66.6**
Micro enterprises (up to 9 employees)	87.1	24.9
Small enterprises (10-49 employees)	10.6	21.8
Medium enterprises (50-249 employees)	2.0	20.0
Large enterprises (250 employees and over)	**0.4**	**33.4**

Source: Swiss State Secretariat for Economic Affairs.

StatLink ᵃᵍᵖ *http://dx.doi.org/10.1787/888932580291*

The share of SME credit used to credit authorised was about 77% over 2007-10, indicating SMEs' need for credit. The share of long-term loans in business loans increased, indicating that investment was still taking place during the recession.

SME credit conditions

There were no data on interest rates or collateral requirements for 2007 and 2008. However, the interest rate spread between large and small enterprises grew slightly between 2009 and 2010. The *Monthly Bulletin of Banking Statistics* showed that the percentage of SME loans requiring collateral increased. The Secretariat of State for Economic Affairs undertook three SME surveys on their opinions on access to finance in spring 2009, fall 2009 and spring 2010. The survey results are contained in Table 4.62 and suggest that SME financing in Switzerland was not in jeopardy. The credit market for SMEs was functioning and further intervention by the government was not needed. In fact, the results are somewhat contradictory. While more SMEs thought that the banks' attitude had not worsened and more SMEs got all the financing they sought, rejection rates still exceeded pre-crisis levels and interest rates were rising.

Table 4.62. **SMEs' access to finance in Switzerland, 2009-10**

% of SMEs surveyed

Survey question	Spring 2009	Fall 2009	Spring 2010
Access deteriorated	45	28	35
Needed external funds	24	21	26
Got all	60	56	64
Rejected	4	9	7
Bank attitude deteriorated	28	35	25
Interest rate increased	7	5	9
Demand for collateral increased	27	18	19

Source: Secretariat of State for the Economic Affairs, Survey of SME Access to Finance, April 2009, November 2009 and April 2010.

StatLink ⟦⟧ http://dx.doi.org/10.1787/888932580310

Between Q4 2008 and Q2 2009, banks reported a slight tightening of their lending standards for SME loans. This is consistent with the presumption that banks tighten their lending standards in recessions in order to protect themselves against higher default risk. However, the somewhat tighter lending standards have hardly affected loan volumes. There were positive, but declining growth rates of SME loans in 2009.

The quarterly *Survey of Bank Lending* confirmed the hardening of credit conditions that started in the third quarter of 2008. SMEs faced difficult conditions because of the downturn in the economy and the continued strengthening of the Swiss Franc vis-à-vis the euro and the US dollar, rather than because of problems in the banking system.

Equity financing

Private equity investment declined between 2008 and 2009 but experienced a solid rebound in 2010. The definition of private equity contains venture capital and later-stage transactions, including buy-outs, buy-ins, replacement capital, and turnarounds. These latter transactions accounted for the rebound in 2010.

Table 4.63. **Private equity investments in Switzerland, 2009-10**

In CHF thousands

	2009	2010
Seed	8 734	6 923
Start-up	229 300	151 410
Later stage venture	100 492	63 859
Growth	115 870	271 828
Sub-total	454 396	494 020
Turnaround, replacement, buyouts	444 155	1 315 528
Buyout	434 717	1 299 930
Total Investments	**898 550**	**1 809 548**

Source: EVCA Yearbook.

StatLink ⟦⟧ http://dx.doi.org/10.1787/888932580329

Other indicators

According to Intrum Justitia, payment delays remained steady from 2007 through 2010. This indicates that SMEs' liquidity problems were not growing or as acute as elsewhere. However, insolvencies or bankruptcies were on the rise (up 23% in 2009 and 20% in 2010). This increase could be attributed in part to a new regulation which simplified the de-registration of inactive firms.

Government policy response

In Switzerland, there are four guarantee co-operatives that help promising SMEs obtain bank loans up to CHF 500 000. Three are regional co-operatives and one national one for women. The guarantee covers 65% of the loan. Loan guarantees increased steadily throughout the period (2007-10). This was largely due to a restructuring of the guarantee programmes. The guarantee programmes increased the amount of risk that they covered, and this in turn increased the demand for guarantees. The Swiss Export Risk Insurance (SERV) programme introduced new products: a) working capital insurance; b) counter guarantees; c) refinancing guarantees; and d) letter of credit confirmation insurance. It increased its cover ratio from 85% to 95% for private buyer risk under the supplier credit insurance. SERV also offered insurance for short term exports to OECD/EU countries, if private insurance companies had rejected the exporter's application.

Table 4.64. **Financing SMEs and entrepreneurs: Scoreboard for Switzerland, 2007-10**

Indicator	Units	2007	2008	2009	2010
Debt					
Business loans, SMEs	CHF millions	285 160	302 088	318 135	322 297
Business loans, total	CHF millions	350 378	371 492	396 048	402 216
Business loans, SMEs[1]	% of total business loans	81.4	n.a.	n.a.	n.a.
Short-term loans, all enterprises	% of total business loans	82.7	78.9	77.1	73.5
Long-term loans, all enterprises	% of total business loans	17.3	21.1	22.9	26.5
Government export-related credits	CHF millions	3 527	2 394	3 529	3 588
Government guaranteed loans, SMEs	CHF millions	104	148	187	215
Loans used, SMEs	CHF millions	220 585	237 423	244 328	250 930
Loans used, SMEs	% of loans authorised	77.3	78.0	77.0	77.6
Interest rate	%	n.a.	n.a.	2.21	2.11
Interest rate spread	%	n.a.	n.a.	0.86	0.88
Collateral, SMEs	%	n.a.	n.a.	77.5	82.1
Equity					
Private equity	EUR millions	2 138	1 641	898	1 810
Private equity	% annual growth rate	n.a.	−23.2	−45.3	101.6
Other					
Payment delays	Days	13.7	12.0	13.0	13.0
Bankruptcies	Number	4 314	4 221	5 215	6 255
Bankruptcies	% annual growth rate	n.a.	−2	24	20
Bankruptcies	% of total enterprises	1.38	1.35	1.67	2.00

1. 2008, 2009 and 2010 not available due to definitional changes.
Sources: Refer to Table 4.65 "Definitions and sources of indicators for Switzerland's Scoreboard".

StatLink ⟪⟫ http://dx.doi.org/10.1787/888932580348

Figure 4.27. **Trends in SME and entrepreneurship finance in Switzerland**

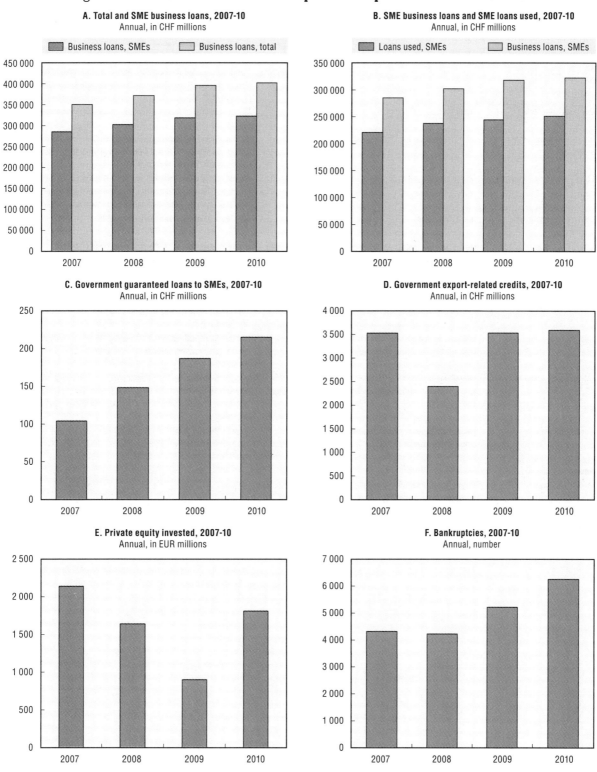

Sources: Charts A and B: Monthly Bulletin of Banking Statistics [www.snb.ch]. Chart C: Administrative data from the guarantee co-operatives. Chart D: SERV Annual Report. Chart E: EVCA Yearbook. Chart F: Creditreform.

StatLink ᴍ⑤ http://dx.doi.org/10.1787/888932579151

Table 4.65. **Financing SMEs and entrepreneurs: Definitions and sources of indicators for Switzerland's Scoreboard**

Indicator	Definition	Source
Debt		
Business loans, SMEs	Credit lines of all SMEs (firms with less than 250 employees).	Monthly Bulletin of Banking Statistics: 3Ca: Total credit lines (1) excl. total credit lines to companies with 250 or more employees (1) [*www.snb.ch*]
Business loans, total	Credit lines of all enterprises.	Monthly Bulletin of Banking Statistics: 3Ca: Total credit lines (1) [*www.snb.ch*]
Short-term loans, all enterprises	Claims against banks, all enterprises.	Monthly Bulletin of Banking Statistics: 1G: Claims against banks with a residual maturity of up to 1 year (15) + (18) + (21) in relation to total claims against banks [*www.snb.ch*]
Long-term loans, all enterprises	Claims against banks, all enterprises.	Monthly Bulletin of Banking Statistics: 1G: Total claims against banks (11) excl. Claims against banks with a residual maturity of up to 1 year in relation to total claims against banks [*www.snb.ch*]
Government export-related credits	New commitments.	SERV annual report [*www.serv-ch.com*]
Government guaranteed loans, SMEs	Four guarantee co-operatives offer loan guarantees for SME of up to CHF 500 000. The federal government covers 65 per cent of the exposure and shares in the administration costs. SMEs defined as firms with up to 250 employees.	Administrative data from the guarantee co-operatives.
Loans used, SMEs	Used credits of all SMEs (firms with up to 250 employees).	Monthly Bulletin of Banking Statistics: 3Ca: Total utilisation (2) excl. total utilisation of lending to companies with 250 or more employees (2) [*www.snb.ch*]
Interest rate	Interest rate at the end of the year for investment loans amounts less than CHF 1 million.	Monthly Statistical Bulletin: E3c: Average Investment loans with fixed interest rates for loan amount between CHF 50 000 and 1 million in December
Interest rate spread	Interest rate at the end of the year for investment loans amounts less than CHF 1 million and equal to greater than CHF 1 million.	Monthly Statistical Bulletin: E3c: Interest rates of investment loans between CHF 50 000 and 1 million (average) minus interest rates of investment loans between CHF 1 and 15 million (average) in December
Collateral, SMEs	Secured demands opposite customers in relation to total demands opposite customers.	Monthly Bulletin of Banking Statistics: 3Ca: secured demands opposite customers (5) in relation to total utilisation of demands opposite customers (4) for SMEs (up to 249 employees)
Equity		
Private equity	Private equity investments including early stage, later stage transactions (buyouts, buy-ins, replacement capital and turnarounds).	EVCA Yearbook
Other		
Payment delays	Business to business.	Intrum Justitia, European Payment Index
Bankruptcies	Number of enterprises.	Creditreform
Bankruptcies	Bankruptcies as a percentage of total enterprises.	Number of enterprises in the Business Census 2008 (*www.bfs.admin.ch*)

Thailand

SME lending

There were 2.9 million SMEs (firms with less than 200 employees) in Thailand in 2010, constituting 99.6% of all enterprises and providing 78% of employment including agriculture. The economy of Thailand was hit by two major events during the period under study: political instability and the financial crisis originating in the West. The OECD publication *Studies on SME and Entrepreneurship: Thailand. Key Issues and Policies* (2011) found that less than half of the 2.9 million SMEs can access formal finance. This problem was compounded in Thailand by systemic volatility in financial markets. The Asian financial crisis and the recent global financial crisis have made it difficult for Thai banks to accept risky loans, not least because they were often burdened with extremely high non-performing loan rates. The lesson learned from the Asian crisis in 1997 was that adequate capital alone cannot encourage bank lending. Banks will only lend when they are comfortable with the level of credit risk.

Table 4.66. **Distribution of enterprises in Thailand, 2010**

By size of enterprise

Enterprise size (employees)	Number	%
All enterprises	2 924 912	100.0
SMEs (50-200 employees)	2 913 167	99.6
Small (less than 50)	2 894 780	99.0
Medium (50-200)	18 387	0.6
Large (200+)	9 140	0.3

Note: Data include the manufacturing, services, wholesale and retail industries.
Source: Thai Office of SME Promotion.

StatLink http://dx.doi.org/10.1787/888932580367

Most banks do not use the national definition for an SME. Instead, they use the size of loan as a proxy, and definitions vary across banks. Total business loans decreased between 2007 and 2010, but the share of SME loans increased from 28.1% (2007) to 38% (2010). Bank lending to businesses in general languished at two-thirds of the 1990s levels. Both SME long-term and short-term loans increased from 2007-09, whilst only the latter continued to grow in 2010. The percentage of SME non-performing loans was high compared to western countries. 7.6% of SME loans were non-performing in 2009, and 7.4% in 2010.

SME loans authorised *vs.* requested

The ratio of loans authorised *vs.* requested rose from 71.54% (2007) to 85.6% (2009), indicating that banks were continuing to provide credit although the terms were tightening. It is likely that more stringent credit requirements could be met by only the best SMEs. However, the ratio in 2010 returned to its previous levels.

SME credit conditions

Interest rates for SMEs continued to climb over the entire period, since Thailand did not engage in monetary easing. Interest rate spreads between small and large enterprises increased slightly. More importantly, the value of collateral required as a percentage of the value of the loan increased from about 60% (2007) to 170% (2010). Nearly all SMEs in Thailand were required to pledge collateral. Banks had a high degree of risk aversion and more stringent SME loan approval procedures. However, this was not entirely unreasonable given the high rate of non-performing SME loans, which exceeded the rate for all business loans.

Equity financing

Scarce supplies of venture capital stifled the business momentum of innovative firms. The venture capital and private equity industry is small in Thailand and has focused on mergers and acquisitions and restructurings, rather than start-up and mezzanine finance. The Market for Alternative Investments was established in 1999. It provides a simpler and lower cost alternative to smaller firms than the Stock Exchange of Thailand (SET). As such, MAI provides an exit point for venture capital investors and facilitates capital raising by firms from institutional and sophisticated investors. As of 2010, the MAI had 62 companies listed; and the market capitalisation of MAI listings was THB 43 billion. There are no official statistics for venture capital, but about 20 venture capital funds were operating in Bangkok in 2005. The median fund size was THB 720 million (USD 20 million). While these funds attracted capital both nationally and regionally, Thai firms had to compete with other Asian firms, particularly Chinese firms, to access these funds. By 2005, the 20 venture capital funds had invested in 101 firms. The major challenge these funds faced was finding good deals. In general, fund managers said that the SMEs were poorly managed and lacked financial transparency. In 2009, there were only 11 members of the Thai Venture Capital Association. In addition, the weak Thai legal system and the underdeveloped capital market made exits difficult (Scheela and Jittrapanum, 2007).

Government policy response

Thailand established a five-year Portfolio Guarantee Scheme for SMEs in February 2008. All local commercial banks signed a Memorandum of Understanding to participate. It was expected that this would assure participating banks an acceptable level of risk. This supplemented the activities of the state-owned banks such as the Small Business Credit Guarantee Corporation (SBCGC).

The SBCGC provides credit guarantees to viable small businesses which do not have sufficient collateral. The SBCGC provides a letter of guarantee for approved applications to the financial institutions after the SME has paid the guarantee fee. In 2009, it had a THB 30 billion loan guarantee facility. In 2007, 2 866 SMEs were accepted for credit guarantees. The total number of loans guaranteed was an average of 7 800. This is a relatively small number compared to the total number of SMEs, pointing to an unexploited potential to ease SMEs' access to credit.

This facility was fully utilised in 2009 but was expected to be increased in the future. This will accommodate the recovery in demand from SMEs in the export and tourism sectors. The SBCGC offers guarantees worth THB 2 million each and can assist a total of 15 000 SMEs. By the end of 2009, THB 21.4 billion in SME loans were government guaranteed. When taking into account the supply chain, where each SME may employ an estimated 20 workers, this scheme might have helped save 300 000 jobs.

In January 2009, the government designed a soft loan package of THB 50 billion for smaller enterprises and SMEs in the South. Commercial banks will distribute these funds at an interest rate of 1.5%. By mid-2009, Thailand was in a severe recession, and the government injected a further THB 4 billion into the private sector through the state-owned banks.

As a result of these programmes, the insolvency rate of 66% was expected to decline below 50% in 2009.

Box 4.8. **Definition of SMEs used in Thailand's SME and entrepreneurship finance Scoreboard**

Country definition

On 11 September 2002, the Ministry of Industry introduced the definition of Thai small and medium-sized enterprises (SME). This definition is based on the number of employees and fixed capital. An enterprise is categorised as an SME if it has less than 200 employees and fixed capital less than THB 200 million, excluding land and properties. SMEs in Thailand are classified in three sectors: production, service, and trading.

Definition of SMEs according to the Thai Ministry of Industry

Type	Small		Medium	
	Employees	Capital (THB million)	Employees	Capital (THB million)
Production	Not more than 50	Not more than 50	51-200	51-200
Service	Not more than 50	Not more than 50	51-200	51-200
Wholesale	Not more than 25	Not more than 50	26-50	51-100
Retail	Not more than 15	Not more than 30	16-30	31-60

The SME definition used by financial institutions

The official definition for SMEs is not used by financial institutions in Thailand. In fact, each financial institution in Thailand is permitted to use their own definition of SMEs, which typically follows criteria such as sales less than THB 400-500 million and/or credit line less than THB 200 million. Therefore, data presented in Thailand's profile does not reflect the above national definition.

Table 4.67. **Financing SMEs and entrepreneurs: Scoreboard for Thailand, 2007-10**

Indicators	Units	2007	2008	2009	2010
Debt					
Business loans, SMEs	THB billions	1 331	1 457	1 565	1 678
Business loans, total	THB billions	4 733	5 471	5 819	4 369
Business loans, SMEs	% of total business loans	28.1	26.6	26.9	38.4
Short-term loans, SMEs	THB billions	578	647	692	973
Long-term loans, SMEs	THB billions	753	810	873	701
Total short and long-term loans, SMEs	THB billions	1 331	1 457	1 565	1 674
Short-term loans, SMEs	% of total SME loans	43.4	44.4	44.2	58.1
Loan guarantees outstanding, SBGC	THB billions	..	..	..	64
Government guaranteed loans, SMEs	THB billions	..	..	21	..
Loans authorised, SMEs	THB billions	217	312	186	392
Loans requested, SMEs	THB billions	304	421	218	536
Ratio of loans authorised to requested, SMEs	%	71.5	74.1	85.6	73.1
Non-performing loans, total	THB billions	453	397	412	..
Non-performing loans, SMEs	THB billions	105	99	119	75
Non-performing loans, SMEs	% of SME business loans	7.9	6.9	7.6	4.4
Non-performing loans, large	% of total business loans	7.3	5.3	5.4	..
Interest rate, SME average rate	%	5.94	6.34	6.52	7.39
Interest rate spread (between average interest rate for loans to SMEs and large firms)	%	1.20	1.30	1.42	..
Collateral, SMEs	THB billions	793	2 201	3 553	2 855
Collateral, SMEs	Value of collateral provided by SMEs over SME business loans, %	59.6	151.0	227.0	170.0
Other					
Payment delays, SMEs	Average number of days	33	..	..	..
Bankruptcies, total[1]	% of insolvencies over total number of SMEs	66	..	..	..

1. According to the Bank of Thailand, Thailand only has data for 2007 due to the financial statement reformat required by the Ministry of Commerce in 2009. Therefore, all financial statement data in 2008 are delayed for submission. In 2007, there were 370 118 insolvent companies in Thailand. In other words, Thailand had 6 600 insolvent companies per 10 000 enterprises. However, it should be noted that while companies shut down very frequently, it is also very easy for them to restart.

Sources: Refer to Table 4.68 "Definitions and sources of indicators for Thailand's Scoreboard".

StatLink ⟨ms⟩ http://dx.doi.org/10.1787/888932580386

Figure 4.28. **Trends in SME and entrepreneurship finance in Thailand**

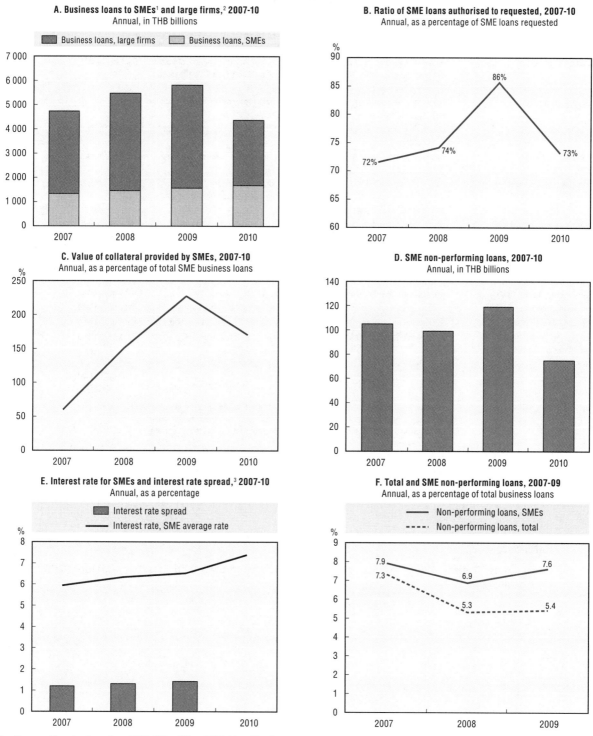

A. Business loans to SMEs[1] and large firms,[2] 2007-10
Annual, in THB billions

B. Ratio of SME loans authorised to requested, 2007-10
Annual, as a percentage of SME loans requested

C. Value of collateral provided by SMEs, 2007-10
Annual, as a percentage of total SME business loans

D. SME non-performing loans, 2007-10
Annual, in THB billions

E. Interest rate for SMEs and interest rate spread,[3] 2007-10
Annual, as a percentage

F. Total and SME non-performing loans, 2007-09
Annual, as a percentage of total business loans

1. Firms with sales less than THB 400 million (EUR 10 million).
2. Firms with sales greater than THB 400 million (EUR 10 million).
3. Spread between average interest rate for loans to SMEs and large firms. Banks did not provide information for 2010.
Sources: Bank of Thailand.

StatLink ≡⊓⊑⊏ http://dx.doi.org/10.1787/888932579170

Table 4.68. **Financing SMEs and entrepreneurs: Definitions and sources of indicators for Thailand's Scoreboard**

Indicators	Definition	Source
Debt		
Business loans, SMEs	Outstanding amount of SME loans provided by bank at the end of period, stocks. Banks in Thailand define SMEs as enterprises with sales less than THB 400 million and/or a credit line less than THB 200 million.	Bank of Thailand
Business loans, total	Outstanding amount of all loans (excluding interbank loans) provided by bank at the end of period, stocks.	Bank of Thailand
Short-term loans, SMEs	Outstanding amount of SME loans provided by bank with the maturity less than 1 year, stocks.	Bank of Thailand
Long-term loans, SMEs	Outstanding amount of SME loans provided by bank with the maturity more than 1 year, stocks.	Bank of Thailand
Loan guarantees outstanding, SBGC	SME loans guaranteed by Credit Guarantee Corporation. SMEs are defined as an enterprise with less than 200 employees and/or has fixed assets (excluding land) of less than THB 200 million.	Bank of Thailand
Government guaranteed loans, SMEs	Guarantees outstanding at the end of the year. SMEs are defined as an enterprise with less than 200 employees and/or has fixed assets (excluding land) of less than THB 200 million.	Small Business Credit Guarantee Corporation, Annual Report
Loans authorised, SMEs	SME loans approved by the banks.	Bank of Thailand
Loans requested, SMEs	SME loans requested for approval.	Bank of Thailand
Non-performing loans, total	Figures cover all enterprises in the Thai banking system.	Bank of Thailand
Non-performing loans, SMEs	SME loans 90 days past due date. Figures cover all SMEs in the Thai banking system.	Bank of Thailand
Interest rate, SME average rate	Average interest rate charged to new SME loans, approved by the bank during a year.	Bank of Thailand
Interest rate spread (between average interest rate for loans to SMEs and large firms)	Average interest rate spread between SME loans and corporate loans.	Bank of Thailand
Collateral, SMEs	Appraisal value of collateral based on market valuation.	Bank of Thailand
Other		
Payment delays, SMEs	Average payment delay in days for trade credit, business-to-business (*i.e.* seller gives credit term to buyer for 30 days but the buyer makes a delayed payment after credit term 15 days. So, the payment delay is 15 days). SMEs are defined according to the national definition contained in Box 4.8.	BOL
Bankruptcies, SMEs	Insolvent SMEs divided by the total number of SMEs, presented as a percentage. SMEs are defined according to the national definition contained in Box 4.8.	BOL

Reference

OECD (2011), *Thailand: Key Issues and Policies*, OECD Studies on SMEs and Entrepreneurship, OECD Publishing.

United Kingdom

SME lending

While the national statistical definition of an SME follows the EU in terms of the number of employees, SME loans are defined by turnover, either up to GBP 1 million or up to GBP 25 million, depending on the source of the data. 94.9% of enterprises have 1-9 employees. Following a period of growth, the stock of lending to SMEs peaked in 2009 and has declined in subsequent years. Lending to large enterprises also peaked in 2008, but declined more sharply than SME lending in 2009. The decline in the stock of lending was affected by both supply-side factors, as well as demand-side factors, with evidence indicating that SMEs were deleveraging and repaying existing bank debt. The SME share in total business lending, for SMEs with less than GBP 1 million turnover, has remained stable but is very small (11.6%) compared to other countries in the OECD Scoreboard on financing SMEs and entrepreneurs, as it does not include all lending to larger SMEs. Other evidence[1] suggests total lending to SMEs (with up to GBP 25 million turnover) accounts for around a quarter of the stock of lending to all UK businesses, which is more in line with other countries.

Table 4.69. **Distribution of enterprises in the United Kingdom, 2007**

By size of enterprise

Enterprise size (employees)	Number	%
All enterprises	**1 670 572**	**100.0**
SMEs (1-249)	**1 664 489**	**99.6**
Micro (1-9)	*1 585 607*	*94.9*
Small (10-49)	*51 449*	*3.1*
Medium (50-249)	*27 433*	*1.6*
Large (250+)	**6 083**	**0.4**

Note: Includes the non-financial business economy (ISIC Rev. 3 Codes C, D, E, F, G, H, I and K). Data include registered enterprises only. It is estimated that there are 4.5 million registered and unregistered SMEs in the United Kingdom. Details are available at: *www.bis.gov.uk/assets/biscore/statistics/docs/b/business-population-estimates–2011_statistical-release.pdf.*
Source: OECD Structural Demographic and Business Statistic Database.

StatLink ᵐˢ▄ http://dx.doi.org/10.1787/888932580405

SME loans authorised *vs.* requested

The Department for Business Innovation and Skills (BIS) periodically conducts a demand survey among SME employers. In its latest survey, it found that the percentage of SME employers seeking finance in the last 12 months rose from 23% (2007-08) to 26% (2010), although there is evidence to show a decline in demand for bank finance.[2] Over half of SME employers that sought finance (56%) were seeking finance for working capital, compared to 21% seeking it for investment purposes.

The majority of those SME employers seeking finance were able to obtain the sum they required. Of those seeking finance, 68% obtained all the finance they needed and 6%

obtained some of the finance they needed in 2010, compared to 89% obtaining all in 2007-08, and 2% obtaining some in 2007-08.[3] Those SME employers that obtained no credit in 2010 (21%) increased almost three fold since 2007-08 (from 8%). Surprisingly, a significant number of SME employers did not know why the bank rejected their application.

SME credit conditions

Despite an increase in margins, most SMEs paid less for finance overall, due to the decline in the Bank of England interest rate, which fell from 5.5% in 2007 to 0.5% in 2009. For instance, the average interest rate on fixed-rate lending was 4.54% at the end of 2008, compared to 3.57% at the end of 2010. Interest rate spreads between large enterprises and SMEs have increased. On the other hand, in 2010, 45% of loans (including commercial mortgages[4]) were required to provide collateral, compared to 50% in 2007.[5]

Figure 4.29. **Lending to SMEs and corporations in the United Kingdom, 2008-11**

Year-on-year percentage change

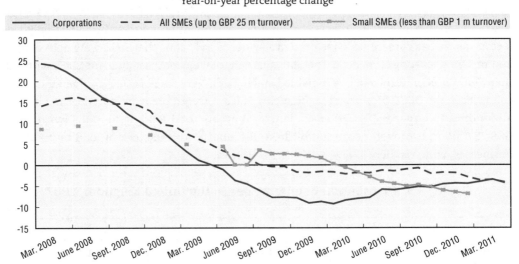

Note: By definition, commercial mortgages are secured. Excluding commercial mortgages, 35% of loans required security.
Source: Bank of England Trends in Lending July 2011.

StatLink ⟲ http://dx.doi.org/10.1787/888932579189

Equity financing

While only a minority of SMEs seek external equity financing, it is an important source of finance to innovative businesses with high-growth potential. There has been a large decline in the number and value of venture and growth capital investments since 2008.

Table 4.70. **Venture and growth capital investment in the United Kingdom, 2008-10**

By stage of development, GBP millions

Stage of development	2008	2009	2010
Seed	12	14	10
Start-up	160	125	46
Early stage	187	164	168
Expansion	2 050	1 055	1 651
Total	**2 409**	**1 509**	**1 964**

Source: British Venture Capital Association.   *StatLink* ⟲ http://dx.doi.org/10.1787/888932580424

Bankruptcies and payment delays

Enterprise liquidations (bankruptcies) peaked in 2009 and declined by 16% in 2010. The current liquidation rate is low by historical standards. In the twelve months ending 2Q2011, 0.7% of all active registered companies went into liquidation, which is substantially lower than the peak of 2.6% in 1993, and the average of 1.3% seen over the last 25 years.[6] Enterprise payment delays, or the average number of days beyond term, were more than 22 days. Survey evidence shows cash flow was the second most important obstacle to the success of the business, just after the economy.

Government policy response

As a result of the economic crisis, the government introduced the Enterprise Finance Guarantee Scheme (EFG) in January 2009, which replaced the Small Firm Loan Guarantee Scheme (SFLG). EFG supports counter-cyclical lending, and assistance is available to viable enterprises that in normal circumstances would be able to secure lending from banks, but which cannot secure bank lending in the credit crunch. The scheme helps enterprises that lack collateral and/or a track record but EFG offers more help to a greater number of enterprises. For instance, while SFLG provided loans of up to GBP 250 000, the EFG has an upper limit of GBP 1 million. The EFG assistance is also available to enterprises with a turnover of up to GBP 25 million instead of the SFLG's GBP 5.6 million. The EFG Scheme can also be used to convert an overdraft into a loan. Consequently, there was a three-fold increase in the volume of guaranteed loans in 2009 compared to 2007/08 under the previous scheme, and the level remains high. Between 83%-90% of the guaranteed loans offered have been utilised. Overall, since its launch in 2009, 15 769 SMEs have been offered EFG loans with a total value of GBP 1.59 billion. Of these, 13 769 SMEs have drawn down loans for a value of over GBP 1.37 billion.

Box 4.9. **Definition of SMEs used in the United Kingdom's SME and entrepreneurship finance Scoreboard**

Country definition

The national statistics definition is based on business size of less than 250 employees.

Financial institutions' definition

Financial institutions' definition is based on turnover of up to GBP 25 million, but the British Bankers Association's current definition covers only SMEs with a turnover of up to GBP 1 million and so it is an underestimate of the full SME population.

Table 4.71. **Financing SMEs and entrepreneurs: Scoreboard
for the United Kingdom, 2007-10**

Indicator	Units	2007	2008	2009	2010
Debt					
Business lending, SMEs	GBP millions	50 460	54 600	55 360	51 960
Business lending, total	GBP millions	478 888	488 803	478 890	446 067
Business lending, SMEs	% of total business loans	10.5	11.2	11.6	11.6
Government loans guaranteed (offered), SMEs	GBP millions	207.0	178.0	759.5	588.6
Government loans guaranteed (drawn), SMEs	GBP millions	..	..	626.6	529.5
Ratio of government loans guaranteed drawn to offered, SMEs	%	..	..	83.0	90.0
Interest rate, SMEs[1]	%	..	4.54	3.46	3.57
Interest rate, UK corporations[2]	%	..	3.71	2.24	2.13
Interest rate spread	%	..	0.83	1.22	1.44
Collateral, SMEs	% of loans requiring collateral	55	..	23	45
Equity					
Venture and growth capital	GBP millions	..	2 409	1 509	1 964
Venture and growth capital	Year-on-year growth rate, %	..	n.a.	−37.4	30.2
Other					
Payment delays, SMEs	Average days beyond term (full year)	..	..	22.80	22.58
Bankruptcies, total (liquidations)	Number	12 507	15 535	19 077	16 045
Bankruptcies, total	Year-on-year growth rate, %	..	24	23	−16

1. Based on Bank of England interest rate.
2. Based on LIBOR.
Sources: Refer to Table 4.72 "Definitions and sources of indicators for the United Kingdom's Scoreboard".

StatLink ᴍᴤᴘ *http://dx.doi.org/10.1787/888932580443*

Figure 4.30. **Trends in SME and entrepreneurship finance in the United Kingdom**

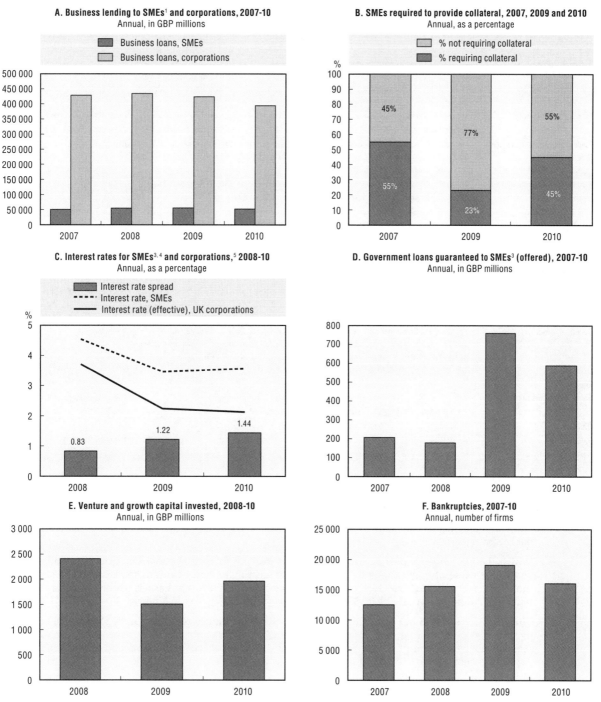

1. SMEs are defined as firms with annual turnover of up to GBP 1 million.
2. For firms with annual turnover of over GBP 1 million.
3. SMEs are defined as firms with up to GBP 25 million annual turnover.
4. Based on Bank of England interest rate.
5. Based on LIBOR.

Sources: Chart A: British Bankers Association (BBA). Chart B: Various surveys. Chart C: Bank of England (BOE). Chart D: BIS. Chart E: British Venture Capital Association (BVCA). Chart F: Insolvency Service.

StatLink ⬛ http://dx.doi.org/10.1787/888932579208

Table 4.72. **Financing SMEs and entrepreneurs: Definitions and sources of indicators for the United Kingdom's Scoreboard**

Indicator	Definition	Source
Debt		
Business lending, SMEs	Value of the stock of bank's term lending and overdrafts to SMEs. BBA defines an SME as having an annual turnover of up to GBP 1 million. BIS defines an SME as having an annual turnover of up to GBP 25 million. Thus, BBA figures do not provide complete coverage of the SME market. It is not possible to provide a break down by size of loan.	British Bankers Association (BBA)
Business lending, total	Stock of outstanding monetary financial institutions' sterling lending to private non-financial corporations.	Bank of England (BOE)
Government loans guaranteed (offered), SMEs	The value of Enterprise Finance Guaranteed (EFG) loans offered to SMEs. EFG covers SMEs up to GBP 25 million annual turnover. Figures for 2007 and 2008 are for the Small Firms Loan Guarantee scheme and relate to financial years.	BIS
Government loans guaranteed (drawn), SMEs	The value of Enterprise Finance Guaranteed (EFG) loans drawn by SMEs. EFG covers SMEs up to GBP 25 million annual turnover. There are no figures for 2007 and 2008.	BIS
Interest rate, SMEs	The Median interest rate by value of new SME facilities by 4 major lenders (for SMEs up to GBP 25 million turnover). Quarterly figures are the prevailing rates in March, June, September and December of each respective year. Based on Bank of England median rate.	Bank of England (BOE)
Interest rate (effective), UK corporations	Effective interest rate on new lending to UK Corporations, non-seasonally adjusted. Quarterly figures are the prevailing rates in March, June, September and December of each respective year. Based on LIBOR.	Bank of England (BOE)
Interest rate spread	Effective interest rate on new lending to Private Non-Financial Corporations – SME interest rate. Quarterly figures are the prevailing rates in March, June, September and December of each respective year.	Bank of England (BOE)
Collateral, SMEs	Percentage of SMEs that were required to provide collateral on bank loans drawn down. The 2009 figure is not comparable with other years due to differences in the way the question was asked between surveys. SMEs are defined as enterprises with less than 250 employees and include non-employer enterprises.	Various surveys
Equity		
Venture and growth capital	Amount of external equity invested in UK enterprises by BVCA members (includes seed, start-up, early stage and expansion capital).	British Venture Capital Association (BVCA)
Other		
Payment delays	Average number of days beyond term for all businesses.	Experian
Bankruptcies, total	Number of companies liquidated (voluntary and compulsory) in England and Wales.	Insolvency Service

Notes

1. Bank of England (2011), *Trends in Lending*, April 2011. Available at: *www.bankofengland.co.uk/publications/other/monetary/TrendsApril11.pdf*

2. Whilst the BIS survey shows an increase in SMEs seeking finance overall, the Bank of England shows the value of applications by SMEs for new term loans and overdraft facilities in the six months to February 2011 was 19% lower than in the same period a year earlier. Lower demand for bank finance, and deleveraging by SME is also impacting on the stock of lending.

3. This is confirmed by other research. For instance the SME Finance monitor survey shows 85% of overdraft applicants and 66% of loan applicants in 20010/11 obtained an overdraft or loan respectively by the end of the borrowing process. 12% of overdraft applicants and 27% of loan applicants were unable to obtain finance

4. By definition commercial mortgages are secured. Excluding commercial mortgages, 32% of loans required security.

5. In 2009 the proportion of loans requiring collateral fell but the figure is not comparable due to differences in the way the question was asked between surveys.

6. *www.insolvencydirect.bis.gov.uk/otherinformation/statistics/201108/index.htm.*

United States

Small business lending

The United States Small Business Administration (USSBA) broadly classifies small businesses as any firm with 500 or fewer employees.[1] These firms account for more than 5 million businesses, or 99% of all firms. They employ slightly over half of the private sector's employees, pay about 44% of the total private sector payroll, generate about 65% of net new private sector jobs, and create more than half of the nonfarm private Gross Domestic Product.[2]

Table 4.73. **Distribution of firms[1] in the United States, 2009**
By size of firm

Firm size (employees)	Number	%
Total firms	**5 088 114**	**100.0**
SMEs (1-499)	**5 067 879**	**99.6**
Micro (1-9)	*3 851 578*	*75.7*
Small (10-99)	*1 130 064*	*22.2*
Medium (100-499)	*86 237*	*1.7*
Large (500+)	**20 235**	**0.4**

1. A firm is a business organisation consisting of one or more domestic establishments that were specified under common ownership or control. The firm and the establishment are the same for single-establishment firms. For more details see: *www.ces.census.gov/index.php/bds/bds_database_list*.
Source: US Census Bureau, *Business Dynamics Statistics*.

StatLink http://dx.doi.org/10.1787/888932580462

A detailed analysis of the changes in demand and supply for small business credit is hampered by a lack of meaningful data. This is especially true for high frequency data on privately held small businesses.[3] This lack of data has significantly impeded an understanding of the impact of the recent credit contraction on small business credit markets.[4] Notwithstanding these data limitations, it became clear that credit to small businesses experienced a pronounced contraction. It is unclear, however, if lending to large firms contracted at the same pace. On the one hand data from the Federal Reserve seem to indicate that the lending contraction to small firms was more pronounced than the lending contraction to large firms. On the other hand data from the Federal Deposit Insurance Corporation (FDIC) seem to indicate that the credit contraction was just as severe for small and large firms.

Unfortunately, these lending statistics are un-weighted diffusion indices, thus do not contain any information on the level of or quantity change in the *volume* of lending supplied by these institutions. At best, a general directional change in the level of credit supply can be inferred.

A rough sense of the lending level supplied to small firms by depository institutions, which provide about 64 per cent of traditional credit to small businesses, can be obtained from the Federal Deposit Insurance Corporation (FDIC) Call Reports.[5] These provide end-of-quarter loan balances held by these institutions. This dataset shows that, as of the second quarter of 2011, depository institutions holdings of small loans declined to USD 607 billion, representing a 15% drop from the peak level of USD 711 billion held at the end of the second quarter of 2008.

Figure 4.31. **Loan balances at depository institutions – commercial and industrial loans under USD 1 million, 1995-2011**

In USD millions

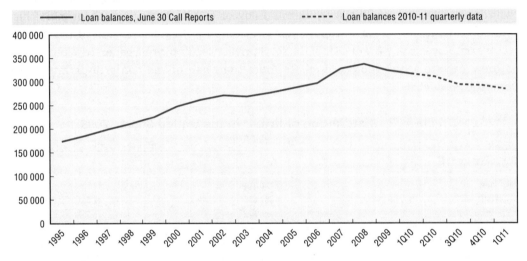

Source: FDIC, *Call Reports.*

StatLink http://dx.doi.org/10.1787/888932579227

This dataset most likely understates the decline in small business lending by these institutions. *End-of-quarter balances* of small loans are not the supply of small loans provided by these institutions *during the quarter*. In essence, these are inventory data that are often erroneously referred to as supply data. Thus, during the pre-crisis period, when the secondary markets were at their peak, financial institutions could easily sell loans they produced during the quarter, thus showing little to no change in their balance positions at the end of the quarter.[6]

Two types of small business loans are reported by the FDIC: 1) loans secured by nonfarm non-residential properties, commonly referred to as *commercial real estate* (CRE) loans; and 2) *commercial and industrial* (C&I) loans.[7] Small business loans are defined as business loans under USD 1 million. These business loans are further separated into three size categories: USD 100 000 or less, USD 100 000 plus through USD 250 000, and USD 250 000 plus through USD 1 million (see Table 4.74).

CRE and C&I small business loans outstanding declined by 8.0% and 4.1%, respectively in 2009-10. This dataset indicates that Large Business Loans outstanding declined 8.9%, while Total Small Business Loans outstanding declined 6.2% during 2009-10.

Table 4.74. **Value of small business loans outstanding for depository lenders, 2005-10**

By loan type and size, USD billions, nominal

Loan type and size at organisation	2005	2006	2007	2008	2009	2010	Change 09-10	
							Difference	%
Commercial real estate								
USD 100 000 or less	29.9	28.7	28.4	28.5	26.4	22.1	−4.3	−16.3
USD 100 000 to USD 250 000	62.4	65	68.8	68.6	67.1	59.6	−7.5	−11.2
USD 250 000 to USD 1 million	222.8	244.2	262.8	277.9	278.4	260.5	−17.9	−6.4
Total commercial real estate	315.1	337.9	360.1	375.0	372.0	342.3	−29.8	−8.0
Commercial and Industrial								
USD 100 000 or less	108.3	117.0	131.2	141.7	134.5	137.2	2.7	2.0
USD 100 000 to USD 250 000	54.5	54.7	57.5	57.3	55.1	21.2	−3.9	−7.1
USD 250 000 to USD 1 million	123.5	124.6	138.0	137.4	133.6	121.6	−12.0	−9.0
Total commercial and industrial	286.4	296.3	326.7	336.4	323.2	309.9	−13.3	−4.1
Total small business loans (USD 1 million and less)	601.5	634.2	686.8	711.5	695.2	652.2	−43.0	−6.2
Total large business loans (more than USD 1 million)	1 223.9	1 386.9	1 536.8	1 797.8	1 755.3	1 599.1	−156.2	−8.9
Total business loans	1 825.3	2 021.0	2 223.5	2 509.3	2 450.6	2 251.3	−199.2	−8.1
Total assets of depository lenders	9 461.7	10 261.3	10 789.9	11 708.4	11 905.1	11 707.5	−197.6	−1.7
Number of BHCs and independent lenders	7 662	7 594	7 456	7 360	7 224	7 023	−201.0	−2.8

Source: Federal Deposit Insurance Corporation, "Statistics on Depository Institutions", June 2005 through June 2010.

StatLink ⏷ *http://dx.doi.org/10.1787/888932580481*

SME lending by lender size

Lenders of all sizes experienced declines in small business loans outstanding from 2009 to 2010 (see Table 4.75). Mega-lenders with USD 50 billion or more in assets had the largest dollar volume decline in small business loans outstanding, with a loss of more than USD 18 billion.

Table 4.75. **Value of small business loans outstanding, 2005-10**

By depository lender size, USD billions, nominal

Loan type and size at organisation	2005	2006	2007	2008	2009	2010	Change 09-10	
							Difference	%
Lenders by total asset size								
Less than USD 100 million	30.9	29.8	27.3	25.3	23.7	21.9	−1.8	−7.6
USD 100 million to USD 499.9 million	129.8	130.8	129.1	130.8	129.8	125.0	−4.8	−3.7
USD 500 million to USD 999.9 million	54.8	59.7	62.0	66.4	65.0	62.7	−2.3	−3.6
USD 1 billion to USD 9.9 billion	120.6	129.1	137.8	145.6	137	127.7	−9.4	−6.8
USD 10 billion to USD 49.9 billion	77.6	76.1	88.1	74.4	69.2	62.7	−6.5	−9.4
USD 50 billion or more	187.8	208.7	242.5	269.0	270.5	252.4	−18.2	−6.7
Total small business loans	601.5	634.2	686.8	700.5	695.2	652.2	−43.0	−6.2

Source: Federal Deposit Insurance Corporation, "Statistics on Depository Institutions", June 2005 through June 2010.

StatLink ⏷ *http://dx.doi.org/10.1787/888932580500*

The number of *Total Small Business Loans* outstanding declined 3.4% during 2009-10, and was driven by the decline in C&I loans of less than USD 100 000, or micro loans (see Table 4.76). These C&I micro loans constituted about 88% of small business loans, and accounted for over 80% of the decline in the number of *Total Small Business Loans*.

Table 4.76. **Number of small business loans outstanding, 2005-10**

By loan type, millions of loans

Loan type and size at organisation	2005	2006	2007	2008	2009	2010	Change 09-10	
							Difference	%
Commercial real estate								
USD 100 000 or less	0.68	0.64	0.71	0.64	0.59	0.56	−0.03	−5.8
USD 100 000 to USD 250 000	0.47	0.72	1.11	0.51	0.51	0.46	−0.05	−9.0
USD 250 000 to USD 1 million	0.57	0.58	0.064	0.7	0.69	0.71	0.02	2.7
Total commercial real estate	1.71	1.95	2.46	1.84	1.79	1.73	−0.06	−3.4
Commercial and Industrial								
USD 100 000 or less	18.37	18.38	20.93	24.37	20.37	19.73	−0.64	−3.2
USD 100 000 to USD 250 000	0.54	0.52	0.62	0.55	0.54	0.51	−0.03	−5.6
USD 250 000 to USD 1 million	0.41	0.41	0.52	0.46	0.47	0.41	−0.06	−12.4
Total commercial and industrial	19.32	19.32	22.07	35.38	21.39	20.66	−0.73	−3.4
Total small business loans	21.03	21.26	24.53	27.22	23.18	22.39	−0.79	−3.4

Source: Federal Deposit Insurance Corporation, "Statistics on Depository Institutions", June 2005 through June 2010.
StatLink ⟐ http://dx.doi.org/10.1787/888932580519

Mega-lenders held more than USD 16 billion or 72% of *Total Small Business Loans* in 2010, and were one of the two groups of lenders to experience growth in the number of small business loans. The increase in loans by mega-lenders has been largely credit card loans.

There are two small business loan concentration ratios. The first of these measures is the ratio of the Total Small Business Loans outstanding to the lender's Total Assets – here referred to as the *Total Assets Ratio*. The Total Assets Ratio declined steadily from 16.9% in 2005 to 15.3% in 2010 (see Table 4.78). The trend indicates that small businesses are somewhat less successful in competing with other uses of the capital held by lending institutions.

Table 4.77. **Number of small business loans outstanding from depository lenders, 2005-10**

By lender size, millions of loans

Loan type and size at organisation	2005	2006	2007	2008	2009	2010	Change 09-10	
							Difference	%
Lenders by total asset size								
Less than USD 100 million	0.49	0.47	0.44	0.41	0.41	0.31	−0.10	−24.7
USD 100 million to USD 499.9 million	1.45	1.66	2.01	1.41	1.38	1.23	−0.15	−10.7
USD 500 million to USD 999.9 million	1.86	2.00	1.86	1.83	1.85	1.94	0.09	4.8
USD 1 billion to USD 9.9 billion	3.05	2.81	4.91	5.17	1.22	1.14	−0.08	−6.7
USD 10 billion to USD 49.9 billion	4.61	2.55	3.03	3.46	3.19	1.56	−1.63	−51.2
USD 50 billion or more	9.57	11.79	12.28	14.95	15.13	16.21	1.08	7.1
Total small business loans	21.03	21.26	24.53	27.22	23.18	22.39	−0.79	−3.4

Source: Federal Deposit Insurance Corporation, "Statistics on Depository Institutions", June 2005 through June 2010.
StatLink ⟐ http://dx.doi.org/10.1787/888932580538

The second ratio is the ratio of the Total Small Business Loans outstanding to Total Business Loans, or the *Total Business Loan Ratio* (see Table 4.79), which corresponds to the SME share in total business loans used in the OECD Scoreboard on SME and entrepreneurship finance. This ratio fell from about 77% in 2005 to under 69% in 2010.

Table 4.78. **Ratio of the value of small business loans outstanding to the value of total assets of depository lenders, 2005-10**

By lender size, ratio (percentage)

Loan type and size at organisation	2005	2006	2007	2008	2009	2010	Change 09-10	
							Difference	%
Lenders by total asset size								
Less than USD 100 million	16.36	16.30	15.77	15.94	15.82	15.36	−0.46	−2.9
USD 100 million to USD 499.9 million	18.78	18.59	18.3	17.94	17.43	16.72	−0.71	−4.1
USD 500 million to USD 999.9 million	15.01	14.82	14.69	14.63	14.06	13.78	−0.28	−2.0
USD 1 billion to USD 9.9 billion	11.35	11.70	11.74	11.48	10.75	10.21	−0.54	−5.0
USD 10 billion to USD 49.9 billion	5.65	5.65	6.33	6.18	6.53	6.07	−0.46	−7.0
USD 50 billion or more	4.42	4.33	4.18	4.48	4.84	4.68	−0.16	−3.3
Total small business loans	16.85	16.72	16.37	16.27	15.89	15.34	−0.55	−3.5

Source: Federal Deposit Insurance Corporation, "Statistics on Depository Institutions", June 2005 through June 2010.

StatLink ᴍᴸᴾ http://dx.doi.org/10.1787/888932580557

Table 4.79. **Ratio of the value of small business loans outstanding to the value of total business loans outstanding for depository lenders, 2005-10**

By lender size, ratio (percentage)

Loan type and size at organisation	2005	2006	2007	2008	2009	2010	Change 09-10	
							Difference	%
Lenders by total asset size								
Less than USD 100 million	89.42	88.73	87.12	85.90	86.29	86.95	0.66	0.8
USD 100 million to USD 499.9 million	74.67	73.62	71.85	69.68	68.03	66.56	−1.47	−2.2
USD 500 million to USD 999.9 million	56.31	55.14	54.72	51.95	49.91	49.02	−0.88	−1.8
USD 1 billion to USD 9.9 billion	42.88	43.32	41.99	40.49	38.48	36.83	−1.65	−4.3
USD 10 billion to USD 49.9 billion	31.36	30.94	33.04	31.44	28.64	26.22	−2.42	−8.4
USD 50 billion or more	25.69	23.59	18.89	18.47	22.10	25.76	3.65	16.5
Total small business loans	77.45	76.09	74.07	71.57	70.02	68.99	−1.03	−1.5

Source: Federal Deposit Insurance Corporation, "Statistics on Depository Institutions", June 2005 through June 2010.

StatLink ᴍᴸᴾ http://dx.doi.org/10.1787/888932580576

SME credit conditions

A close analysis of the Federal Reserve's Senior Loan Officer Opinion Survey on Bank Lending practices indicates that during this cycle, financial institutions tightened credit to small firms for five quarters longer than credit to large firms (see Figure 4.32).[8] This pattern is the opposite of one set during the 2000-01 credit tightening cycle, when financial institutions tightening focused on large firms.

Interest rates declined on small and large loans but the spread in 2010 was 1.2%. The percentage of small business loans that had to provide collateral increased from 84% (2007) to 89% (2009). However, only 48.5% of large business loans had to provide collateral in 2009.

Figure 4.32. **Senior loan officer opinion survey on bank lending practices, 1990-2011**

By size of firm, net percentage of banks tightening standards for C&I loans

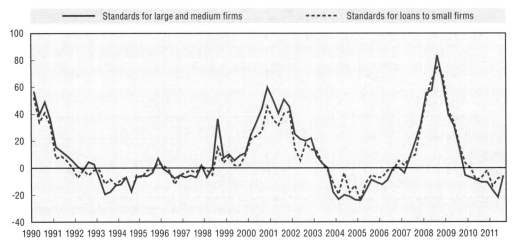

Source: Federal Reserve, "Senior Loan Officer Opinion Survey on Bank Lending Practices".
StatLink http://dx.doi.org/10.1787/888932579246

Small business credit demand

Data availability on small business credit *demand* is just as, if not more limited. Whatever data are available, indicate that demand did contract significantly during the recession (see Figures 4.33 and 4.34). The two major data sources on small business credit demand, however, portray a contradictory picture as to whether small business credit demand rebounded after the recession ended in July 2009. The Federal Reserve data indicate that credit demand by small, as well as large, firms followed a typical cyclical contraction-pattern and rebounded after the recession ended. Data from the National Federation of Independent Business (NFIB), however, indicate that small business credit demand continued to decline after the recession ended.

Figure 4.33. **Demand for commercial and industrial loans, 1992-2011**

By size of firm, net percentage of responders reporting stronger demand

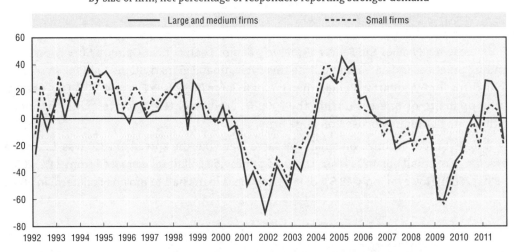

Source: Federal Reserve, "Senior Loan Officer Opinion Survey on Bank Lending Practices".
StatLink http://dx.doi.org/10.1787/888932579265

Figure 4.34. **Per cent of small firms borrowing at least once during the quarter, 1986-2011**

Monthly (seasonally adjusted), as a percentage

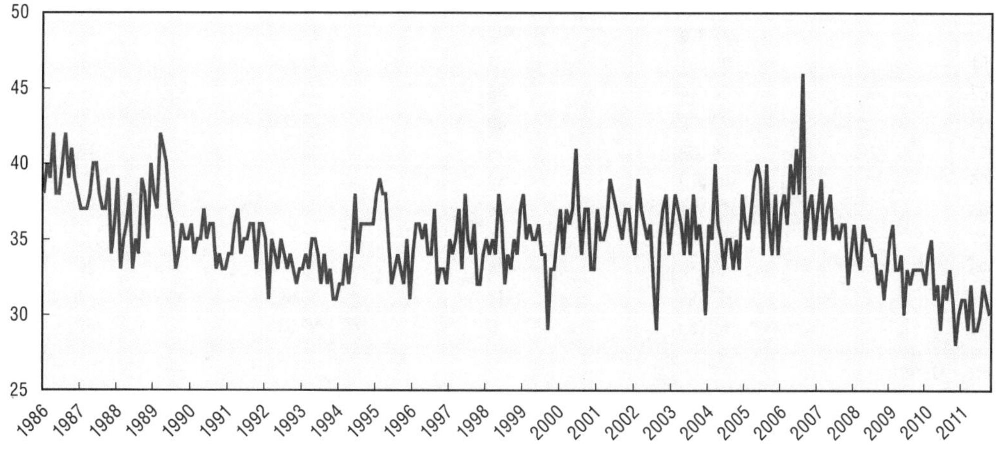

Source: National Federation of Independent Business (NFIB), "Small Business Economic Trends".

StatLink http://dx.doi.org/10.1787/888932579284

Other indicators

Bankruptcies more than doubled between 2007 and 2009 when they reached a peak of 60 837. They were still abnormally high in 2010 with 56 282 business failures.

Private equity financing

Given the dot.com bubble in 2001 and the losses incurred by private investors, both business angels and venture capital fell off sharply and did not recover in 2010.

Government policy response

The USSBA works with approximately 5 000 banks and credit unions, some 250 Community Development Corporations (CDCs), over 170 non-profit financial intermediaries and Community Development Financial Institutions (CDFIs), and approximately 300 small business investment companies (SBICs). The USSBA Capital Access Program has several major sub-programmes that provide guarantees and co-funding for a wide range of products designed to meet the diverse financial needs of small firms throughout their life cycle, starting from small start-ups to established firms.[9]

The largest of these, the *7(a) Loan Program*, provides guarantees for working capital loans up to USD 5.0 million to new and existing small businesses. The second largest sub-programme, the *Certified Development Corporation 504 Loan Program*, provides guarantees and co-funding for loans up to USD 5.0 million used for the purchases of fixed assets.

The financial and economic crisis of 2008-09 had a pronounced impact on the USSBA's Capital Access Programs. The volume of its two largest loan guarantee programmes declining from a monthly average of USD 1.7 billion during the 2005-07 period to a low monthly level of USD 687 million, an approximate 60% decline. The average dollar volume for these two programmes rebounded to USD 1.4 billion after major interventions by the federal government.

Table 4.80. **SBA 7a and 504 loan guarantees, 2000-10**

Various

	Number	Year-on-year, %	Dollar value (USD million)	Year-on-year, %
2000	47 369	−4	11 903	−4
2001	49 551	5	12 670	6
2002	60 844	23	14 573	15
2003	79 369	30	15 380	6
2004	94 069	19	18 147	18
2005	103 370	10	20 534	13
2006	109 941	6	20 236	−1
2007	107 567	−2	20 611	2
2008	65 519	−39	16 064	−22
2009	57 020	−13	15 366	−4
2010	66 059	16	22 536	47

Source: USSBA.

StatLink http://dx.doi.org/10.1787/888932580595

Figure 4.35. **Gross loans guarantees, total 7(a) and 504 programs, 1990-2011**

In USD thousands

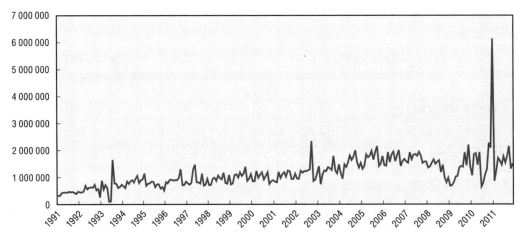

Source: USSBA.

StatLink http://dx.doi.org/10.1787/888932579303

To achieve this rebound in volume, the USSBA first provided additional incentives to financial institutions, and second it assisted in the unfreezing of the secondary market for USSBA loans.

The Agency employed additional funding received from Congress to temporarily increase its guarantees from around 75% to 90% of each loan for which USSBA provided guarantees.[10] The USSBA also temporarily reduced or eliminated the fees it charges financial institutions participating in its loan guarantee programmes. The Agency also increased its loan limits.

The second problem facing the USSBA was that, due to the sharp drop of interbank confidence, the volume in the secondary market for SBA (7a) backed loans dropped sharply just as it did in the commercial paper market. About 40% of 7(a) guaranteed loans are sold in the secondary market.

This market experienced a sharp drop during the second half of 2008, moving from an average monthly level of about USD 328 million to approximately USD 100 million during the first month of 2009. In response, on March 16, 2009 the President announced that as part of the *Financial Stability Plan* (FSP), the Department of Treasury would purchase USD 15 billion of USSBA loans on the secondary market.[11] Through this programme the government promised to be a buyer of last resort for these recent loans.

Table 4.81. **Financing SMEs and entrepreneurs: Scoreboard for the United States, 2007-10**

Indicators	Units	2007	2008	2009	2010
Debt					
Business loans, SMEs	USD millions	686 760	711 453	695 227	652 259
Business loans, total	USD millions	2 280 385	2 572 667	2 517 001	2 251 300
Business loans, SMEs	% of total business loans	30.1	27.7	27.6	29.0
Short-term loans, SMEs	% of credit market debt	31.1	31.6	26.7	23.5
Government sponsored Enterprise loans	USD billions	28.5	53.4	56.4	57.7
Government guaranteed loans, SMEs	USD billions	20.6	16.1	15.4	22.5
Ratio of loans authorised to requested, SMEs	%	71.8	66.6	. .	. .
Non-performing loans, total	% of loan stock	1.22	1.89	3.90	3.47
Interest rate, loans < USD 100 000	%	7.7	5.8	5.3	5.4
Interest rate, loans between USD 100 000-499 000	%	7.1	5.2	4.5	4.7
Interest rate, loans between USD 500 000-999 999	%	7.8	4.3	3.8	4.2
Collateral, loans < USD 100 000	% of loans secured by collateral	84.2	84.7	89.2	. .
Collateral, loans USD 100 000-USD 999 999	% of loans secured by collateral	76.4	70.9	77.6	. .
Collateral, loans USD 1 000 000-USD 999 999 999	% of loans secured by collateral	46.7	42	48.5	. .
Equity					
Venture capital	USD billions	30	28	18	22
Venture capital	Year-on-year growth rate, %	. .	−6	−35	19
Other					
Bankruptcies, total	Number	28 322	43 546	60 837	56 282
Bankruptcies , total	Year-on-year growth rate, %	. .	53.8	39.7	−7.5

Sources: Refer to Table 4.82 "Definitions and sources of indicators for the United States' Scoreboard".

StatLink ᵐˢᴾ *http://dx.doi.org/10.1787/888932580614*

Figure 4.36. **Trends in SME and entrepreneurship finance in the United States**

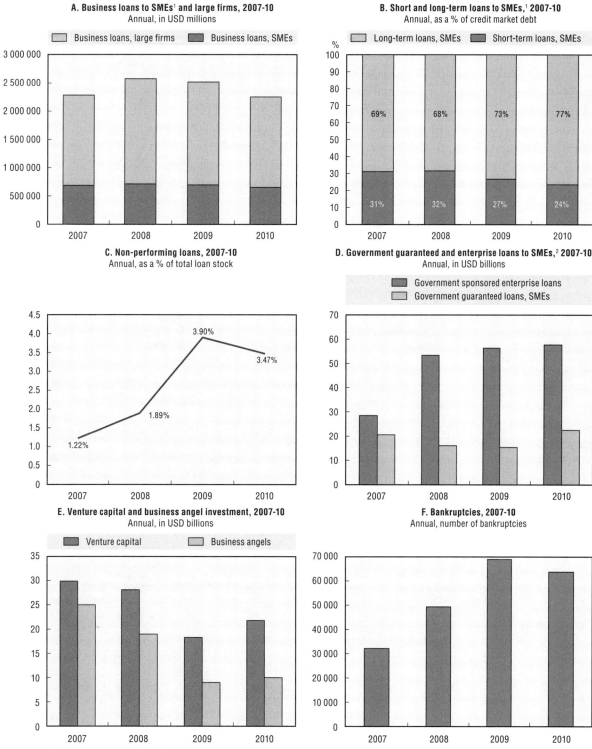

1. For loans up to USD 1 million.
2. Proxied by loans sponsored by the Small Business 7(a) loan program.

Sources: Chart A: FDIC, Consolidated Reports of Condition and Income for US Banks and thrift institutions. Chart B: Federal Reserve, Flow of Funds Accounts of the United States. Chart C: Federal Reserve Board. Chart D: Federal Reserve and USSBA. Chart E: PwC Money Tree Survey, Venture Capital Association and Center for Venture Research. Chart F: Adm. Office of US Courts: Business Bankruptcy Filings.

StatLink 🔗 *http://dx.doi.org/10.1787/888932579322*

Table 4.82. **Financing SMEs and entrepreneurs: Definitions and sources of indicators for the United States' Scoreboard**

Indicators	Definitions	Sources
Debt		
Business loans, SMEs	Loan balances held at financial institutions, loans to non-financial firms, loans up to USD 1 million.	FDIC, Consolidated Reports of Condition and Income for US Banks and thrift institutions, June 30 reports.
Business loans, total	Loan balances held at financial institutions, loans to "Commercial Real Estate", "Commercial and Industrial Loans", and "Commercial real estate loans not secured by real estate".	FDIC Call reports
Short-term loans, SMEs	Loans to non-financial corporations with a duration of less than one year, loans up to USD 1 million, flows.	Federal Reserve, Flow of Funds Accounts of the United States, Table L102, line 43, "Short-term debt/credit market debt".
Government sponsored Enterprise loans	Government sponsored enterprise loans to non-corporate partners.	Federal Reserve, Flow of funds reports.
Government guaranteed loans, SMEs	Full value of guaranteed loans outstanding for working capital and fixed assets. Government guaranteed loans to SMEs by the Small Business 7(a) loan program, which are the most basic and most commonly used type of loans.	USSBA, 7(a) and 504 loan guarantee program
Ratio of loans authorised to requested, SMEs	Approval rate.	Kauffman Foundation, Firm Survey Micro data
Non-performing loans, total	CandI bank loans, 30 days past due, all sizes, as a percentage of loan stock.	Federal Reserve Board
Interest rate, loans < USD 100 000	Annual average from quarterly data.	Fed. Res. Board, Survey of Terms of Business Lending, E2 Release
Interest rate, loans between USD 100 000-499 000	Annual average from quarterly data.	Fed. Res. Board, Survey of Terms of Business Lending, E2 Release
Interest rate, loans between USD 500 000-999 999	Annual average from quarterly data.	Fed. Res. Board, Survey of Terms of Business Lending, E2 Release
Collateral, SMEs	The percentage of loans secured by collateral.	Fed. Res. Board, Survey of Terms of Business Lending, E2 Release
Equity		
Venture capital	Investment in all enterprises.	PwC Money Tree Survey, Venture Capital Association
Other		
Bankruptcies, total	Bankruptcy data are 12 month numbers for 30 September of each year, all enterprises.	Adm. Office of US Courts: Business Bankruptcy Filings

Notes

1. The USSBA has two different approaches for defining small firms. The first approach is to define any firm with less than 500 employees as "small". This practice was first established by the Small Business Act of 1953. However, the same Act required the USSBA to establish a size standard that "should vary to account for differences among industries". Second, the Act called on the USSBA to "assist small businesses as a means of encouraging and strengthening their competitiveness in the economy". These two considerations are the basis for the SBA current methodology for establishing small business size standards. For further details see The US Small Business Administration (2009) SBA Size Standard Methodology.

2. For more details on the importance of small businesses in the US economy see The US Small Business Administration, Frequently Asked Questions.

3. For example, the Federal Financial Institutions Examination Council (FFIEC), as part of the Community Reinvestment Act of 1977, once a year publishes loan-origination data, including business loans, reported by various financial institutions. For further detail see FFIC *www.ffiec.gov/*.

4. For a detailed discussion on the lack of data on small business credit markets and its impact on the policy making process, see (Congressional Oversight Panel, 2010).

5. For data on balances held by depository institutions see FDIC, Call Reports. For data and discussion on the share of credit supplied to small businesses see US Small Business Administration (2009) Small Business in Focus: Finance.

6. For example, an institution may underwrite USD 100 million in small business loans in one quarter, and sell USD 50 million of those loans on the secondary market. As a result, the institution's balance sheet would increase by USD 50 million. In the following quarter, the same institution may underwrite only USD 75 million in small business loans, and sell only USD 25 million of these loans on the secondary market. Once again, the institution's balance sheet would increase by another USD 50 million. Hence, the balance sheet position continues to expand at the same USD 50 million pace, when in fact there was a USD 25 million reduction in its underwriting.

7. This section is based on US Small Business Administration Office of Advocacy, *Small Business lending in the United States*, 2009-10.

8. See Board of Governors of the Federal Reserve System, "Senior Loan Officer Opinion Survey on Bank Lending Practices".

9. For further details on the SBA's Capital Access Programs see *www.sba.gov*.

10. The USSBA provides a range of guarantees through its various guarantee products. For a quick reference on the details of its loan guarantee programs see the US Small Business Administration, Quick Reference to SBA Loan Guarantee Programs.

11. The Federal Reserve had already started to purchase some SBA guaranteed loans under the Term Asset-Backed Securities Loan Facility (TALF). For more details see Board of Governors of the Federal Reserve System, Term Asset-Backed Securities Loan Facility (TALF) Terms and Conditions, and the (White House Office of the Press Secretary 2010).

References

Board of Governors of the Federal Reserve System, "Senior Loan Officer Opinion Survey on Bank Lending Practices".

Congressional Oversight Panel, (2010) The Small Business Credit Crunch and the Impact of the TARP. *http://cybercemetery.unt.edu/archive/cop/20110402035902/http://cop.senate.gov/documents/cop-051310-report.pdf*.

Federal Deposit Insurance Corporation, *Call Reports, www.fdic.gov*.

Federal Financial Institutions Examination Council (FFIEC), *www.ffiec.gov/*.

National Federation of Independent Business (NFIB), *Small Business Economic Trends*.

US Small Business Administration, Frequently Asked Questions, *www.sba.gov/advocacy/7495/8420*.

US Small Business Administration, "Quick Reference to SBA Loan Guarantee Programs", *www.sba.gov/sites/default/files/files/LoanChartHQ20110728.pdf*. Accessed October 10, 2010.

US Small Business Administration (2009), "SBA Size Standard Methodology", *www.sba.gov/content/size-standards-methodology*, Accessed October 10, 2010.

US Small Business Administration Office of Advocacy, *Small Business lending in the United States*, 2009-10.

US Small Business Administration (2009), "Small Business in Focus: Finance", *http://archive.sba.gov/advo/research/09finfocus.pdf*.

The White House Office of the Press Secretary, Remarks by The President to Small Business Owners, Community Lenders and Member of Congress, 16 March 2009, *www.whitehouse.gov/the_press_office/Remarks-by-the-President-to-small-business-owners/*.

ANNEX A

Methodology

Introduction

Financing SMEs and Entrepreneurs: An OECD Scoreboard provides a framework to monitor trends in SMEs' and entrepreneurs' access to finance – at the country level and internationally – and a tool to support the formulation and evaluation of policies. This framework is currently built around 13 core indicators, which tackle specific questions related to SMEs' and entrepreneurs' access to finance. At the country level, this framework allows indicators to be examined as a set and to draw a more coherent picture of SME access to finance, governments' responses and the impact of those responses on SME survival.

The indicators have been developed using a "target" SME population which consists of non-financial "employer" firms, that is, firms with at least one employee besides the owner/manager. This is consistent with the methodology adopted by the OECD-Eurostat Entrepreneurship Indicators Programme, which also calculates its indicators on the basis of "employer" enterprises (OECD, 2009; OECD, 2011).

Most of the indicators in this report are built on supply-side data; financial institutions and other government agencies represent the main source of information. Over time, quantitative demand-side data, as collected by SME surveys, should complement the picture and improve the interpretative power of this framework. However, whereas a plethora of *qualitative* SME surveys (*i.e.* opinion surveys) exist, *quantitative* demand-side surveys are rare. Experience shows that *qualitative* information based on opinion survey responses must be used cautiously. Furthermore, comparability of national surveys is limited, as survey methodologies differ from country to country.

Criteria for the selection of the core indicators on SME financing

The pilot phase of development of the OECD Scoreboard on SME and entrepreneurship finance, conducted in 2009-10, established the following criteria for the selection of the core indicators: *usefulness, availability, feasibility, timeliness* and *comparability*:

- The SME financing indicators should be *useful*, in the sense that the indicators must be an appropriate instrument to measure how easy or difficult it is for SMEs to access finance and to help policy makers formulate or adjust their policies and programmes.

- The data for constructing the indicators should be *readily available* in order not to impose new burdens on governments.

- If the information for constructing the indicator is not publicly available, it should be *feasible* to make it available at a modest cost, or to collect it during routine data exercises or surveys.

- The information should be collected in a *timely* manner so that the evolving conditions of SME access to finance can be monitored. This means that annual or quarterly data are needed. In many cases, turning points can be better captured by quarterly data. In fact, annual data might not be appropriate to understand when a trend has changed and intervention is necessary. Some countries are downsizing their periodic surveys so that they can be administered on a quarterly basis.

- The indicators should be *comparable*. In particular, they should be relatively uniform across countries in terms of the population surveyed, content, method of data collection and periodicity or timeliness.

Thirteen indicators were identified in the course of the pilot project that fulfil most of the five criteria (Table A.1).

Table A.1. **Core indicators of the OECD SME and entrepreneurship finance Scoreboard**

1   SME loans/all business loans
2. SME short- term loans/SME loans
3. SME government loan guarantees
4. SME government guaranteed loans
5. SME direct government loans
6. SME loans authorised/SME loans requested or SME loans used/SME loans authorised
7. SME non-performing loans
8. SME interest rates
9. Interest rate spread between SMEs and large enterprises or the difference between the interest rate charge on loans and prime base
10. SMEs (%) required to provide collateral
11. Venture and growth capital
12. Payment delays
13. Bankruptcies

Each of the core indicators are *useful* to policy makers in that they measure or gauge the impact of the SME financing "gap". The individual indicators, and their interpretation as a set, therefore contribute to addressing key policy questions, such as:

- What is the allocation of credit in the country by size of firm?

- How much credit goes to investment (growth) *vs.* operational expenses (survival)?

- Does the supply of credit match the SME demand for credit?

- How large is the unmet demand for credit and does this represent a "serious" financing gap?

- Do SMEs face tighter credit conditions than larger firms? Are credit conditions becoming more onerous for them?

- What percentage of SMEs loans are government guaranteed?

- What is the uptake of government guarantee programmes by banks? What is the leverage ratio of such programmes?

- What role does venture and growth capital play in SME financing?

- What do payment delays and bankruptcies indicate in terms of the ability of SMEs to survive economic downturns and credit crunches?

The core indicators

Share of SME loans in total business loans: This ratio shows how well SMEs are doing in accessing finance compared to larger firms.

Share of short-term loans in SME loans: This ratio shows the debt structure of SMEs or whether loans were being used to fund current operations or were for investment and growth. A ratio greater than 50% suggests that loans were being used to stay afloat rather than investing in expansion.

SME government loan guarantees, SME government guaranteed loans, SME direct government loans: These indicators show the extent of public support for the financing of SMEs. They can be interpreted in various ways. When combined with SME loans, a high ratio could indicate that the banks are making use of government guarantee programmes to decrease their risk and increase lending to SMEs. An increase in the ratio could measure the government response to a credit crunch. In the future, the OECD Scoreboard on SME and entrepreneurship finance will collect information on the amount of the partial guarantees; this will capture the impact of increasing guarantee coverage, as experienced during the recent financial crisis.

SME authorised loans/SME requested loans: This indicator shows the tightness of the financial market and the willingness of banks to lend from the point of view of the SMEs. A decrease in the ratio indicates a tightening in the market. It also shows the "rejection" rate for SME loans. A limitation in this indicator is that it omits the impact of "discouraged" borrowers. However, discouragement and rejection are closely correlated. During economic downturns, as SME turnover declines and loans become riskier, loan authorisations decrease. At the same time, SME loan requests could also decrease because of the discouraged borrower effect. However, surveys seem to suggest that discouraged borrowers are only a small share of the SME population, so that in difficult times the ratio would still decline.

SME loans used/SME loans authorised: This ratio is used as a proxy by some countries for the above indicator. It shows the willingness of the banks to provide credit. However, in contrast with the above ratio, a decrease in this ratio indicates that credit conditions are loosening because not all credit authorised is being used.

SME non-performing loans/SME loans: This indicator shows the ability of the bank to manage its portfolio and its willingness to take on risks. It can be compared with the overall ratio of non-performing loans to all business loans to determine whether SMEs are less creditworthy.

SME interest rates and interest rate spreads: These indicators describe the tightness of the market and the (positive or negative) correlation of interest rates with firm size.

Collateral required: This indicator shows tightness of credit conditions. It is based on demand-side surveys where SMEs report if they have been required to provide collateral for their last loan. It is not available from supply-side sources, as banks do not generally divulge this information.

Venture capital and growth capital: This indicator shows the ability to access external equity in the form of seed, start-up, early stage venture capital as well as expansion capital. It excludes buyouts, turnarounds and replacement capital, as these are directed at restructuring and generally concern larger enterprises.

SME payment delay in days: This indicator contributes to assess SME cash flow problems. If the delay is business-to-customer (B2C), it reveals difficulties in SMEs being paid by their clients; if it is business-to-business (B2B), it shows supplier credit delays and how SMEs are coping with cash flow problems by delaying their payments. The higher the B2B delay compared to B2C, the more relief to cash flow problems. At present, the detailed distinction is not made in the report, but in the future both indicators will be collected in order to allow this comparison.

SME bankruptcies or bankruptcies per 10 000 or 1 000 SMEs: This indicator is a proxy for SME survival prospects. Abrupt changes in bankruptcy rates demonstrate how severely SMEs are affected by economic crises. The indicator likely underestimates the number of SME exits, as some SMEs close their business before being in financial difficulties.

Process of data collection

Four years were chosen for data collection: 2007 (benchmark year), 2008, 2009 and 2010. The analysis of the annual and quarterly changes allowed to determine the impact of the 2008-09 financial crisis on SME financing and the extent of the recovery.

Generally, data on SME financing are sourced from quantitative data collected by the financial regulatory authorities. In other cases, data can be obtained from tax records or from quantitative surveys undertaken by government agencies or statistical authorities.

There exist also numerous surveys of SMEs (demand-side surveys) and bank loan officers and equity fund members (supply-side surveys), undertaken by government agencies, business associations and investors' associations. This information is usually qualitative and is based on estimates or opinions, although some governments and regional banks do undertake quantitative demand-side surveys.

Experience shows that *qualitative* information based on opinion survey responses must be used cautiously as they often appear to be inconsistent. For example, surveys of senior loan officers sometimes show demand for credit decreasing, while at the same time surveys of SMEs show the SMEs' need for credit increasing. Furthermore, across surveys there is little standardisation in terms of the timing, the sample population, the sampling method, the interview method, and the questions asked.

This problem was recognised at the Brasilia Conference on SME Financing (2006). It recommended a quantitative … "survey of SMEs and suppliers of finance on a regular basis to provide policy makers with more accurate and detailed information". Both sources of information (*i.e.* transaction-based data and opinion survey responses) were used in developing the OECD Scoreboard on SME and entrepreneurship finance, but preference was given to transaction-based data, and survey responses were used to provide additional information.

The role of country experts

Eleven countries participated in the development of the pilot phase of the OECD Scoreboard on financing SMEs and entrepreneurs: Canada, Finland, France, Italy, Korea, the Netherlands, New Zealand, Sweden, Switzerland, Thailand and the United States. During the second stage of the project, Chile, Denmark, Hungary, Portugal, the Slovak Republic, Slovenia and the United Kingdom also joined and provided data. Each participating country nominated a country expert, who had access to the information needed from a variety of supply-side and demand-side sources.

The Pilot exercise started off with a long list of over 25 potential indicators. With the limitations of availability and feasibility in mind, the 11 original country experts specified for which indicators they had information, along with their source (supply- or demand-side). Canada volunteered to be a test case and provided quantitative and qualitative information for as many of the indicators as possible. Based on the Canadian test case and the other country indications of availability, it was possible to reduce the list of indicators to a set of 13 core indicators which met the five criteria.

Data issues

There are several areas where improvements are needed to better monitor SMEs' access to finance, and to increase the usefulness of this exercise as a framework for policy makers. There is a need for OECD and non-OECD countries to collect data on SME finance in a more timely fashion. In addition, to enable better cross-country comparisons, it is necessary for countries to advance in the harmonisation of data content and in the standardisation of methods of data collection. The following paragraphs highlight key challenges and directions for improved collection and harmonisation.

Differences in the statistical and financial definitions of an SME

The biggest challenge in creating the OECD Scoreboard on SME and entrepreneurship finance was the lack of comparability across countries in the statistical definitions of an SME itself. Greater harmonisation in this sense continues to prove difficult due to the different economic, social and political concerns of individual countries (see Box A.1). The EU SME definition is the most commonly used, although this definition is set to be reviewed in 2012.

Box A.1. **What is an SME?**

There is no single definition of an SME, and employee numbers need not be the sole defining criterion. However, SMEs are generally considered to be non-subsidiary firms which employ less than a given number of employees. This number varies across countries. The most frequent upper limit designation of an SME is 250 employees, as in the European Union. However, some countries set the limit at 200, while the United States consider SMEs to include firms with fewer than 500 employees. Small firms are mostly considered to be firms with fewer than 50 employees while micro-enterprises have at most ten, or in some cases, five employees. Financial assets are also used to define SMEs: in the EU, the turnover of medium-sized firms (50-249 employees) should not exceed EUR 50 million; that of small enterprises (10-49 employees) should not exceed EUR 10 million; and that of micro firms (< 10 employees) should not exceed EUR 2 million.

Source: OECD (2006), *The SME Financing Gap (Vol. I): Theory and Evidence*, Paris.

Furthermore, the national statistical SME definition often differs from the one used by banks and financial institutions to collect data on SME financing. Table A.2 illustrates the differences between the national statistical SME definitions and those used by financial institutions in the same country.

The process of developing this Scoreboard suggests that the main source of inconsistency is the difference in the definitions used by the banks and financial institutions, which define an SME loan either by the firm size or by loan size. Ideally, countries should define an SME loan by firm size, using the same size subgroups. This would allow data to be aggregated in a uniform way, for instance conforming to the EU definition of an SME, while still leaving the possibility to aggregate the data in other ways to suit various national purposes. It should be noted, however, that at the present time some banks and other creditors are reluctant to switch from reporting based on authorisation levels to reporting based on the number of employees unless required to do so by regulators.

Table A.2. **Difference between national statistical and financial definitions of SMEs**

Country	National statistical definition of SMEs	Indicator	Definition of SMEs used
Canada	Size of firm: 1-499 employees	Business loans, SMEs	Size of loan: amounts up to CAD 1 million
		Short and long-term loans, small businesses	Size of firm: enterprises with 1-99 employees
		Government guaranteed loans, SMEs	Size of firm: annual sales (turnover) lower than CAD 5 million
		Direct government loans, SMEs	Size of firm: annual sales (turnover) less than CAD 25 million
		Risk premium for small businesses	Size of firm: enterprises with 1-99 employees
		Loans authorised and requested, small businesses	Size of firm: enterprises with 1-99 employees
		Collateral, small businesses	Size of firm: enterprises with 1-99 employees
Chile	Annual sales of firm: up to UF 100 000	Business loans, SMEs	Size of loan: amounts up to UF 18 000
		Short and long-term loans, SMEs	Size of loan: amounts up to UF 18 000
		Government guaranteed loans, SMEs	Size of firm: annual sales up to UF 100 000 or annual exports up to UF 400 000
		Direct government loans, SMEs	Less than 12 hectares and capital up to UF 3 500
		Loans authorised and requested, SMEs	Size of firm: annual sales up to UF 100 000
		Non-performing loans, SMEs	Size of loan: amounts up to UF 18 000
		Short-term interest rate, SMEs	Size of loan: amounts up to UF 18 000
		Payment delays, SMEs	Size of loan: amounts up to UF 18 000
Denmark	Size of firm: less than 250 employees	Business loans, SMEs	Size of loan: amounts up to EUR 1 million
		Short and long-term loans, SMEs	Size of loan: amounts up to EUR 1 million
		Government loan guarantees, SMEs	Size of firm: up to 250 employees
		Interest rate, SMEs	Size of loan: amounts up to EUR 1 million
Finland	EU definition (less than 250 employees and annual turnover below EUR 50 million and/ or balance sheet below EUR 43 million)	Business loans, SMEs	Size of loan: up to EUR 1 million
		Short and long-term loans, SMEs	Size of firm: less than 250 employees
		Value of government guaranteed loans, SMEs	Size of firm: less than 250 employees
		Loans authorised and requested, SMEs	Size of loan: up to EUR 1 million
		Interest rate, SMEs	Size of loan: up to EUR 1 million
		Collateral, SMEs	Size of firm: less than 250 employees
France	EU definition (less than 250 employees and annual turnover below EUR 50 million and/ or balance sheet below EUR 43 million)	Business loans, SMEs	Firm size: number of employees (less than 250), turnover (less than EUR 50 million), total assets of legal units (less than EUR 43 million) and independent
		Short, medium and long-term loans	Firm size: number of employees (less than 250), turnover (less than EUR 50 million), total assets of legal units (less than EUR 43 million) and Independent
		Share of the outstanding loans of failing companies, SMEs except micro-enterprises	Firm size: number of employees (less than 250), turnover (less than EUR 50 million), total assets of legal units (less than EUR 43 million) and independent
		Interest rate, SMEs	Size of loan: less than EUR 1 million
		Bankruptcies, SMEs	Firm size: number of employees (less than 250), turnover (less than EUR 50 million), total assets of legal units (less than EUR 43 million) and independent

Table A.2. **Difference between national statistical and financial definitions of SMEs** (cont.)

Country	National statistical definition of SMEs	Indicator	Definition of SMEs used
Hungary	EU definition (less than 250 employees and annual turnover below EUR 50 million and/ or balance sheet below EUR 43 million)	Business loans, SMEs	Firm size: number of employees (less than 250 employees), turnover (less than EUR 50 million) and total assets (less than EUR 10 million).
		Overdraft loans, SMEs	Firm size: number of employees (less than 250 employees), turnover (less than EUR 50 million) and total assets (less than EUR 10 million).
		Investment loans, SMEs	Firm size: number of employees (less than 250 employees), turnover (less than EUR 50 million) and total assets (less than EUR 10 million).
		Direct government loans, SMEs	Firm size: number of employees (less than 250 employees), turnover (less than EUR 50 million) and total assets (less than EUR 10 million).
		Government guaranteed loans, SMEs	Firm size: number of employees (less than 250 employees), turnover (less than EUR 50 million) and total assets (less than EUR 10 million).
		Non-performing loans, SMEs	Firm size: number of employees (less than 250 employees), turnover (less than EUR 50 million) and total assets (less than EUR 10 million).
		Average interest rate, SMEs	Size of loan: amounts up to EUR 1 million
Italy	EU definition (less than 250 employees and annual turnover below EUR 50 million and/ or balance sheet below EUR 43 million)	Business loans, SMEs	Firm size: less than 20 workers
		Short and long-term loans, SMEs	Firm size: less than 20 workers
		Government guaranteed loans, SMEs	Size of firm: less than 250 employees
		Direct government loans, SMEs	Size of firm: less than 250 employees
		Loans authorised and used, SMEs	Firm size: less than 20 workers
		Non-performing loans, SMEs	Firm size: less than 20 workers
		Interest rate, average SME rate	Firm size: less than 20 workers
		Collateral, SMEs	n.a.
		Venture and expansion capital, SMEs	Size of firm: less than 250 employees
		Payment delays, SMEs	Size of firm: turnover of up to EUR 50 million
Korea	Varies by sector	Business loans, SMEs	The definition of SMEs differs according to sector.
		Short and long-term loans, SMEs	The definition of SMEs differs according to sector.
		Government loan guarantees, SMEs	The definition of SMEs differs according to sector.
		Direct government loans, SMEs	The definition of SMEs differs according to sector.
		Loans authorised and requested, SMEs	The definition of SMEs differs according to sector.
		Non-performing loans, SMEs	The definition of SMEs differs according to sector.
		Interest rate spread, SME and large firm rates	The definition of SMEs differs according to sector.
		Payment delays, SMEs	The definition of SMEs differs according to sector.
Netherlands	EU definition (less than 250 employees and annual turnover below EUR 50 million and/ or balance sheet below EUR 43 million)	Business loans, SMEs	Size of loan: up to EUR 1 million
		Short and long-term loans, SMEs	Size of loan: up to EUR 1 million
		Government loan guarantees, SMEs	Size of firm: up to 250 employees
		Loans authorised and requested, SMEs	Size of firm: up to 250 employees
		Collateral, SMEs	Size of firm up to 250 employees
New Zealand	Size of firm: less than 20 employees	Interest rates, SMEs	Size of loan: up to NZD 1 million
Portugal	EU definition (less than 250 employees and annual turnover below EUR 50 million and/ or balance sheet below EUR 43 million)	Business loans, SMEs	Size of firm: EU definition (less than 250 employees and annual turnover below EUR 50 million and/ or balance sheet below EUR 43 million, Com Recommendation 2003/361/EC)
		Short and long-term loans, SMEs	Size of firm: EU definition (less than 250 employees and annual turnover below EUR 50 million and/ or balance sheet below EUR 43 million, Com Recommendation 2003/361/EC)
		Government guaranteed loans, SMEs	Size of firm: EU definition (less than 250 employees and annual turnover below EUR 50 million and/ or balance sheet below EUR 43 million, Com Recommendation 2003/361/EC)
		Loans authorised and requested, SMEs	Size of firm: EU definition (less than 250 employees and annual turnover below EUR 50 million and/ or balance sheet below EUR 43 million, Com Recommendation 2003/361/EC)
		Non-performing loans, SMEs	Size of firm: EU definition (less than 250 employees and annual turnover below EUR 50 million and/ or balance sheet below EUR 43 million, Com Recommendation 2003/361/EC)
		Interest rates, SMEs	Size of loan: up to EUR 1 million (prior to 2010) and loans up to EUR 0.25 million (in 2010)
		Collateral, SMEs	Size of firm: EU definition (less than 250 employees and annual turnover below EUR 50 million and/ or balance sheet below EUR 43 million, Com Recommendation 2003/361/EC)

Table A.2. **Difference between national statistical and financial definitions of SMEs** (cont.)

Country	National statistical definition of SMEs	Indicator	Definition of SMEs used
Slovak Republic	EU definition (less than 250 employees and annual turnover below EUR 50 million and/ or balance sheet below EUR 43 million)	Business loans, SMEs	Size of firm: less than 250 employees (including natural persons)
		Short and long-term loans, SMEs	Size of firm: less than 250 employees (including natural persons)
		Government loan guarantees, SMEs	Size of firm: less than 250 employees (including natural persons)
		Government guaranteed loans, SMEs	Size of firm: EU definition (less than 250 employees and annual turnover below EUR 50 million and/ or balance sheet below EUR 43 million, Com Recommendation 2003/361/EC)
		Direct government loans, SMEs	Size of firm: less than 250 employees (including natural persons)
		Collateral, SMEs	Size of firm: EU definition (less than 250 employees and annual turnover below EUR 50 million and/ or balance sheet below EUR 43 million, Com Recommendation 2003/361/EC)
		Venture capital, SMEs	Size of firm: EU definition (less than 250 employees and annual turnover below EUR 50 million and/ or balance sheet below EUR 43 million, Com Recommendation 2003/361/EC)
Slovenia	EU definition (less than 250 employees and annual turnover below EUR 50 million and/ or balance sheet below EUR 43 million)	Short and long-term loans, SMEs	Size of firm: less than or equal to 250 employees and asset value less than or equal to EUR 17.5 million.
		Direct government loans, SMEs	Size of firm: less than or equal to 250 employees and asset value less than or equal to EUR 17.5 million.
		Interest rate, SMEs	Firm and loan size: enterprises with less than 250 employees and amounts less than EUR 1 million.
Sweden	EU definition (less than 250 employees and annual turnover below EUR 50 million and/ or balance sheet below EUR 43 million)	Business loans, SMEs	Size of firm: 1-249 employees
		Short and long-term loans, SMEs	Size of firm: 1-249 employees
		Government guaranteed loans, SMEs	Size of firm: 0-249 employees
		Government loan guarantees, SMEs	Size of firm: 0-249 employees
		Direct government loans, SMEs	Size of firm: 0-249 employees
		Loans authorised, SMEs	Size of firm: 0-249 employees
		Interest rates, SMEs	Size of loan: up to EUR 1 million
Switzerland	Size of firm: less than 250 employees	Business loans, SMEs	Size of firm: less than 250 employees
		Government guaranteed loans, SMEs	Size of firm: less than 250 employees
		Loans used, SMEs	Size of firm: less than 250 employees
		Collateral, SMEs	Size of firm: up to 249 employees
		Interest rates, SMEs	Size of loan: less than CHF 1 million
Thailand	Number of employees and fixed capital: less than 200 employees and fixed capital less than THB 200 million	Business loans, SMEs	Size of firm: sales less than THB 400 million and/or a credit line less than THB 200 million
		Short and long-term loans, SMEs	Size of firm: sales less than THB 400 million and/or a credit line less than THB 200 million
		Government guaranteed loans, SMEs	Size of firm: sales less than THB 400 million and/or a credit line less than THB 200 million
		Loans authorised and requested, SMEs	Size of firm: sales less than THB 400 million and/or a credit line less than THB 200 million
		Non-performing loans, SMEs	Size of firm: sales less than THB 400 million and/or a credit line less than THB 200 million
		Interest rate, SME average rate	Size of firm: sales less than THB 400 million and/or a credit line less than THB 200 million
		Payment delays, SMEs	The National definition of SMEs differs according to sector
		Bankruptcies, SMEs	The National definition of SMEs differs according to sector
United Kingdom	Size of firm: less than 250 employees	Business lending, SMEs	Size of firm: turnover of up to GBP 1 million
		Interest rates, SMEs	Size of firm: turnover up to GBP 25 million
		Collateral, SMEs	Size of firm: less than 250 employees, including non-employer enterprises
United States	Size of firm: less than 500 employees	Business loans, SMEs	Size of loan: up to USD 1 million
		Short-term loans, SMEs	Size of loan: up to USD 1 million
		Government guaranteed loans, SMEs	n.a.
		Collateral, SMEs	n.a.

Deviations from preferred definitions

In a number of cases it was not possible to adhere to the preferred definition of the core indicators (Table A.3). In these instances a "proxy" was used by country experts.

Table A.3. **Preferred definitions for core indicators**

Indicator	Definition/Description	Sources
SME loans	Bank and financial institution loans to SMEs, amount outstanding (stocks) at the end of period OR new loans (flows); by firm size using the national definition of SME or if necessary, loan amounts less than EUR 1 million	Supply side data from financial institutions
Total business loans	Bank and financial institution business loans to all non-financial enterprises, amount outstanding (stocks) or new loans (flows)	Supply side data
SME short-term loans	Loans equal to or less than one year; outstanding amounts or new loans	Supply side data
SME long-term loans	Loans for more than one year; outstanding amounts or new loans	Supply side data
SME government loan guarantees	Guarantees available to banks and financial institutions, either new or outstanding	Supply side data
SME government guaranteed loans	Loans guaranteed by government, stocks or flows	Supply side data
SME government direct loans	Direct loans from government, stocks or flows	Supply side data
SME loans authorised	Stocks or flows	Demand side survey
SME loans requested	Stocks or flows	Demand side survey
SME non-performing loans	SME non-performing loans out of total SME loans	Supply side data
SME interest rate	Average annual rates for new loans, base rate plus risk premium; for maturity less than 1 year; and amounts less than EUR 1 million	Supply side data
Interest rate spreads	Between small and large enterprises; for maturity less than 1 year; amounts less than EUR 1 million and equal to or greater than EUR 1 million	Supply side data
Collateral	Percentage of SMEs that were required to provide collateral on latest bank loan	Demand side survey
Venture and growth capital	Seed, start-up, early stage and expansion capital (excludes buyouts, turnarounds, replacements)	VC association (supply side)
Payment delays	Average number of days delay beyond the contract period for Business to Business (B2B) and Business to Customer (B2C)	Demand side survey
Bankruptcy	Number of enterprises ruled bankrupt; and No. bankrupt per 10 000 or 1 000 enterprises	Administrative data

SME loans

The OECD Scoreboard on SME and entrepreneurship finance aims to collect business loan data that includes overdrafts, lines of credit, short-term loans, and long-term loans, regardless of whether they are performing or non-performing loans. Additionally, it aims to exclude personal credit card debt and residential mortgages. However, for some countries, significant deviations exist from this preferred SME loan definition.

In some countries, central banks do not require *any* reporting on SME lending. In these cases the SME loans were estimated from SME financial statements available from tax authorities. In other cases credit card debt was included in SME loans, and it could not be determined which part was consumer credit card debt and which was business credit card debt. In one case, lines of credit and overdrafts were excluded.

The report includes data on government loan guarantees. Supply-side data is the best source of information on loan guarantees, because SMEs are not always aware that their loan is backed by a government guarantee. There are many sources for such guarantees: local, regional or central governments and the guaranteed loans are not always consolidated to obtain national figures.

The indicator on SME loans authorised *vs.* SME loans requested is obtained from demand-side surveys. However, not all countries undertook such a survey, or if they did, the results were not comparable. Several countries had information on SME loans used *vs.*

requested. They produced a proxy consisting of SME loans used divided by SME loans authorised. While this does not provide the identical information as the preferred definition, a decline in the ratio showed that the credit market was easing, or that banks were willing to provide more credit than was being used.

There is also a great deal of latitude in how banks define "non-performing" loans. Some use a cut-off of 90 days, and others a longer period. However, if the changes in this ratio are analysed, the indicator can be used for cross-country comparisons.

SME credit conditions

The calculation for SME interest rates is still a matter of debate, and significant differences exist across countries. While there is agreement that "fees" should be included in the "cost" of the SME loans, it appears to be particularly difficult to determine which "fees", among the various charges applied to firms, to include in the interest rates. Only one country included this element in interest rate.

Central banks usually do not collect key pieces of information on SME access to finance, such as the collateral required for SME loans. Banks consider this to be confidential information. A rough approximation can be obtained from demand-side information, that is, the percentage of SMEs required to provide collateral on new loans. The country experts considered that this was the most expedient way to obtain information on collateral for the OECD Scoreboard on SME and entrepreneurship finance until there is more transparent reporting by banks on the terms of their SME lending.

Equity financing

The present report monitors venture and growth capital. Venture capital is usually reported by stage of development: seed, start-up and early expansion capital. It was decided to include later stage expansion capital as well, referred to as growth capital. Excluded from venture and growth capital were buyouts, turnarounds and replacement capital. Country classification systems do not always break down private equity data. Most do not break it down by size of firm. Venture capital data are collected by private venture capital associations which rely on voluntary reporting and whose membership may be incomplete. There is also no standard method to value venture capital.

There is a need for greater standardisation of venture capital data reporting, in terms of both the definition used for the different stages of investment, and the methodology employed to collect data. In the future, the equity dimension is expected to be better addressed, taking into account additional forms of external and internal equity used by SMEs.

Payment delays and bankruptcies

Payment delays and bankruptcy data are usually collected for all enterprises and not broken down by firm size. Since SMEs account for more than 97% of the enterprises in the participating countries, the national figures for payment delays and bankruptcy rates were used in this report. However, bankruptcies are hard to compare across countries because of different bankruptcy costs, legislation and behaviour in the face of bankruptcy.

Impact of the diversity in definitions

Despite the diversity in definitions and missing data, it was possible in most cases to identify sufficient data which would allow core indicators or reasonable proxies to be constructed. Cross-country comparisons are still difficult and only a few of the indicators can be compared in a meaningful way. However, when analysing trends, the differences in the exact composition of the indicators are muted by the fact that the *changes* in the indicators between the pre-crisis, crisis and recovery periods are considered.

Harmonisation of data on the supply and demand sides

While considerable work to harmonise the indicators has been conducted, more work needs to be done in the harmonisation of data collection. What is needed is better data collection, rather than more data collection. For example, some governments, in order to have more precise and timely information, are reducing the size of their surveys so that they can be conducted more frequently and they are harmonising the questions asked with other national surveys.

As a complement to such improved supply-side information, short, comparable demand-side surveys focusing on the key indicators could be developed, such as the one undertaken by the European Central Bank and the European Commission. This provides a good example of the benefits that can come from standardised definitions and methodology across countries. At the country level, the experience of Canada shows that demand-surveys can have good coverage, be limited in the number of questions and relatively inexpensive to carry out, while yielding high quality data.

References

OECD (2006), *The SME Financing Gap*, Volume 1, Theory and Evidence, OECD Publishing.

OECD (2009), *Measuring Entrepreneurship: A Collection of Indicators*, 2009 Edition, OECD-Eurostat Entrepreneurship Indicators Programme, OECD Statistics Directorate, OECD Publishing.

OECD (2011), *Entrepreneurship at a Glance 2011*, OECD Publishing.

ANNEX B

Surveys and Statistical Resources on SME and Entrepreneurship Finance

Surveys represent an important source of information and data for monitoring the state of financing available and used by SMEs and entrepreneurs, as well as for assessing appropriateness and effectiveness of government policies in this area. A large number of supply-side and demand-side surveys are conducted at the national level by government agencies, national statistical offices, central banks and, in some cases, business associations and private organisations.

Survey-based evidence, on both the demand and the supply side, can complement the quantitative data collected from supply-side sources and improve the understanding of business financing needs. Survey data are particularly useful for assessing credit conditions when relevant data are not easily accessible or produced in a timely manner. This is the case, for instance, of information on collateral requirements for SME loans, which are treated as confidential by most banks.

However, harmonisation is urgently needed in the design and implementation of surveys. At present, there is little standardisation across countries in terms of the timing, the sample population, the sampling method, the interview method, and the questions asked. To address this issue, governments are encouraged to increase co-operative efforts between public and private institutions in order to increase coverage and comparability of results of different surveys covering the same phenomenon. The ECB/EC's survey on SME access to finance uses a standardised methodology and provides a good example of the benefits that can come from standardised definitions and methodology across countries.

The OECD can serve as a clearinghouse for national and multilateral efforts to improve the knowledge base on SME finance, by fostering international dialogue on this issue, and collecting and diffusing information on the statistical resources and survey practices and methodologies developed in OECD and non-OECD countries. The list below represents a first step in this direction, providing links to relevant sources for the countries in the Scoreboard on SME and entrepreneurship finance and at the international level.

Canada

SME Financing Data Initiative – *Survey on Credit Condition*,
www.sme-fdi.gc.ca/eic/site/sme_fdi-prf_pme.nsf/eng/h_02192.html.

SME Financing Data Initiative – *Survey on Financing of Small and Medium Enterprises*,
www.sme-fdi.gc.ca/eic/site/sme_fdi-prf_pme.nsf/eng/h_01570.html.

SME Financing Data Initiative – *Survey of Suppliers of Business Financing*,
www.sme-fdi.gc.ca/eic/site/sme_fdi-prf_pme.nsf/eng/h_01569.html.

SME Financing Data Initiative – *Survey of SME Needs and Satisfaction*,
www.sme-fdi.gc.ca/eic/site/sme_fdi-prf_pme.nsf/eng/h_01571.html.

Chile

Central Bank of Chile – *General Conditions and Standards in the Credit Market*, June 2011,
www.bcentral.cl/estadisticas-economicas/credito-bancario/index.htm.

Central Bank of Chile – *Working Papers*,
www.bcentral.cl/eng/studies/working-papers/.

Denmark

Danmarks Nationalbank – *Lending Survey*,
http://nationalbanken.dk/DNUK/Statistics.nsf/side/Danmarks_Nationalbanks_lending_survey!Open Document.

European Commission

DG Enterprise and Industry's Survey on the Access to Finance of SMEs,
http://ec.europa.eu/enterprise/policies/finance/data.

European Central Bank

Euro Area Bank Lending Survey,
www.ecb.int/stats/money/surveys/lend/html/index.en.html.

Survey on the Access to Finance of SMEs in the Euro Area,
www.ecb.int/stats/money/surveys/sme/html/index.en.html.

European Investment Bank Group

European Investment Fund – *Working Papers*,
www.eif.org/news_centre/research/index.htm.

Finland

Bank of Finland – *Finnish MFI new business on euro-denominated loans to euro area non-financial corporations by loan amount*,
www.suomenpankki.fi/en/tilastot/tase_ja_korko/Pages/tilastot_rahalaitosten_lainat_talletukset_ja_korot_lainat_lainat_uudet_sopimukset_yrityksille_en.aspx.

Bank of Finland, the Confederation of Finnish Industries and the Ministry of Employment and the Economy – *Business financing surveys*,
www.suomenpankki.fi/en/julkaisut/selvitykset_ja_raportit/Pages/default.aspx.

Confederation of Finnish Industries EK – *EK´s longitudinal financing surveys*,
www.ek.fi/ek/en/news/eks_financial_surveys_provide_an_accurate_picture_of_economic_situation_among_smes-5367.

Federation of Finnish Enterprises and Finnvera – *SME-Barometer (in Finnish)*,
www.yrittajat.fi/fi-FI/uutisarkisto/a/uutisarkisto/pk-yritykset-varautuvat-uuteen-taantumaan-6.

Financial Supervisory Authority – *Nonperforming assets and impairment losses by sector and industrial category*,
www.finanssivalvonta.fi/en/Statistics/Credit_market/Nonperforming_assets_by_sector/Pages/Default.aspx.

Finnish Venture Capital Association – *FVCA industry statistics*,
www.fvca.fi/en/knowledge_centre/statistics.

Finnvera – *Annual reviews*,
www.finnvera.fi/eng/About-Finnvera/Publications.

Statistics Finland – *StatFin online service*,
www.stat.fi/tup/statfin/index_en.html.

France

Banque de France – *Monthly report on the Financing of SMEs in France* (Le financement des PME en France),
www.banque-france.fr/economie-et-statistiques/entreprises/credits-par-type-dentreprise.html.

Banque de France – *SME finance "Webstat"*,
http://webstat.banque-france.fr/fr/browse.do?node=5384417.

Banque de France – *Enterprise data homepage*,
www.banque-france.fr/economie-et-statistiques/entreprises.html.

Banque de France – *Quarterly Bank Survey on the Distribution of Credit* (Enquête trimestrielle auprès des banques sur la distribution du crédit),
www.banque-france.fr/statistiques/titres/titres-credits-distribution.htm.

Ministry of the Economy, Finance and Industry – *Report of the Firms Financing Observatory*,
http://mediateurducredit.fr/site/content/download/444/2637/file/RapportObsfi%20.pdf.

Hungary

Hungarian Financial Supervisory Authority – *Credit Institution data*,
www.pszaf.hu/en/left_menu/pszafen_publication/creditdata.html.

Italy

Bank of Italy – *Bank Lending Survey*,
www.bancaditalia.it/statistiche/indcamp/bls;internal&action=_setlanguage.action?LANGUAGE=en.

Bank of Italy – *Survey of Industrial and Service Firms*,
www.bancaditalia.it/statistiche/indcamp/indimpser/boll_stat;internal&action=_setlanguage.action?LANGUAGE=en.

Bank of Italy – *Business Outlook Survey of Industrial and Service Firms*,
www.bancaditalia.it/statistiche/indcamp/sondaggio;internal&action=_setlanguage.action?LANGUAGE=en.

Bank of Italy – *Survey of Banks*,
www.bancaditalia.it/pubblicazioni/econo/ecore/2011/analisi_m/domanda_e_offerta_di_credito_2010.pdf.

ISAE – *Monthly ISAE Survey on Manufacturing and Mining Enterprises November 2010* (Inchiesta Mensile Isae Sulle Imprese Manifatturiere ed Estrattive),
www.isae.it/not_ind_ita_11_10.pdf.

Korea

Financial Supervisory Service – *Bank Management Statistics*,
www.fss.or.kr/fss/kr/bbs/list.jsp?bbsid=1207396624018&url=/fss/kr/1207396624018.

Financial Supervisory Service – *Financial Statistics Information System*,
http://fisis.fss.or.kr/

The Netherlands

Central Bank of the Netherlands (De Nederlandsche Bank) – *Domestic MFI Statistics*,
www.statistics.dnb.nl/index.cgi?lang=uk&todo=Banken.

New Zealand

Reserve Bank of New Zealand – *Financial Stability Report*,
www.rbnz.govt.nz/finstab/fsreport/.

Small Business Advisory Group – *various reports*,
www.med.govt.nz/business/business-growth-internationalisation/small-and-medium-sized-enterprises/previous-small-business-advisory-group-reports.

Statistics New Zealand – *Business Operations Survey*,
www.stats.govt.nz/methods_and_services/information-releases/business-operations-survey.aspx.

Slovak Republic

National Agency for Development of SMEs – *State of Small and Medium Enterprises Survey*,
www.nadsme.sk/en/content/state-small-and-medium-enterprises.

Slovenia

Bank of Slovenia – *Financial Stability Review*,
www.bsi.si/en/publications.asp?MapaId=784.

Sweden

ALMI – *Reports on Business Financing*,
www.almi.se/Finansiering/Dokumentarkiv/.

Statistics Sweden – *Structural Business Statistics*,
www.scb.se/Pages/Product____130402.aspx.

Statistics Sweden – *Financial Market Statistics*,
www.scb.se/Pages/Product____37274.aspx.

Switzerland

Secrétariat d'État à l'économie (SECO) – *Survey of Swiss SME Finance 2010*,
www.seco.admin.ch/aktuell/00277/01164/01980/index.html?lang=fr&msg-id=33346.

Swiss National Bank – *Monthly Bulletin of Banking Statistics*,
www.snb.ch/en/iabout/stat/statpub.

Swiss National Bank – *most recent survey releases*,
www.snb.ch/en/iabout/stat/collect/id/statpub_coll_aktuelles.

United Kingdom

Bank of England – Credit Conditions Survey,
www.bankofengland.co.uk/publications/other/monetary/creditconditions.htm.

Department for Business, Innovation and Skills (BIS) – *SME data portal,*
http://stats.bis.gov.uk/ed/sme/.

BIS – *Reports on SME-related issues including finance,*
http://bis.ecgroup.net/Publications/EnterpriseBusinessSupport/EnterpriseSmallBusiness.aspx.

BIS – *Results from the 2009 Finance Survey of SMEs,*
www.bis.gov.uk/assets/biscore/enterprise/docs/10-636-2009-finance-survey-smes-results.

BIS – *Small Business Surveys, SME Business Barometers and Household Surveys of Entrepreneurship,*
www.bis.gov.uk/policies/enterprise-and-business-support/analytical-unit/research-and-evaluation/
cross-cutting-research.

United States

Federal Reserve Board – *Senior Loan Officer Opinion Survey on Bank Lending Practices,*
www.federalreserve.gov/boarddocs/snloansurvey/.

Federal Reserve Board – *Survey of Terms of Business Lending,*
www.federalreserve.gov/releases/e2/current/.

US Census Bureau – *Business Dynamics Statistics,*
www.ces.census.gov/index.php/bds/bds_database_list.

US Department of the Treasury – *Monthly Lending and Intermediation Snapshot,*
www.treasury.gov/initiatives/financial-stability/results/cpp/snapshot/Pages/default.aspx.

Federal Financial Institutions Examination Council (FFIEC) – loan-origination data,
www.ffiec.gov/.

Intrum Justitia

Intrum Justitia – *European payment index 2007-10,*
www.intrum.fi/1429_FIN_R.asp.

ANNEX C

Example of a Simplified Quantitative Demand-side Survey

Survey on Small Business Credit Conditions 2010 by Industry Canada

Number of questions:	
Section A (Screening):	4
Section B (General Financing):	4
Section C (Debt Financing):	6
Section D (Lease Financing):	2
Section E (Equity Financing):	2
Section F (General Business Information):	5
Section G (Owner Information):	4
Total:	**27**

Expected time: 15 minutes

Target respondent: owner, chief financial officer, accountant or person in charge of corporate finances

SCREENING QUESTIONS

The following are screening questions to determine if the business is in scope.

A.1. Just to confirm, are you: *(Note: Read all)*

a) The Business Owner?

b) The person in charge of finance in your business?

c) Other?

> **If A.1 = "c" —> Go to A.2**,
>
> **Else —> Go to A.3**

A.2. We are looking to speak with the person who is knowledgeable about the business characteristics finances. Are you the correct person?

Yes [Continue]

No [Ask to speak to the correct person]

A.3. Is your business classified as a non-profit organisation, a co-operative, a joint venture or a government agency?

Yes____ No____

If "yes" or "don't know/refused" —> **READ:** Since this survey is for private for-profit businesses, we will not need to proceed with the survey. Thank you for your participation.

A.4. Excluding the owner(s) of the business, how many paid full-time and part-time employees did the business have in 2010?

Full-time _____ Part-time_____

[Do not include contractors or sub contractors, *e.g.* in construction industry builders use sub contractors, plumbers, etc. who have their own business they are not employees and should not be counted}

If 0 < A.4 ≤ 100, continue to B.1

If A.4 = "0" or A.4 >"99" —> **READ:** Since this survey is for small businesses with 1 to 99 employees, we will not need to proceed with this survey. Thank you for your participation.

Note: This question is used as a screening question and is also a key question of the survey.

GENERAL FINANCING

B.1. What types external financing did your business seek in the 2010 calendar year?

(Note: MARK ALL THAT APPLY. The respondent is to reply with YES/NO/Refused/Don't Know after hearing each option.)

a) Did not seek any external financing

b) New mortgage or refinancing of an existing mortgage

c) New term loans

d) New line of credit or increase in existing line of credit

e) New credit card or increase in existing credit limit

f) Leasing

g) Trade Credit

h) Equity

i) Other, please specify:_____

If B.1 = "a" —> **Go to B.2**

Else —> **Go to B.3**

B.2. What was the main reason why your business did not seek external financing in the 2010 calendar year?

[*Read list and mark only one main reason*]

a) Financing not needed

b) Investment project postponed

c) Thought the request would be turned down

d) Applying for financing is too difficult

e) Cost of financing is too high

f) Other, (Please specify)_____ [*Do not read*]

   —> **Go to F.1**

B.3. What was main intended use for the financing requested that was requested in the 2010 calendar year? Was it for:

(*Note: Read list and mark only one main intended use*)

a) Fixed asset?

   (**Prompt:** Fixed assets are assets that the business expects to use for an extended period, such as land, buildings, vehicles, machinery and equipment)

b) Working capital/operating capital such as inventory or paying suppliers?

   (**Prompt:** Funds used to finance the day-to-day operations of the business such as the purchase of inventory or paying suppliers)

c) Research and development?

   (**Prompt:** R&D expenditures refers to expenditures meant to bring a new product to market or to improve an existing product)

d) Debt consolidations?

e) Enter a new domestic market?

f) Enter a new global market?

g) Other? (Please specify): _____ [Do not read Probe for other reason if nothing provided above]

B.4. What is your main supplier of finance?

(*Note: Read list and mark only one main supplier of finance*)

a) Domestic chartered bank (specify): _____

b) Foreign bank or subsidiary of a foreign bank (specify): _____

c) Credit union/ Caisses populaires (specify): _____

d) Leasing company

e) Government institution, for example BDC, EDC, FCC (specify):

f) Other (specify): _____ [Do not read]

(*Note:* Alberta Treasury Branches (ATB) should be considered a domestic chartered bank)

DEBT FINANCING

     If B.1b, B.1c, B.1d or B.1e = "YES"—> Go to C.1

     Else —> Go to Section D

C.1. In the most recent debt financing request in the 2010 calendar year, what was the dollar amount requested?

   (**Prompt:** Please provide your best estimate)

a) $_____

b) Don't know

c) Refused

C.2. What was the amount that was authorised as a result of your 2010 request?

a) $_____

   Note: Write $ 0 if the loan was rejected

b) Request is still under review

c) Don't know

d) Refused

   If C.2a = "$ 0", —> Go to C.3

   If $ 0 < C.2a —> Go to C.4

   If C.2 = b —> Go to Section D

C.3. Which of the following reasons were given as to why the loan was rejected?

   [Read list and mark all that apply]

a) No reason given by credit supplier

b) Insufficient sales or cash-flow

c) Insufficient collateral or security

d) Poor credit history or lack of credit history

e) Project was considered too risky

f) Other reason

   —> **Go to section D**

C.4. What was the annual interest rate on the loan?

a) _____%

b) Don't know

c) Refused

C.5. What was the length of term of the loan?

a) _____months

b) Not applicable

c) Don't know

d) Refused

C.6. What collateral were you asked to provide to obtain the loan?

(Note: MARK ALL THAT APPLY. The respondent is to reply with YES/NO/Refused/Don't Know after hearing each option.)

   (**Prompt:** Collateral are any assets pledged as security for the payment of a debt)

a) None

b) Business Asset (including land, buildings, materials and equipment, inventories, accounts receivable, financial assets)

c) Personal Assets

d) Intellectual Property

(**Prompt:** Intellectual Property is intangible property that is the result of intellectual activity and includes patents, trademarks or copyrights)

e) Other (Please specify: _____) [Do not read]

LEASE FINANCING

If B.1f = "YES", —> Go to D.1

Else —> Go to Section E

D.1. In the most recent lease financing request in the 2010 calendar year, what was the dollar amount requested?

(**Prompt:** Please provide your best estimate)

a) $_____

b) Don't know

c) Refused

D.2. What was the amount that was authorised?

a) $_____

b) Don't know

c) Refused

EQUITY FINANCING

If B.1h = "YES", —> Go to E.1

Else —> Go to Section F

E.1. In the most recent equity financing request in the 2010 calendar year, how much financing was requested?

(**Prompt:** Please provide your best estimate)

a) $_____

b) Don't know

c) Refused

E.2. What was the amount that was authorised?

a) $_____

b) Don't know

c) Refused

GENERAL BUSINESS INFORMATION

F.1 In which sector does your business primarily operate?

Goods-Producing Sector:

a) Agriculture, Forestry, Fishing and Hunting (NAICS 11)

b) Mining and Oil and Gas Extraction (NAICS 21)

c) Construction (NAICS 23)

d) Manufacturing (NAICS 31-33) Please specify:_____

Services-Producing Sector:

e) Wholesale Trade (NAICS 41)

f) Retail Trade (NAICS 44-45)

g) Transportation and Warehousing (NAICS 48-49)

h) Professional, Scientific and Technical Services (NAICS 54)

i) Accommodation and Food Services (NAICS 72)

j) Other Services Please specify _____

k) Other, (Please specify :_____)

F.2. How many years has the company been in existence?

_____year(s)

F.3. What was the value of the following business financial figures for your 2010 fiscal year?

(**Prompt:** Please provide your best estimate)

a) Total business revenues $_____

b) Profit/net income, before taxes $_____

c) Total Assets $_____

(**Prompt:** What is the approximate total amount of all financial and non-financial assets that the business owns?)

d) Total Liabilities $_____

(**Prompt:** What is the approximate total amount of all short-term and long-term debt that the business owes to its creditors?)

F.4. In 2011, estimate the percentage of the total sales that came from the following geographic market regions:

(**Prompt:** Please provide your best estimate)

(**Note:** Should add up to 100%, but if it does not, do NOT correct this with the respondent as it can easily become too time consuming)

a) Your market (same municipality or region) ____%

b) Rest of your province/territory ____%

c) Rest of Canada _____ %

d) United States _____ %

e) Rest of the World _____ %

F.5. In the 2010 calendar year has the business developed or introduced:

(Note: Read every option and mark all that apply. The respondent is to reply with YES/NO/Refused/ Don't Know after hearing each option)

a) Product innovation: [Prompt if necessary a new or significantly improved good or service to the market?]

b) Process innovation: [Prompt if necessary a new or significantly improved production process or method?]

c) Organizational innovation: [Prompt if necessary A new organisational method in your business practices, workplace organisation or external relations?] (Prompt: It must be a result of strategic decision taken by management)

d) Marketing innovation:[Prompt if necessary A new way of selling your goods or services?] (Prompt: this requires significant changes in product design or packaging, product placement, product promoting or pricing)

OWNER INFORMATION

G.1. What is the age of the majority owner?

(**Prompt:** In the case of equal partnership, please report the average age of the partners)

_____years

G.2. How many years of experience does the majority owner have in owning or managing a business?

_____years

G.3. What is the gender of the majority business owner?

a) Male

b) Female

c) Equal ownership (50-50 ownership)

G.4. What is the highest level of education attained by the majority owner?

a) Less than high school diploma

b) High school diploma

c) College/cegep/trade school diploma

d) Bachelor degree

e) Master degree or above

QUESTIONNAIRE CONCLUSION

H.1. In the event that we conduct a short follow-up questionnaire in the next two years, would you be willing to complete it?

Yes_____ No_____

If H.1. = yes —> Go to H.2

If H.1. = no —> Go conclusion text

H.2. As the follow-up survey will be electronic, could you please provide us with your e-mail address?

ORGANISATION FOR ECONOMIC CO-OPERATION AND DEVELOPMENT

The OECD is a unique forum where governments work together to address the economic, social and environmental challenges of globalisation. The OECD is also at the forefront of efforts to understand and to help governments respond to new developments and concerns, such as corporate governance, the information economy and the challenges of an ageing population. The Organisation provides a setting where governments can compare policy experiences, seek answers to common problems, identify good practice and work to co-ordinate domestic and international policies.

The OECD member countries are: Australia, Austria, Belgium, Canada, Chile, the Czech Republic, Denmark, Estonia, Finland, France, Germany, Greece, Hungary, Iceland, Ireland, Israel, Italy, Japan, Korea, Luxembourg, Mexico, the Netherlands, New Zealand, Norway, Poland, Portugal, the Slovak Republic, Slovenia, Spain, Sweden, Switzerland, Turkey, the United Kingdom and the United States. The European Union takes part in the work of the OECD.

OECD Publishing disseminates widely the results of the Organisation's statistics gathering and research on economic, social and environmental issues, as well as the conventions, guidelines and standards agreed by its members.

OECD PUBLISHING, 2, rue André-Pascal, 75775 PARIS CEDEX 16
(85 2012 01 1P) ISBN 978-92-64-02802-9 – No. 59813 2012-02